On Being At Work

Inspired by the work of the philosopher Judith Butler, influenced by Marx's theory of alienation and intrigued by theories of death, this book develops an anti-methodological approach to studying working lives. Distinctions are drawn between labour (the tasks we do in our jobs) and work (self-making activities that are carried out at the workplace): between the less than human, zombie-like laborer and the working human self. Nancy Harding argues that the experience of being at work is one in which the insistence on practising one's humanity always provides a counterpoint to organizational demands.

Nancy Harding is Professor of Organization Theory at Bradford University School of Management. She is currently writing a series of books on the social construction of, respectively, the manager (Routledge, 2003), the employee (Routledge, 2013) and the organization (forthcoming).

Routledge Studies in Management, Organizations, and Society

This series presents innovative work grounded in new realities, addressing issues crucial to an understanding of the contemporary world. This is the world of organised societies, where boundaries between formal and informal, public and private, local and global organizations have been displaced or have vanished, along with other nineteenth century dichotomies and oppositions. Management, apart from becoming a specialized profession for a growing number of people, is an everyday activity for most members of modern societies.

Similarly, at the level of enquiry, culture and technology, and literature and economics, can no longer be conceived as isolated intellectual fields; conventional canons and established mainstreams are contested. Management, Organization and Society addresses these contemporary dynamics of transformation in a manner that transcends disciplinary boundaries, with books that will appeal to researchers, student and practitioners alike.

For a full list of titles in this series, please visit www.routledge.com

On Being At Work
The Social Construction
of the Employee

Nancy Harding

Routledge
Taylor & Francis Group

NEW YORK AND LONDON

First published 2013
by Routledge
711 Third Avenue, New York, NY 10017

Simultaneously published in the UK
by Routledge
2 Park Square, Milton Park, Abingdon, Oxon OX14 4RN

*Routledge is an imprint of the Taylor & Francis Group,
an informa business*

© 2013 Taylor & Francis

The right of Nancy Harding to be identified as the author of the editorial material has been asserted in accordance with sections 77 and 78 of the Copyright, Designs and Patents Act 1988.

Trademark Notice: Product or corporate names may be trademarks or registered trademarks, and are used only for identification and explanation without intent to infringe.

Library of Congress Cataloging-in-Publication Data

Harding, Nancy, 1952–
    On being at work : the social construction of the employee / by Nancy Harding.
        p. cm. — (Routledge studies in management, organizations, and society ; 21)
    Includes bibliographical references and index.
    1. Work—Social aspects—History—21st century.   2. Women professional employees—History—21st century.   3. Women employees—History—21st century.   I. Title.
    HD6955.H3527   2012
    306.3'61—dc23
    2012038919

ISBN: 978-0-415-57971-1 (hbk)
ISBN: 978-0-203-55903-1 (ebk)

Typeset in Sabon
by Apex CoVantage, LLC

This book is dedicated to my siblings:
Dawn Mary Parkes
Robert Davies
Julie Davies
Shan Stockwood
Fiona (Fifi) Wake
Adrian (Adey) Davies

And to the memory of our parents
William (Bill) Davies (1920–2010) and
Bessie Davies (1925–2003)

And, as always, to the lights of my life, Brychan and
Dylan Harding, their parents, Iorwerth and
Clare Harding, and their Uncle Gareth
and his partner, Cerys.

Contents

Acknowledgements

Firstly, to Sandra Thomas (1948–2011), a Valleys intellectual, fount of wisdom, giggles and fun, who has left a big gap in many people's lives.

I am grateful to Bradford School of Management, which has given me a congenial place in which to work for the past five years, as well as my first ever sabbatical (yippee!), in which I was able to finish a book that I had started eight years previously. I have been able to discuss aspects of the work with various colleagues, and Anna Zueva-Owens and Rob Wapshott commented on early ideas. The wonderful Eva Niemann has taken too much of the load of the DBA while I've been completing this book.

I owe more than can be said to my 'virtual university' of people who are friends more than colleagues and whose willingness to comment on draft chapters has far surpassed the call of duty. Marianna Fotaki of Manchester Business School has seen drafts of every chapter and provided congenial company, insightful comments, scintillating conversation and Greek sunshine in the early summer of 2012. She has challenged my thinking and made me push my ideas beyond what would have been possible without her care and friendship. A day and more in deep conversation with Sarah Gilmore of Portsmouth Business School brought Chapter Five, on gender, to life. Numerous long conversations with Sarah buoyed up my spirits when I thought I'd never finish writing the manuscript, and she is a constant source of new ideas, intellectual inspiration and 'wow' moments. Kate Kenny of the University of Galway has provided extremely insightful comments in regard to Butler's work, along with a magical evening in an Irish pub, an introduction to several Irish restaurants, an opportunity to rehearse Chapter Three in public (thank you to her colleagues for listening and for generating a very lively debate) and much more beside. Mark Learmonth's paper with Patrick Reedy on death and organizations was the original stimulus for Chapter Six; Mark read a draft of that chapter, and his challenge to my thinking helped develop Chapter Seven. Mark's influence goes way beyond a single chapter, although I never got to grips with Derrida. Jackie Ford has been there through bad times and good, keeping me on track when I needed a shove, ensuring the light of the 'Foucault and lippie' conversations never went out, commenting on drafts, pointing me to literature, giving me far more than I can ever put down in words and generally living and breathing the ideas I discuss in Chapter 4. Finally, major thanks must go to my chief nag, the force of nature that is Hugh Lee. Our long discussions mean that it is difficult sometimes to know whose idea is whose, although the jokes are usually Hugh's. The discussion of violence in this book reflects aspects of our joint work. Hugh has been responsible not only for commenting on most chapters in this book but also for helping the ideas develop and for cutting through weaknesses in my arguments. His friendship defines what friendship should be.

Introduction: Inspirations, Aims, Debates, Reflexivity and Anti-Methodology

This book seeks to develop a theory of being at work in the 21st century: what does work mean for us, what does it do to us and what sort of persons does it allow us to become? It has three interrelated arguments. First, in Western societies we grow up with dreams of the person we will one day be, dreams we do not necessarily abandon as we get older. Work is one of the major forums in which we believe we will constitute those future, dreamed-of selves. Second, labour, or the tasks we perform in fulfilling the terms of the employment contract, should therefore be distinguished from work, which involves processes of self-making over and above the 'mere' doing of labour. Third, the organization's desire is that we be reduced to zombie-machines which labour and that are less than human, and although we try to circumvent this desire in various ways, organizations always limit the possibilities for achieving the self I/we wish to be(come). The dreams of the me-I-might-become through work are therefore shattered by the organiza-tion's compulsion that forces me to labour. In brief, the thesis of this book is that organizations murder the me's-that-might-have-been.

I borrow the term 'less than human' from the philosopher Judith Butler, whose work provides much of the theoretical frame for the book's argu-ments. In 'Butler-speak', the questions I am seeking to answer are: what does it mean to be a being doing paid work in/for that thing we call 'an or-ganization', who is this being that is doing the doing and how is this subject brought into being through the doing?

BEYOND THE CONTROL/RESISTANCE BINARY

Although this work emerges out of both Marxist and Foucauldian labour process theory's hugely significant analysis of managerial control and em-ployee resistance (Braverman, 1974; Littler and Salaman, 1982; Knights and Willmott, 1989; Alvesson and Willmott, 1996; Cooper and Burrell, 1998), its trajectory is somewhat different in that it investigates what goes on beyond the control/resistance binary. The control/resistance coupling ineluctably ties the working self into a relationship with management, so that staff are management's other and therefore can know one another only through a managerial lens. Although that is an important aspect of what it is to be a being at work, there are spaces and places where management is not omnipresent, where selves are constructed not only in resistance to or conformity with management but also beyond the purview of management. In this book I conceive of employees, not managers, making a working *place* out of the *space* in which work is carried out (Lefebvre, 1991). So, rather than starting from the position of management organizing and controlling work in ways that result in more or less resistance from employees, that is, locating management as the powerful and the normative, I am starting from a perspective that regards the workplace as a social sphere where life, in all its glory, is lived by beings who are seekers after dreamed-of selves and into which management intrudes. In this reading, a social workplace is the norm, and management, or 'the organization', transgresses the norm.

Alongside Butler's work, the inspiration for this book was a somewhat un-nuanced reading of Marx's theory of alienation (Marx 1988, originally published in 1844). In that early work (which I discuss in more depth in Chapter Six), Marx argued that the employee is alienated within capitalism in four ways: from the product, from the self, from the social and from nature. Turning this on its head suggests that the non-alienated employee is someone who is engaged meaningfully in producing a product or service they value, who works in a social environment where they can develop a strong sense of self and in conditions that are aesthetically pleasing (and obviously not controlled by capitalism). In contemporary parlance, we can envisage a utopia in which people constitute confident, fulfilled workplace selves through the work they do and the people they do it with. This changes the focus so that economic exploitation and the managerialist compulsion to maximise productivity are somewhat decentred. Although these must, of course, remain highly pertinent, there are other conditions in 21st-century workplaces that require our attention. A brief detour through some of Bauman's work and his articulation of a major change between early and late modernism will explain.

In *Consuming Life* (2007), Bauman proposes that we live in an era of a society of consumers, in which the boundary between commodities and consumers is effaced. That is, in order to have selfhood, individuals must work on *themselves*, must indeed manufacture themselves, become a commodity that is to be 'consumed' by self and others. How one looks, how one behaves and how one develops one's skills and expertise must add up to a package (the self) that can be 'sold' to an employer or be judged by oneself and fellow citizens in much the same way as we judge objects offered for sale in shop windows. In Bauman's words (2007:12), 'no one can become a subject without first turning into a commodity, and no one can keep his or her subjectness secure without perpetually resuscitating, resurrecting and replenishing the capacities expected and required of a sellable commodity. . . . The "subjectivity" of the "subject", and most of what that subjectivity enables the subject to achieve, is focused on an unending effort to itself become, and remain, a sellable commodity'. When one looks in the mirror, one judges what one sees as if it were offered in a marketplace. Subjects must turn themselves into commodities so as to lift themselves out of a 'grey and flat invisibility and insubstantiality, making themselves stand out from the mass of indistinguishable objects' (12). Bauman argues that whereas, in the society of producers that previously held sway, commodity fetishism hid from view the human substance involved in the production of objects (Marx's thesis), in its successor, the society of consumers, subjectivity fetishism hides this new, commoditised reality. Now the emotions are dominated by the constantly revivified abilities of wanting, desiring and longing that have become the 'principal propelling and operating force of society' (28).

In the society of producers, Bauman argues, work played the lynchpin role in organizing society. Now, he argues, work is secondary, and consumerism has become not only the lynchpin but an attribute of society: it is consumerism that holds society together and provides the 'specific parameters for effective individual life strategies' (29). Rather than gratification of needs, there is an ever-increasing volume and intensity of desires and a belief, always impossible to prove, that commodities will satisfy insatiable needs. The supreme value of such a society is happiness (44), and there is a promise that happiness is available through the consumption of objects, but this promise is always unfulfilled, the pursuit of yet more objects to consume must be continuously repeated and so the promise of happiness brings only unhappiness.

Moreover, and importantly for this book, in the society of consumers the self becomes an object for consumption by both self and others: the self is commoditised, has to be worked on and made into a sellable commodity. To be 'fully and truly human' requires making the self into both an ideal commodity (59 et passim) *and* a competent consumer (64): failure results in exclusion and 'Promethean shame' (59 et passim).

Although Bauman captures extremely well the importance of working on the self so that it becomes a commodity to be consumed by both self and others, I diverge from his thesis on two points. The first is his sharp distinction between work and consumerism. We do not compartmentalise our lives so neatly, so the work we do is and indeed must be a major aspect of the selves we constitute, as the vast literature on identities in organizations testifies (see Alvesson, Ashcraft and Thomas, 2008, for a review). Work on constituting the self, on identity-making, is another way in which organizations may seek to control us (Alvesson and Willmott, 2002). But, although there is increasing pressure to turn ourselves into the sort of workplace commodity that the organization will desire to hire (Sabath, 2007), the workplace is also a social world, so we may constitute ourselves as commodities for consumption by ourselves and our fellow employees. This work, in which recognition is given, is productive and may (or should) be pleasurable. Second, and relatedly, Bauman's pessimism can be parried with Foucault's exploration of the ethics of working on the self, that is, 'an exercise of the self on the self by which one attempts to develop and transform oneself, and to attain to a certain mode of being' (Foucault, 1997a:282). This is a 'practice of freedom' (not of liberation) that should be conducted ethically (ibid.:283). In other words, whilst work on the self is in many ways concerned with commoditisation of the self, it does not have just that one, singularly pessimistic, interpretation. There are other explanations and other possibilities, and Foucault's thesis brings with it implications of an ethical duty to constitute workplace selves that nourish other workplace selves.

In summary, the earliest inspiration for this book's arguments was Marx's theory of alienation within modern capitalism. Its more recent inspiration is Judith Butler's analyses of abjection in postmodern capitalism's conditions of subjection and subjectification. We move, it seems, from alienation to abjection. This book takes Butler into the workplace, along with an unemployed person, a boss, a manual worker, an archaeologist and two academics, so as to explore the forms that alienation and abjection may or may not take in 21st-century working lives.

ON THE OTHER HAND . . .

Those are the academic inspirations for the arguments in this book. There are other, more personal reasons for needing to write it. I have been immersed in 'critical management studies' for a quarter of a century, and what *bothers* me in many of its debates is the absence of explorations of work other than through the lens of control and resistance. Much working life goes on despite, rather than because of, management, and there is much about the sense of a working self that is not encapsulated within concepts of control and resistance. The conditions of possibility that led this particular, authorial 'I' to be concerned with how organizations render subjects abject, nonhuman, beyond the reach of ethics and within the reach of only limited definitions of justice, arise from memories of my life before I became an academic, a life in which I took for granted my feelings of inferiority. I was a working-class girl who was told subtly when I watched films or television or read a novel or a newspaper that I was, in my class and gender status, inferior. That inferiority penetrated the psyche. I swam in inferiority like a fish swims in water: it was so much a part of my sense of self I hardly noticed it, although I constantly felt it. It fuelled resentment and despair and a sense of the impossibility of ever being good enough to pass as 'normal'. Marx's theory of alienation, when I encountered it as a mature student, described some of this experience, but I have found it explained best by postcolonial theory, notably Said's *Orientalism* (1978) and Fanon's *Black Skin, White Masks* (2008). These authors articulate in a way that theories of economic exploitation never do the subjective experience of being an abjected (inferior, despised) self.

A sense of the injustices of what labouring (and thus class identity) does to people seems, looking back on my childhood and early adulthood in a coal-mining village, so deeply part of the mining quotidian, of the sense of a community that defined itself as 'not-manager', that this need to explore the different forms by which work oppresses us is part of my personal always-already there, waiting only for me to gain knowledge of the language necessary for the undertaking of such an exploration. On the other hand, the 'I' referred to throughout this text, that is, 'I' the author, is an academic sitting at her desk typing, referring to texts, evading the direct gaze of a managerial other although indirectly measured by it. There are many frustrations in this job, but in many ways it is a dream job, one with status and self-respect. I have become in some ways the me I dreamed of being when I made the first, faltering inquiries about the possibilities of going to university as a mature student. This book is therefore an attempt in some ways to understand my own experiences; it is the personal become philosophical.

My aim, therefore, is to develop a theory on what it is to *be* at work, that is, to be engaged in workplace activities (the doing of work) in which the ongoing processes of the becoming of the workplace self simultaneously take place. I will appropriate Butler's arguments, weaving them through the work of some other theorists and individual's accounts of their working lives, all the time delighting in the licence she gives to meld together different theoretical perspectives when so doing facilitates explanation and understanding. There is also some optimism in Butler's later work in which she develops a new form of left-wing politics based on ethical relationships. It is that optimism that I want to use in order to avoid a patriarchal pessimism that otherwise could emerge from a study such as this one.

ESTABLISHING TERMS

Social Constructionism

This is the second book in a planned trilogy that focuses on the social constructions of management (2003), the employee (2013) and the organization (as soon as possible). As in the first book, I am using the term 'social constructionism' very broadly, to refer to a critical, relativist, interpretivist position (Burrell and Morgan, 1979; Crotty, 1998) that adapts itself as new theoretical positions become available or as authors become tired of methodolatry (Janesick, 1994).

The Zombie-Machine

I am using the term 'zombie-machine' as shorthand to capture that form of the self which organizations seem to prefer in their employees: devoted to the work, devoid of any objectives or pleasures save those which relate to the organization's purpose and little more than extensions of organizational technologies—that is, computerised machines made out of human flesh but without any desire for agency save that which is required to fulfil organizational objectives. This description emerges out of four decades of antiperformative (Fournier and Grey, 2000) approaches to understanding management and organizations, inspired notably by Braverman's seminal *Labor and Monopoly Capital* (1974), taken forward in various forms of labour process theory (see Littler and Salaman, 1982, for a review) and in the various antiperformative approaches more or less encapsulated in the category 'critical management studies' (see Grey and Willmott, 2005, for 'classic' papers, and O'Doherty and Willmott, 2001, for an analysis of the relationship between labour process theory and critical management). I will use the phrase 'zombie-machine' throughout the book, relying on these four decades of work by academics major and minor to justify its use.

The Human and Less-than-Human

Implicit in Butler's body of work on abjection and her more recent development of a new, left-wing politics is a concept where all people are born into the human and into an ethical domain arising from recognition. Some have that humanity taken away from them because of the absence or refusal of recognition. This allows others to treat them as if they were inanimate rather than sensate beings. I equate zombie-machines with the status of the less-than-human, because the zombie-machine is an organic tool designed to achieve organizational ends.

A RATHER LONG NOTE ABOUT METHODOLOGY, OR, TOWARDS A SOCIOCULTURAL PHILOSOPHY OF MANAGEMENT AND ORGANIZATION STUDIES

When I started writing this Introduction, I aimed to keep it as succinct and to the point as possible. The discussion of 'methodology', however, betrays this aim. Rather than justifying the choice of methodology (using one person's working-life story), I want to critique the limitations to thinking that a focus on methodology brings with it, and this cannot be done in just a few paragraphs. It requires first setting out my unease about regarding management and organization studies (MOS) as a social science and second the articulation of an alternative means of understanding the world of work. Chapters One to Four of this book are each based on an 'interview' with one person about his or her working life, and Chapter Five is based on an 'interview' with two people. I will start this section by outlining the reasons for putting scare quotes around the word 'interview' and the related term 'data gathering'.

The interview is the most popular and widely used method in qualitative research in management and organization studies. Its use is advocated by positivist and postpositivist researchers alike, and increasingly sophisticated methodologies of interview data analysis are generating what seem to be more insightful understandings of what goes on in organizations. This is perhaps aided by the development of technology for recording interviews. It is only in the past 20 or 30 years that portable tape recorders have become available; before that time, the researcher made written notes of the conversation, and it was those notes which were analysed. Today we can work with transcripts that note every pause, cough and stammer, and correspondingly sophisticated methods of analysis have emerged. And yet there are many flaws in interviews.

One of the most obvious is problems of recall and bias in interviewees' accounts. With Jackie Ford and Brendan Gough (2010), I sought to overcome problems of recall by asking interviewees to keep a diary of one day in their lives, which we used as an aide-memoire for interviews held a week or so later. What we saw was a process of condensing and forgetting. The diaries were a maximum of about 1,000 words, so the complexities of 12 to 16 hours in a person's life were fundamentally reduced. Interviews lasted between 60 and 90 minutes, so those hours were again shoehorned into some proportion of the actual time we were exploring. Much must have been left out of each person's description of the working day, but we cannot know what was omitted in this condensation, because only a week after keeping the diary many of the interviewees reported their surprise at being reminded of things they had already forgotten. This leads to the question of the relationship of an interview account to the experiences that are supposedly reported: what is omitted, and what forgotten? It is well known that the people we interview may censor what they tell us, sometimes because they are striving to give us the information they think we need, sometimes because of their needs for privacy. However, problems of recall, selectivity and bias are only the most obvious of problems.

If we look at the context of interviews, then what we have is a somewhat peculiar social practice involving an encounter between two strangers in which one is licensed to ask the other questions that in other social encounters might be regarded as rude and intrusive. The participants speak from the subject position of interviewer and interviewee, constituting these identities through their interactions (Harding, 2007), so the record of the interview, the transcript, may in some ways be little more than an account of the social encounter we call 'the interview' (Alvesson, 2003). Further, participants move between subject positions, sometimes because of the language used by the interviewer (Alvesson, 2003), leading to the question not only of which version of the self is speaking at any specific point in the interview but which version of the self is *allowed* to speak. Various versions of the 'I' and the 'me' may be ready to appear (Harding, 2008), but only one can have control of the tongue at any one moment (Lee, 2005).

So, we engage in discussion with another person whose account may already be greatly edited. But much more happens besides this that is problematic. We use interviews as a means of discovering something about the subjectivities of participants. However, the 'interviewee' has to translate complex realities into language, and language can convey only a limited sense of one's experience. Bollas (1995:147) articulates this through a small experiment. Try to describe your mother, he suggests: you will find it impossible to ever reach a point at which you are satisfied you have conveyed 'that inner presence which you carry within you and which is evoked by her name'. Rather, she is 'a complex inner constellation always sponsored by the name . . . but with discrete representations emerging upon each rethinking' (ibid.). This is not unique to our parents: in all of our encounters, we are immersed in a 'matrix beyond representation'. So the interview's access to subjectivities is limited by the difficulty for interviewees of translating thoughts and experiences into words. Relatedly, these words then come up against the problem of the listener's interpretation, leading to much discussion about the need for reflexivity and reflection about the researcher's influence upon data analysis.

Further, the analysis is normally restricted to the words contained in the transcript that is laboriously typed up after the interview. The living, breathing human being who has sat opposite us is progressively reduced to about 10,000 words in a computer file. The individual's 'idiom', 'itness' or 'aesthetic of being'; his or her 'own very unique configuration in being' (Bollas, 1989; 1993); the ways in which the person interacts, consciously and unconsciously, with others; the response the person evokes in others; the texture the person adds to the room while in it and the shape of the person's absence after s/he leaves—all of these important features of unconscious communication (Bollas, 1993) are lost, and we work with only the words spoken in the fleeting hour of the interview.

These 10,000 words are only that—words; they are not discourses, as all images and pictures are removed from them. We then reduce them further, to major themes. If we have interviewed, say, 25 people and produce 250,000 words, then these quarter of a million words are successively reduced to a small number of major themes—perhaps six words. All 25 people disappear into, are reduced to this small number of words. There is nothing left of them save a small number of words that we then proceed to analyse in huge depth. What we are studying, therefore, is not a phenomenon, or subjectivities or understandings of the world of work but words to which we have given the label 'data'. We have persuaded ourselves (perhaps through operations of power) that these words represent the phenomenon we are studying. In some ways, this reduction of reports of experience to a limited number of words parallels that of quantitative research's reduction of the complexities of the social world to numbers (Valsiner, 2006).

In short, when we interview people, we engage in a process that systematically strips their account of any relationship to the social world and the subjectivities we are ostensibly exploring. By reducing to nothing but a few words the full humanity of the people who give us their time and their accounts of that social world, we decaffeinate them. This is my concern about the interview as a research tool—it is a process of aetiolation that reduces complex, multidimensional people involved in multilayered social worlds to nothing more than a few words. At the same time, the requirement that we write ever more sophisticated accounts of our research methods seems to be intensifying: methodolatry (Janesick, 1994) rules. There is something unethical about this: we have to give ever more rigorous accounts of our research methods and, in so doing, have to maintain the impression that we are exploring subjectivities, understandings and interpretations held by real, fully formed human beings when many of us recognise that we do no such thing.

There has been much discussion about epistemology and ways of working with, if not overcoming, such limitations and problems. However, these discussions are always located within a scientific discourse: MOS is located in the social sciences, and the lens through which we understand our subject is therefore scientific. The label 'science' brings with it scientistic demands so that even poststructural researchers who abhor such grand theories as 'the scientific method' are caught in its net. But why is MOS regarded as a social science, and could there be other ways of knowing? The reasons *why* MOS is located in the social sciences can be traced to the struggle for legitimizing its domain of study and its recommendations, even though much that was claimed by management researchers to be 'scientific' is dubious (Harding, 2003). This is in the context of a birth myth of the social sciences (Jovanovic, 2011:17), in which can be seen a cascading series of binary categories: science is defined as separate and distinct from and superior as a form of knowing to all that is nonscience; under the category of 'science', the physical sciences are separated from the social sciences; under the category of social science, the quantitative are separated from the qualitative; and under the category of the qualitative, the positivist becomes separated from the postpositivist. Such processes of categorisation inhibit the potential for thought, as Foucault has argued, because they prevent our thinking about what has been left outside these categories. In MOS, one of the things left outside is the arts and humanities.

By categorisation Foucault means the discursive compulsion to sort things into groups. He argues that the criteria by which we catalogue and categorise may seem superficially self-evident and obvious but that what falls logically into categories in one episteme may differ from what seems rational in another (Foucault, 1966). Categorisation and classification facilitate control and discipline (Foucault, 1977) and refuse the possibility of difference (Foucault, 1994:357). In preventing a 'univocity' of being wherein each thing can be different and distinct from all others and thus in some ways beyond the purview of control, the possibilities for selfhood are stifled. In terms of qualitative studies in MOS, to be categorised as social scientists makes academics knowable and controllable, reduced to nonbeing and the 'dissolution of the Me' (Foucault, 1994:357) who has forfeited the right to individuality. We *know* this—when we rail against the need to limit our aspirations within unexciting and unchallenging parameters so as to win research grants, we know we are conforming to the demands of a scientistic approach. There is little chance that we will foment any revolution against capitalism—we are too busy conforming to the requirements to publish in the best journals whilst also being evaluated highly by our students for the quality of our teaching *and* carrying out one of the many administrative tasks that permeate every level of university life. Conforming to rules set by a seemingly apolitical scientistic agenda is therefore one symptom of ways in which academics are controlled/fail to resist.

Further, the question of what science *is* must be posed. Arguing from the basis of research within the sociology of scientific knowledge, Law (2004) launches a devastating attack on the Euro-American metaphysics of knowledge that is encapsulated in the term 'science'. He argues that the world is a 'generative flux that *produces* realities' (7) but that research 'attends to, amplifies and retransmits only a few while silencing the others' (144). Many realities are therefore rendered invisible to the researching eye. Not only do research methods construct the realities they attempt to describe, he argues; they also (1) enact presence and (2) manifest an absence that is understood to be relevant to understanding presence but also (3) produce absence as Otherness, that is, that which is absent because presence enacts it as irrelevant, impossible or repressed. In terms of MOS, research methods enact: the *presence* of organizations; the *manifest absence* of any activities not related to 'the organization'; and absence as Otherness, or workplace cultures not recognised as part of 'the organization' which are therefore placed outside existence. Law's argument is that

> Euro-American (research) manifests a world in its depictions that is ontologically single, and therefore inhabited by a finally limited number of objects, forces and processes that may be more or less well known. . . . [T]he possibility of a practice for knowing which recognises that entities are being endlessly enacted and (as a part of this) are being differently enacted in different locations and in different contexts, is repressed. . . . . In the midst of representational singularity there is multiplicity. But this is not seen. The multiple or the fractional, the elusive, the vague, the partial and the fluid are being displaced into Otherness. (Law, 2004:137)

He argues (2006:10) that what we can *see* involves ontological politics: in terms of this discussion, to regard MOS as a social science is an ontological politics that limits the possibilities of understanding which unwittingly represses anything that 'fails to fit the standard package' of scientific regulations (ibid). In such a context, Law argues (2004:148), 'imaginaries, fluxes, indefinitenesses and multiplicities' are regarded as the domain of the arts rather than being aspects of 'serious research methods'. He concludes that such a division of labour is no longer tenable.

If 'imaginaries, fluxes', and so on are the domain of the arts, then it may be useful to have aspects of MOS that are located in the arts and humanities rather than in the social sciences. However, the arts and humanities explore the works of great novelists, filmmakers, playwrights and philosophers to give insights about 'the world', and in privileging the few they silence the voices of the 'ordinary' citizens who participate in social scientific research.

A Sociocultural Philosophy for MOS

There are currently two approaches to (categories for) developing understanding within MOS: empirically based (as discussed here) and purely theoretical, in which the academic follows a long philosophical tradition of developing ideas through interaction with other thinkers (Alvesson and Skoldberg, 2009). These two approaches can be regarded perhaps as the social scientific, which uses empirical material, and the philosophical, which does not. This binary closes possibilities for different ways of developing understanding of organizations, a problem which Parker in his recent book (2011) struggles with but has to gloss over if he is to achieve his aim of articulating how motifs from within popular culture inform and articulate people's feelings about their working lives. What I am proposing is that we can break out of this binary by adding an alternative way of studying organizations, that is, through MOS as a sociocultural philosophy. I am not suggesting anything very revolutionary, merely pointing out that the taken-for-grantedness of MOS as a social science, the impossibility of thinking otherwise because of the lack of awareness of other possibilities, has political consequences that call for a different form of reflexivity beyond that which has become de rigueur in qualitative research. As well as exploring how our subjectivities have influenced how we have done our research, we should also explore how that research has become an aspect of our subjectivities and identities and how it has restricted the possibilities for academic thought.

The method I am proposing involves dismantling the boundary between the social sciences and the arts and humanities through regarding the qualitative interview as a boundary object that is applicable to both social science and the arts and humanities, although its analysis will differ according to the disciplinary focus. That is, the interview-provided account of a single employee would, following the example of the social sciences, privilege the voice of the 'ordinary' citizen but, following the example of the arts and humanities, would regard their account as containing their theory of the issue being explored. Rather than the six metaphors of the social science interview outlined by Alvesson (2003), there would be one metaphor for what I am calling a sociocultural philosophy of MOS, that is, the metaphor of theory. This theory can then be interrogated in similar ways to, say, the theory contained in a novel or in a philosopher's works. Each person would be regarded as a theorist of his or her own experiences, and our role as researchers becomes that of interrogators of those theories. We thus become concerned with a poetics of organizational analysis that combines elements of the social sciences, arts and humanities and which relishes that which is non-sense (or outside the parameters of what the disciplinary gaze judges as sense) (Linstead, 2000).

We qualitative researchers are convinced of the value of qualitative methods compared to quantitative methods, because the latter ignore subjectivities, lived experiences, and so forth. Despite the problems of interviews, good interview-based research studies produce exciting, thought-provoking insights that can, at best, change the world for the better. This *sociocultural philosophy of* MOS would retain the value of the interview but, in abandoning claims to be a science, thus moving away from the worship of methodology (methodolatry), would open up possibilities for using them differently.

These thoughts about anti-methodology inform the ways in which I have discussed their working lives with a small number of people, and later sat down and worked with the recording of each interview. This takes us neatly to a summary of the structure of this book.

STRUCTURE OF THIS BOOK

In Chapter One, using the contrast between the lives of two sisters (myself and my sister Julie) and Butler's recent work on recognition, I argue that we desire (paid) employment not only because it provides the means of sustenance but also because it is one of the primary locations where work on the self is undertaken. I distinguish in this chapter between labour (the tasks of doing the job) and work (the possibility of developing a self through the doing of the job). Chapter Two explores how managers themselves, the people who do the work of management, are as caught up in this desire as are other staff. Using a discussion of the working life of the owner of a small business which I read through the account of the master/slave dialectic in Butler's work, this chapter argues that the 'boss' is as controlled by the title 'boss' as is staff. The argument is that the will of the manager requires, for that person to know that s/he is a manager, that staff be reduced to the status of zombie-machine. I therefore trace through the psyche and desires of one manager the inscription of centuries of capitalism, colonialism, class and hierarchy that constitute the speaking subject as 'manager'. The paradox of this is explored in Chapter Three, the Bondsman's Tale, in which I use Butler's *Antigone's Claim* (1997) to explore the working life of a male manual worker, Shakeel. In that chapter we, in the guise of a male manual worker, go into the cave where Antigone was to die and see how arbitrary is the division between management and staff. Shakeel despises managers even as he speaks the idiom of management.

Chapter Four builds further on Butler's thesis on kinship in *Antigone's Claim* to analyse the working life of an archaeologist. This illuminates the distinction between labour and work and argues that the friends with whom we work provide that recognition through which we become human. Chapter Four is therefore a thesis on friendship and work. Chapter Five turns to Butler's early work and explores organizations and gendering. It argues that we are surprised into gender, with labour requiring a compulsory gendering of the subject and work allowing (some of us, some of the time) to escape from the pall that gender casts on the psyche and on selves. Chapter One therefore articulates a desire to constitute a self through the work we aspire to, and the succeeding four chapters explore how that desire is frustrated by the organization's proscriptions so that, even though self-making is undertaken, circumstances limit the possibilities for being selves. Chapter Six argues that this is a form of murder, of the me's-I-might-have-been. Rather than Butler's work, which says little directly about death, I turn in this chapter to Jonathon Dollimore's book *Death, Desire and Loss in Western Culture* (2001). Similarly, where other chapters work with interviews with one or two people, this chapter deviates from that modus operandi in that it draws on a cultural product, the whodunit, to help articulate and expound its arguments. I return to Marx's theory of alienation in that chapter. Finally, the book concludes, in Chapter Seven, with an exploration of the ethics of organizational self-making.

1 What Is 'Work'? A Tale of Two Sisters

I am writing this opening paragraph on a July night in 2009. As I type, there is a thunderstorm raging outside my window, a window that looks, from its fifth-floor vantage point, over the rooftops of a city in northern Sumatra. I am here to do research, and the hotel in which I am staying has a swimming pool, a gym and all the accoutrements of a four-star business hotel anywhere in the world. It is a Saturday night: I have spent the morning exploring the working lives of women in the emerging industrial powerhouse that is Indonesia and the afternoon being treated like royalty by schoolchildren keen to rehearse their English with a native English speaker. Is this work, and, if so, what is it about it that qualifies it as 'work'?

Figure 1.1   Five siblings (Mary, Shan, Robert, Fifi, Julie, and with apologies to Adey who had wandered off)

In contrast, my sister Julie will have spent today much as she has spent every day for the past 15 years. She will have walked to our father's house in the village a mile from where we grew up, will have lit his fire, cooked his breakfast, done his shopping and cleaning, and gone back to her own home to cook the midday meal for her sons before continuing with the chores necessitated by caring for a frail elderly relative. Her day is full of what she describes as drudgery. Is what Julie does 'work', and, if so, what is this thing called 'work' that encompasses two such very different ways of employing one's time?

Here are two sisters carrying out very different forms of labour for which the rewards are hugely different: Julie receives in return for her labours minimum state benefits, while I receive the salary of a senior academic, which is extremely generous in contrast to my sister's income. My job allows me to travel; Julie has never been out of the UK and has not had a holiday for 15 years. My working life is adventurous, challenging, stimulating, rewarding, prestigious and (save for time spent in meetings) extremely interesting; my sister's, as we will see, is full of unremitting toil, care and responsibility and deprives her of 'a life'. In this chapter I am using this account of two sisters whose destinies have diverged so greatly to develop the thesis that, in the 21st century, labour and work are two very different, albeit conjoined, things: labour refers to the tasks that one does as part of one's job; work to the aspects of one's job through which the (working) self, that ongoing project through which one constructs the 'me', is constituted. This, of course, is only one of the forums in which the self is constructed, but my focus in this book is on working lives and workplace selves. I introduce in this chapter the thesis that the desire for *work* is a desire to construct the 'me' I wish to be. I will argue in Chapter Six that these future me's are killed, or murdered, by organizations.

My inspiration in this chapter is what was at the time of writing Judith Butler's most recent book, *Frames of War* (FW, 2009), and the related *Precarious Lives* (PL, 2004). *Frames of War* is Butler's response to the violence perpetrated on Moslem and other cultures by the US and its allies following the 9/11 atrocities in New York. In it, she calls for a revivified left politics based on a new ontology of the body. Her analysis focuses on how atrocities may be freely committed upon some people by others because those upon whom violence is visited are not recognised as living human beings. This requires Butler's development of a thesis of what is 'a life' and what is 'a human being', with the first being a condition for but not a guarantor of the latter. In other words, the very fact of being born into the species *Homo sapiens* does not necessarily allow the individual to become human. The questions to which she pursues answers are therefore:

- What are the conditions that facilitate the recognition of some people as human and others as less than human?
- What forms are taken by the violence enacted in and as a consequence of the process of exclusion from the categories of the human?

Butler's distinction between 'a life' and 'a human being' set me wondering if such a distinction could be usefully transposed to the workplace. Critical analyses of management and organizations that focus on management's desire to control every aspect of working lives (see Jermier and Knights [1994] for an overview, Thomas and Davies [2005] for an insightful discussion and other recent useful analyses in Fleming and Spicer [2003; 2008]) suggest the utility of such a distinction in that it offers ways of thinking through the effects on the person of being treated like some recalcitrant and particularly complicated piece of machinery. This leads to the distinction in this chapter between labour and work. My thesis is that it is 'a life' (or what I am calling a zombie-machine) that labours, but 'work' elevates that life to the status of the human; management[1] requires that we labour (as material objects that are alive but not human), but we, as living, breathing, emoting human subjects, desire to *work* and, through so doing, constitute a sense of self. Labour is carried out by zombie-machines who are denied access to the human; work encompasses activities over and above labour so that selves which are human are performatively constituted. In other words, paraphrasing Butler, my questions are:

• What are the organizational conditions that distinguish between the human and the less than human?
• What are the forms of that organizational violence which places labourers outside the categories of the human? and
• In what ways do we evade that violence and constitute ourselves as human while at work?

These questions will not be answered in this chapter alone but will be developed as the book progresses. The book's thesis is that organizational violence takes the form of the murder of the selves who might have been had they been nurtured through work rather than suffocated by labour.

Butler seeks to explore in *Frames of War* two problems, one epistemological and the other ontological. The epistemological problem concerns the issue of framing, or how we develop the politically saturated 'frames through which we apprehend or, indeed, fail to apprehend the lives of others as lost or injured (lose-able or injurable)' (2009:1). The ontological issue is: what is a life? Questions about how 'life' is defined and understood and what brings into visibility those who are regarded as alive, rendering others invisible, never having lived, arise, she argues, from operations of power. Her thesis concerns the wars that the American state and its allies have perpetrated since 9/11, but similar questions can be asked about organizations. I am thinking particularly of abuses in workplaces, some of which critical theorists are very much aware of (such as the pain experienced by many people following mergers and acquisitions 'justified' on the grounds of competitiveness [Ford and Harding, 2003]) and others that are so taken for granted they are regarded as 'normal' or as impediments to productivity (for example, the relentless tedium of many jobs [George and Jett, 2003]). What frames are used when organizing people at work, and how are the lives of working people defined and understood?

However, in turning the lens away from war and towards organizations, the ontological and epistemological questions I must pursue involve not only what is life but its very necessary other: what is 'death'? In arguing that death takes forms other than that of biological death, as I will do in Chapter Six, I would seem to be traducing Butler's intent, while at the same time predisposing my arguments towards an angry denunciation of workplaces. In doing this, am I not stealing a necessary spotlight away from where it matters, those injured and killed in wars, so as to shine it, again, on the privileged West?

My answer to the first charge is that I am borrowing the questions posed by Butler and asking them of my own field of interest because such an acute thinker as Butler facilitates our *reframing* our thoughts and asking questions which otherwise lie dormant, albeit waiting to be asked, at the very tips of our tongues. And indeed Butler provides a licence for the extension of her arguments to the field of work. She calls, in *Frames of War*, for a new bodily ontology that would imply 'the rethinking of precariousness, vulnerability, injurability, interdependency, exposure, bodily persistence, desire, *work* and the claims of language and social belonging' (FW:2, emphasis added). She thus calls specifically for a rethinking of work, providing a licence for the arguments in this book. We must rethink work: what would be a rethought bodily ontology of work in which the structure of bodies is 'socially ecstatic' (FW:33):

> We can think about demarcating the human body through identifying its boundary or in what form it is bound, but that is to miss the crucial fact that the body is, in certain ways and even inevitably, unbound—in its acting, its receptivity, in its speech, desire, and mobility. It is outside itself, in the world of others, in a space and time it does not control, and it not only exists in the vector of these relations, but as this very vector. In this sense, the body does not belong to itself. (FW:52–53)

The body is given over to others, cannot exist without others—and in workplaces another dimension is added to this ek-stacy, that of giving over one's body to labour for a certain time each day in exchange for a wage or salary. It is this condition of interdependency that is, in my reading, the most important aspect of *Frames of War*, for Butler's arguments in this book form a sustained and profound critique of individualism and the Western cult of the self. Her argument is that the self can exist only through its connectivity with others. She develops a thesis on modalities of violence, and in this book my intention is to use Butler's thesis on one modality of violence to think through another such modality, that is, the violence that organizations do in inhibiting the constitution of aspired-to selves. This may occur when recognition is refused or when the only recognition that is forthcoming is that of a denigrated identity; it may arise when possibilities for flourishing are so restricted that only stunted forms of the self can live; it may just be the casual destruction of dreams and aspirations.

That my 'empirical data' in this chapter come from the life story of one of my sisters is not self-indulgence nor guilt nor gloating at being the one who has escaped from the working-class poverty of our childhood. Rather, it is a recall of the feminist slogan of, as we might term it nowadays, the imbrications of the personal and the political: that two sisters who are in many ways similar could live such different lives and have such divergent experience of their selves as a result of the occupations they follow reveals much about the labour/work split, as the chapter will show. I am the oldest of the seven siblings, Julie the middle child (there are almost four years, as well as a brother and a sister, between us). We are about the same height, weight and shape, and our hair colouring is similar, although Julie was the pretty one of the family, while I was the brainy one, with Mary not far behind. We had similar childhoods: ate the same food, wore similar clothes, shared a bed with a third sister, Mary, quarrelled over toys, went to the same village school until we were 11, and grew up with a love of reading and writing (Julie nearly published children's books when she was younger). We each suffered from crippling shyness as children and young adults, had our first children in our late teens and settled into relationships at what seems, in hindsight, like a precocious age. We are both now divorced (and very proud) grandmothers, and each of us lives days bursting with activity. So, to tease out a thesis of what 'work' is, this chapter draws on two hard-working women whose life trajectories would seem to have been destined to run in parallel but whose positions are now fundamentally different. I will first summarise Julie's story of her life, told to me using the interview format followed when gathering the other working—life stories found in this book, interposing some aspects of my own life as I do so. That will provide the focus for the introduction of Butler's thesis of what it is that defines the human at and through work.

TWO SISTERS

In contrast to my own memories of a tough childhood, Julie's are of a happy time when

> *'we didn't have much but there was always things going on'* . . . *I knew [emphasis on 'knew'] we didn't have the money other people had, we didn't have all the clothes and that, but when I look back I remember the nice things like going to chapel in our new dresses, all looking the same.*[2]

The little mining village in which we grew up, surrounded by farms, was an idyllic place for this animal lover, and she spent as much time as possible riding a friend's horses and smuggling a menagerie of pets into the bedroom we five sisters shared. (Because of these activities, I always saw her as confident and outgoing: not until I used a formal interview format for our talk did I find out that we had shared a crippling shyness.) She left school at the first opportunity when she was 15, after having opted out of education at 13 because of that overwhelming shyness, which made her feel as if she didn't and couldn't fit in. Julie's first job was 100 miles away from home, working at a zoo, but she left after six or nine months because she couldn't stand the cruelty of keeping animals in cages. Her next job was at a kennel about 40 miles from home, but she was expected to spend the nights alone in a remote mansion, so one night she left, walked miles to the nearest bus stop and, having missed the last bus home, waited until daylight in the women's toilets at the bus station. Her next job was in a local dry cleaners where she ironed clothes all day. She remembers hating the work but loving the camaraderie of her colleagues. She worked there for two and a half years and left to have the first of her four sons, just before her 19th birthday. Apart from some part-time work as a barmaid she has not been in paid employment since. At the time of our discussion she was 52, living on an £85-a-week[3] carer's allowance paid by the State.

I, meanwhile, left school at 16 with a clutch of G.C.E certificates, and went to work in London as a trainee typist. I returned to Wales nine months later and worked on the lines in a factory, making condensers for the insides of radios, experiencing at first hand what I was to learn much later were Taylorist principles of production. I married at 18, had my two sons within 15 months of the marriage, worked part time in the factory for a while, was registered as unemployed for a short period, got onto a government-run course to learn shorthand and refresh my typing skills, and then worked as a secretary for two years, studying 'A' level G.C.E's at evening class, until, at 27, I went to university. It is at this point that our lives diverged, so that my income is now ten times that of my sister, and the other rewards of my job (despite its many frustrations [Willmott, 1995; Harding, Ford and Gough, 2010; Fotaki, 2011; Clarke, Knights and Jarvis, 2012]) are inestimable. I need not describe the life of an academic, familiar to most readers. What follows is an account of the life of a carer.

Julie's first experience of caring was for our widowed aunt, Ethel, who shared her house with Julie and her four sons after Julie's marriage broke down. As Auntie Eth grew older and more frail, Julie, who was then in her late 30s,

> *had to bathe her . . . and then when she had cancer was down [the specialist hospital] everyday and then it was the worry then, cos I mean not only is she going to die but it was was I doing everything right for her, so er [pause] you know it was, it's hard because you've got that focus, that's your focus, even though you've got the boys, you've got to focus*

on make sure she's alright, as you know she was back and fore hospital, she'd broke her hip and um and then she was in [the specialist hospital] and it was always, got to do this, got to do that, so you forget about yourself. . . . I worry so much if I had a chance of a night out I'd worry about leaving her.

But eventually Auntie Eth became very confused and needed to go into a home, where she was happy, but, Julie said,

I always feel guilty about it, and I will say I will go to my grave guilty.

A few years later our mother's health deteriorated. Julie, now in her mid-40s, took on more and more responsibility for her care.

I started coming up quite a few times a week, and then when she was really ill I was up every day then, and sometimes twice, twice a day from Aberbargoed [two miles away, up a very steep hill], walking up, cos they would phone me, I'd come up, do what I had to do, go home, and then they'd phone me that they didn't have no milk, . . . so I'd have to come all the way back up, so through all winds and weathers, every day then.
N: That was walking?
J: That was walking, yeah.

Our mother died four years before this interview, when our father was 84, after which Julie became his carer. I asked her to describe a typical week:

A typical week apart from being boring, it's, it's just [coughs] it's coming over, doing his tablets, every morning and every evening, do his lunch and cook his dinner, do his shopping for him, get his prescriptions, go up [to the local town, five miles away] get his prescriptions, um. . . . .
N: That's on the bus?
J: Yeah, on the bus there and back, and that's twice in a week that is, because the prescription ends so I go up and get it. Um, do his shopping, keep him company, listen to him whinging, so that's a typical week, and it's always like, it's never ending, it's Christmas Day it doesn't matter. It's 24 hours he's on your mind and if he's ill and if he's at the hospital you're back and fore there, the same as it was with Mam, it was always back and fore the hospital, and the same now if like oh, everybody's going out but I can't go out cos I've got to do this for Dad, and er that's a typical, a typical week that is. Every day, seven days a week, yeah, and it's boring inasmuch as you are tied, it's tied down, you've got to be there, you've got to do this, to make sure he's alright, and that's that's my typical time.

Caring combined with money worries from living on such a small income takes over her emotions and controls her mind:

> *If the money was better it could be fair enough, but the money is poor . . . you're full of worry all the time, and believe me it is when you've no money and that you're worrying from one day to the next, you just can't get in that frame of mind to [return to the writing for which she showed an early talent]. . . . You just haven't got that bit of, it's not get up and go, it's the frame of mind, you've got to be in that frame of mind to write and when you've got constant worries you just can't get into that frame of mind.*
>
> *It's not just physically hard, it's mentally challenging, it does get on top of you, and like I say when you see the other sisters and they have their hair nice and have nice clothes and you're in hand-me-downs, it is hard.*

This is not a study of 'informal' carers but a comparison of two contrasting working lives that aims to use the differences to tease out answers to the question of what is work in an epoch when the self is a project that is worked on for consumption by the self and others. I will develop the thesis in this chapter, through interweaving Julie's story through Butler's analysis of what it is to be human, that labour and work should be distinguished from each other: labour involves the tasks that are done as a means of sustaining life or fulfilling the conditions of one's job and is carried out by the nonhuman (the zombie-machine). Work encompasses workplace possibilities, over and above labouring, of constituting selves recognised as human.

Having introduced the sharp differences between two sisters whose working lives have taken very different paths, I now turn to a question that needs clarification if my arguments, and the borrowings from Butler, are to make sense: what do we mean by 'the human'?

WHAT IS 'THE HUMAN'?

At first sight this would appear to be a ridiculous question, but it is one that haunts popular culture and therefore circulates throughout the wider culture. Zombie films, for example, revolve around the suggestion that the body of a human being, although it may be capable of motion, may not be human: there is something missing, some spark of life which animates the body so as to define it as human, and without this spark the body is horrendous. Zombies, Webb and Byrnand (2008) write, are 'disturbingly like us'; not an actuality but a trope, they tell us something of the ontology of the subject, and the something they tell is that there is a 'zombie' in each of us. They are not radically Other but remind us of the inaccessible aspects of the self that are beyond laws of language, culture and society. Their 'remarkable similarity' to 'us', that is, the human, means they can be used in helping our understanding of '*embodied* knowledge, *embodied* cognition, *embodied* identity' (ibid.:95) and so turn us towards an aesthetics of ourselves as human. They tell us of the 'unendurable, unending story of otherness . . . and bring our attention to the limit and the boundary of life and meaning in part because they themselves have escaped this Other' (96). They tell us of the fragility of the boundary between the human and the nonhuman and so return us to Butler's thesis and that of the distinction between the human and the nonhuman, between labour and work.

Science fiction is replete with explorations of the precarious status of the human. Its popularity suggests that at some level it is articulating for us an otherwise unvoiceable question: what is it that marks us out as 'human' (Parker, 2011)? In the highly popular *Star Wars* films and in the cult classic *Star Trek* television series, it is often visual appearance, together with being born on Earth, that distinguishes the human from the nonhuman. Other science fiction films and television series play upon a fear that merely looking the way a human should look is insufficient to qualify one as human, for looks (and other attributes) can be deceiving. Because there is something that looks like a human, talks, feels, thinks and emotes like a human, does that mean it is human? What if it has been manufactured and should therefore be classified as a robot or a cyborg? This is the premise explored in the classic sci-fi story by Philip K. Dick (2007/1962), *Do Androids Dream of Electric Sheep?* and the film of that story, *Blade Runner*, where Harrison Ford's character is responsible for eradicating replicants that are indistinguishable from human beings and which do not know they are not human, for they have (implanted) memories, are intelligent and experience emotions. The horror at the heart of *Blade Runner* is in Ford's slow realisation that his memories may have been implanted—or were they? How can he know if he is cyborg or human? The most successful science fiction series of the first decade of the 21st century, *Battlestar Galactica*, similarly explores the diffuse and inarticulable dividing line between the 'machine' and the human. In zombie movies and science fiction films and programmes, the nonhuman has to be eradicated, even though it is the nonhuman, as its Other, that defines the human. Our cultural unconscious (Jameson, 1991) seems to want to defeat that very thing against which we might define ourselves as human.

The issue of what it is to be human therefore circulates in and through popular culture and also, of course, in academic theory, most influentially perhaps in Donna Haraway's 'A Manifesto for Cyborgs' (1985), in which Haraway describes a globalised world that resembles more and more an integrated circuit, where individuals can be read off and understood as technological (Parker, 1998), so the human/machine distinction breaks down. She argues for a celebration of the cyborg: it shatters the old binary dualisms that gave the illusion of autonomy of the self but delivered domination. Indeed, while at work, we interact with people and artefacts and so become 'cyborg—a temporary assemblage of person and things' (Parker and Cooper, 1998), and the boundary between the metal of the machine and the flesh of the body is overcome (Parker, 1998:511). As I tap the keyboard, writing these words, and see the contents of my thoughts appearing on the screen, where is the line that distinguishes 'me' from the technology I am using? I have a strong sense of myself as human, but is it not in capitalism's interests that that part of me that is human recedes in favour of the zombie-machine that churns out products and services?

In other words, the question of what it is to be human, although seemingly outrageous, circulates throughout culture and, we will see, is echoed in Julie's account. In the Introduction I argued for a sociocultural philosophy of organization studies in which the theories that 'lay philosophers' hold about their lives should be interrogated in much the same way that we interrogate the works of 'great philosophers'. This approach is supported both by Sedgwick's (2003:145) suggestion that there may be far less 'ontological distinction between academic theory and everyday theory' and by a comparison between Butler's and Julie's theses of what is 'life' and 'the human'. Although Butler's is couched in far more complex language, the ideas are very similar.

Julie's Theory about What It Is to Be Human

Julie's answer to my question of what she would do when her caring responsibilities come to an end was given without hesitation:

> *Somebody said to me weeks and weeks back what will you do when your Dad's eyes close? And I looked at them and said 'get a life', and that's the first thing that came to my mind. Without even thinking about it, get a life, that's what I'm going to do.*

She uses that familiar phrase, sometimes used as an insult: 'get a life'. She does not have to think about it; her response speaks for her before she can think: she will 'get a life'. 'Life', it seems, is somewhere out there, something that has to be 'got', something she does not have at the moment. To be alive is therefore commonly distinguished from having a life. Julie's account is reminiscent of zombie films—what are portrayed in films such as *The Cat and the Canary* (1939), *Night of the Living Dead* (1968)[4] and *Shaun of the Dead* (2004) are living beings who do not have lives but go through their days doing the tasks required of them by their controllers. These mindless creatures labour but cannot think or emote or have relationships, pleasure or fun. This is how Julie describes her existence—she does not have 'a life', and thus she has few of those rights which attach to being human.

Butler's Theory about What It Is to Be Human

Butler poses her question starkly: what is it that defines the human? She argues (FW:76) that the human is a 'differential norm' in that what is human is defined by what it is not at the same time as it governs what should be 'human'. The human can be thought of as

> a value and a morphology that may be allocated and retracted, aggrandized, personified, degraded and disavowed, elevated and affirmed. The norm continues to produce the nearly impossible paradox of a human who is no human, or of the human who effaces the human as it is otherwise known. (FW:76)

For there to be a 'human who is no human', there have to be living beings who cannot or do not fulfil the norms that would allow them to be classified as human. In Butler's words (FW:95), 'There are instances where human life— a human animality—exceeds and resists the norm of the human'. This leads to the further question of what is meant by 'a life', and again the definition rests upon both norms and the existence of an opposite: that which is a life is known through its difference from that which is not-life. Butler states:

> The epistemological capacity to apprehend a life is partially dependent on that life being produced according to norms that qualify it as a life or, indeed, as part of life. (FW:3)

Life is therefore something that is recognised by other living beings as fulfilling the criteria for 'being alive'. An immediate response might be (to Julie as well as to Butler): but surely every living creature is/has a life! Isn't it easy to distinguish between a pebble, which is inanimate, and a human being, which is animate and to all intents and purposes is alive/has life? I have to admit that this was the naïve question I asked when I first read Butler's statements about the less-than-human. Then Foucault's remarkable Preface to *The Order of Things* (1966) came to mind: this shows the arbitrariness of all classification systems. His laughter at a passage in a story by Borges, Foucault writes, shattered 'all the familiar landmarks of my thought' (xvi). This passage contains a quotation from a Chinese encyclopaedia:

> animals are divided into: (a) belonging to the Emperor, (b) embalmed, (c) tame, (d) sucking pigs, (e) sirens, (f) fabulous, (g) stray dogs, (h) included in the present classification, (i) frenzied, (j) innumerable, (k) drawn with a very fine camelhair brush, (l) *et cetera*, (m) having just broken the water pitcher, (n) that from a long way off look like flies.

The strangeness of the categories in this list caused Foucault to ponder how systems of categorisation work so as to make it possible for us to 'name, speak, and think' (xxi). Clearly, Butler is pointing out how difficult it can be to identify categories that pertain within one's own culture. It follows that it is possible to be categorised as a human *animal*, something that would be radically different from a human *being*. Butler distinguishes between life, the animal organ upon which the human is inscribed, and the human, so it is possible to, indeed we must recognise that we do, exist as both at one and the same time: the vulnerable flesh of the animal can be excised from the mind but not separated from the actuality of the human being. However, the human animal/life that is not yet human or whose humanness is denied, in Butler's thesis, can be regarded as somewhat akin to pebbles—inanimate, anonymous objects that we may walk over and use as we may. Should they be destroyed, we cannot grieve for them because we do not know even that they have lived.

Importantly, for Butler, judgements are made about who is and who is not human:

> The epistemological capacity to apprehend a life is partially dependent on that life being produced according to norms that qualify it as a life or, indeed, as part of life. (FW:3)

In *Frames of War*, the judge that apprehends a life is the privileged West, with its riches, its weapons of war, its power and its desire to control the world. In other words, life is defined by those with the power to define it. In organizations, we will see as the arguments in this book progress, that although it may be management's desire that staff be less than human, staff themselves disagree and find ways of circumventing that desire.

This leads to the question of how one becomes human/not-human, a living being that has or does not have a life.

HOW DOES ONE BECOME 'HUMAN'?

Julie and Butler again have similar ideas, albeit couched in very different language. Both refer to the face and the importance of recognition.

Julie said that to have a life:

> *I'd have to get a job but it would be nice to go and do something, have money, have my hair cut and buy some nice clothes, and just do what I want to do. If I want to go out for the day, get on the bus and go somewhere I could do it. Just simple things like that.*

A job is something to be deeply desired because it would give her not only 'a life' but the life she dreams of having. To have a life means having paid employment that provides the money to work on one's appearance (have my hair cut and buy some nice clothes) and to have the freedom and resources to do 'simple things'. In Butler's terms, these are not simple things at all, for they all involve *being made visible* (working on one's appearance, travelling in the public domain) for

> the norms that would allocate who is and is not human arrive in visual form. These norms work to *give face* and to *efface*. Accordingly, our

capacity to respond with outrage, opposition, and critique will depend in part on how the differential norm of the human is communicated through visual and discursive frames. (FW:77)

Butler, grounded in Hegelian philosophy, argues that one becomes human through acts of recognition, as articulated through the master/slave dialectic (see Chapter Two for explication and a discussion). She distinguishes between 'apprehend' and 'recognise'. Recognition, with its connotations of an act, practice or scene between subjects, is, Butler points out, the stronger term, but the master and slave did not appear from nowhere—they were already constituted as master and slave before their encounter. It is necessary therefore to examine the stage that facilitates this first encounter: what are the conditions of possibility which instigate the scene in which recognition takes place? In Butler's words, 'We do not simply have recourse to single and discrete norms of recognition, but to more general conditions, historically articulated and enforced, of "recognisability"' (FW:5). There are 'categories, conventions and norms' which induce a subject, make it ready for recognition and therefore capable of being recognised as more than a life, as human. Apprehension, on the other hand, falls short of recognisability and thus of recognition; it is a way of knowing that does not institute a subject, so that 'something is not recognized by recognition' (FW:5). This 'something', this 'figure of the non-human' (FW:64), cannot be recognised because it falls outside the field of what is perceived as reality. We must therefore

understand the differential of power at work that distinguishes between those subjects who will be eligible for recognition and those who will not. In other words, what is the norm according to which the subject is produced who then becomes the presumptive 'ground' of normative debate? (FW:138)

In Butler's thesis, those who are invisible, who do not enter the scene of recognition, can be trampled on, disposed of, destroyed at will, with no one speaking on their behalf because no one (with power) is aware of their existence, and thus they cannot be recognised as human. They are apprehended, that is, it is known that they exist, but without recognition they are not categorised as human and so are not accorded rights to be represented and defended. My sister says something similar: her current labours, as a carer, render her invisible. Trudging the roads of the village each day, she is *apprehended* (one of the many millions of carers in the UK), but she is invisible and not marked out as human (a living, breathing, emoting being) and thus the category 'carer' is overdetermining. The strong theme about freedom in Julie's narrative emphasises the need to be able to go out in the world. In remembering the jobs she held in her teens, she constitutes a human self: as an animal lover with high ethical standards (she left the zoo because of its cruelty in caging animals); presenting a strong articulation of how staff should be treated (not left alone miles from anywhere at dead of night); and enjoying the pleasures of companionship (while ironing clothes). In thinking about what paid work would allow her to do, she has a dream of that earlier freedom: she could 'go out for the day . . . and go somewhere'. She knows that if she can buy clothes, have her hair done and travel out into the world, she will be made visible and thus recognisable. That is, she could go out in the world where, having worked on herself (new haircut and clothes), she would be recognizable as human.

My sister's life is similar in many ways to those of the housewives of the East London working-class community studied by Michael Young and Peter Willmott in 1957 (Young and Willmott, 1969). Her days revolve around the family and the related tasks of caring and housework. Travel remains a distant prospect, and shopping for anything other than day-to-day necessities is a rare luxury. The satisfaction in being a housewife at the centre of a family and kinship circle 50 years ago was in the doing of the activities pertaining to that position. Times have changed: identity has shifted from *doing* to *being*, and doing as an end in itself has switched to doing as the means by which being may be facilitated (Butler, 1990; 1993). Julie, unlike her predecessors, is constantly bombarded with injunctions of how to work on the self: the television in the corner of her living room, the magazines she leafs through at the doctor's surgery, the conversations with sisters who are able to participate in the project of the self—these all bring with them instantiations of the norms of the human in a culture of consumption. That Julie cannot participate renders her a failure in her own eyes: she is not working on the self. Julie's own theory is thus that work will allow her to work on herself so that she can make herself visible and thus *recognisable*. Her desire for *work* is therefore a desire for recognition, because through work one attains 'a life' or, in Butler's terminology, becomes human. It is a dream of the self I wish to construct, the me I want to be.

The very paragraph with which I opened this chapter shows that I, on the other hand, am engaged actively in this project of the self. Not only did I show that I travel to seemingly exotic locations, I could also look at myself in that location, comment to myself on my being there and project myself forward (Fuery and Wagner, 2003) to the accounts I would tell family and friends of my being there—Nancy Harding, world traveller, and therefore a self in process. I have the photographs to prove it.

DISCUSSION: DISTINGUISHING BETWEEN LABOUR AND WORK

The argument so far is this: I have taken two sisters whose lives have deviated in ways that could not have been foreseen in our childhoods. Each of us works long hours, but only one of us in a job that enables working on, constructing, the self as human and fully alive (although the managerialisation of higher education threatens this [Prichard and Willmott, 1997;

Chandler, Barry and Clark, 2002]). The sister whose labours do not facilitate such work on the self classifies herself as outside life. In Butler's terms, she is outside the human. She labours but does not work, so cannot even get to the scene where the master and slave encounter each other to receive, or not receive in the master's case, recognition. She cannot therefore enter the frame of visibility, and so she cannot enter the category of the human, for to be human is to work actively on the self so that the self becomes visible.

When I have discussed this thesis with friends and colleagues, they have pointed out examples of friends and family who choose not to work; how can I, they ask, say that such people are removing themselves from the human? This is to misread my thesis, or, rather, I have not articulated it sufficiently clearly, for someone who chooses not to work will have other fora and other activities in which they prefer to spend their time, and in which they will be able to work on, and thus constitute, a self, because in those places they are visible, have a face. Indeed, the majority of the population will have spaces and places separate and apart from their labouring and working lives in which they are able to work on the self.

What I am focusing upon here is the position in which many of us find ourselves: we have little choice about whether or not we should be in paid employment, and much of our time is therefore taken up in labouring, but our labours do not allow us to participate in the construction of anything other than an abject self. This clarifies the distinction I am drawing between labour and work, where 'work' involves the possibility of working on the self as part of the process of being engaged in a job. My sister is therefore akin to a Weberian 'ideal-type'; she labours but cannot work on the self. By focusing on someone whose labour does not allow work on the self, I can make a clear distinction between labour and work, between a life and being alive. The body while labouring becomes that of the zombie-machine: alive but without life, outwith the human. *The body that labours* is little more than a machine for doing work, and as machine it is without recognition. *The body that works* is involved in working on itself, constituting identity or selfhood. Julie exists as the former, labouring body (as zombie-machine) and dreams of a job that will allow her to do more than labour: to work on the self or selves she aspires to be.

I move on now to exploring how recognition requires a face and how labour renders labourers faceless. That is, I will pick up Julie's discussion about how work would give her the chance to change her appearance and Butler's development of Emmanuel Levinas's thesis on 'the face' in *Frames of War*.

BUTLER AND JULIE ON THE FACE

I have put a photograph of my siblings at the top of this chapter so as to make them visible—to give them faces by which they become recognisable.

In this section I will take forward the distinction between labour (where one is a zombie-machine who carries out the tasks required) and work (where, over and above the tasks one does, one can constitute a self that is human) through arguing that one is rendered invisible (faceless) as a labourer and thus emphasising the importance of 'the face' to the becoming human afforded by work.

I am made visible to many people through my School's web pages, where there is a photograph of me, looking for all the world like my father in drag, plus a summary of my career and a list of my responsibilities and accomplishments. There are similar pages for my academic colleagues, most of which have a photograph attached. However, colleagues with whom I work closely and who are vital to the efficient running of the School, colleagues whose job title is 'administrator', are listed with no more than a name, a phone number and an e-mail address: they appear interchangeable. Other staff at the School—the cleaners, porters, maintenance staff and others without whom things would grind to a halt—have neither photos nor names on the site. They are invisible to us except when we bump into them during the daily round (and often they work outside normal office hours, so we may rarely see them). My School is not unusual—I have looked through a variety of websites, and this, it would appear, is the norm. Even Schools that are proud of their radical traditions feature only the images of academic and senior managerial staff. Academia is not alone in this: there are photos of senior staff on many company websites, but everyone else remains faceless. This is in huge contrast to the social networking sites now springing up, such as Facebook, where people are encouraged to upload photos of themselves, making themselves visible to friends and family. Butler shows that it is necessary to be recognised, that is, to have a 'face' that can be recognised, so as to participate in the social world in which work on the self is undertaken. My sister argues something very similar. The argument I will develop here is that to labour is to be rendered invisible, to be denied a face and thus recognition. To work (on oneself while at work) renders one visible, that is, as having a face that is discernibly human.

In Butler/Levinas's view, the face may not be an actual face but a projection of one; it can both humanise and dehumanise: some faces are recognised as human and worthy of care, while others are demonised and deemed best destroyed. To recognise and be recognised is to give and receive acknowledgement that one is human; failure to do so renders one abject. The reference to recognition is an allusion to Hegel's master/slave dialectic, a mythical scene that establishes the importance of intersubjective recognition for subjectivity, which is a major influence on Butler's work and thus also the arguments developed in this book. She notes in *Frames of War* that for Hegel's master-slave encounter to take place a stage must already have been set: there must already have been people allocated the names of 'master' and 'slave', with the positions from which they can speak already clarified. This encounter is foundational to much Western thinking about how selves come into being, that is, they emerge not fully formed from the womb, as it were, but are ongoing accomplishments constituted in interactions with others (see Chapter Three for a fuller discussion). It seems to me that Butler's work is developing an intense account of what went on in that seminal encounter, through which she weaves her evolving reading of Althusser's myth of being hailed. The latest evolution in this account is the insights she draws from Levinas's thesis on the face.[5]

Her articulation of the master-slave encounter in Chapter Five of *Precarious Lives* is of the demand for recognition as an ethical scene focusing on the responsibility each has to all others. That is

> The structure of address is important for understanding how moral authority is introduced and sustained if we accept not just that we address others when we speak, but that in some way we come to exist, as it were, in the moment of being addressed, and something about our existence proves precarious when that address fails. More emphatically, however, what binds us morally has to do with how we are addressed by others in ways that we cannot avert or avoid; this impingement by the other's address constitutes us first and foremost against our will or, perhaps put more appropriately, prior to the formation of our will. So if we think that moral authority is about finding one's will and standing by it, stamping one's name upon one's will, it may be that we miss the very mode by which moral demands are relayed. That is, we miss the situation of being addressed, the demand that comes from elsewhere, sometimes a nameless elsewhere, by which our obligations are articulated and pressed upon us. (PL, 2004:130)

We must therefore, she goes on, think seriously about modes of address and moral authority. By the very fact of being in the world, one has a responsibility to all others who, even if we do not hear or see them, address us and allow us our selfhood. Levinas's value for Butler is linked to this development of responsibility in the scene of recognition. He first provides a way of thinking 'about the relationship between representation and humanization', the aspect I draw on in this book, and, second, offers Butler an ethics of Jewish nonviolence that she uses to develop her new political theory. Levinas (in my interpretation of Butler's interpretation) argues that slaughter of the masses becomes possible when they are *faceless*, that is, anonymised beings without identity and for whom, therefore, neither compulsion to care nor responsibility for their flourishing is forthcoming. That is, in seeing people's faces we accord them recognition that they are human, and after recognition is given different imperatives arise in regard to what can be done with and to them. When we do not see people's faces, when they are anonymous crowds, they are like pebbles on the beach: we can trample all over them because they have no humanity. I am arguing that the labourer is faceless, that is, management feels free to use labourers to churn out products and services as if they were machines because their faces are not seen and they are therefore not accorded recognition as being human.

Julie's theory of the face expounds this notion from the perspective of someone who has no recognizable face. Her understanding of herself includes a theory of being rendered faceless, and this self-understanding arises, I suggest, from her current position of being a labourer who cannot work on the self. Her desire to earn sufficient money to work on her appearance becomes a desire to have a face, for being faceless, having no face, places one outside the human. Working on the self, constituting an identity, involves making oneself visible to those who can grant recognition. This is Julie's theory of the difference between two sisters, one who has a public face and one who doesn't. I did not ask her a specific question on this but made a narcissistic statement that stimulated her theory of why our lives are different:

> N: *I'm fascinated by how my life has taken such a different trajectory, and we are so similar. I was painfully, cripplingly shy as a child in school. And we had such a similar childhood, and are so similar, but we've had such different experiences.*
>
> J: *But I think, like Dad used to say, you were always determined. If you were going somewhere when they were going out, you knew where you were going and you were ahead and you were gone. With me, I would be around the back. I knew the back. Where you had determination I was the day-dreamer dragging behind. So that's the big big difference. Having it in your mind and doing it, rather than just dreaming about it, like I was a dreamer and you were the doer, and that's what it was, cos I was always hiding behind mam's skirts, but you were in front all the time, I'd see that, and I'd say well I'd come but I'll stay by here behind. So I think that's the difference between us.*

I suggest that this is not a memory of an event but a theory of the present, one in which a light is retroactively shone upon what may be an imagined past so as to understand what is understood as the present. As Lacan observes, there is no present, only a remembering of the past and a projection into the future:

> What is realized in my history is not the past definite of what was, since it is no more, or even the present perfect of what has been in what I am, but the future anterior of what I shall have been for what I am in the process of becoming. (Lacan, 1977:86; 2002:300)

Julie presents a complex theory in which a present-day sense of self is projected into a past self and that self is then projected forward into the future. She draws a sharp divide between the mind and the (active) body: there are things in the mind (dreams) that can be achieved through the actions of the body (doing it). The person who does is 'ahead' and 'gone'. This person is at the front and is visible to anyone she meets. The dreamer, on the other hand, 'drags[s] behind' and 'stays here behind', hiding behind her mother's skirts where she cannot be seen. Julie's theory is that from a very young age one sister had effaced herself (literally, here, denied herself the possibility of having a face), while the other had strode out and shown her face to the world. Her own early experiences belie the foundations of this theory: she'd gone to work in a zoo, hundreds of miles from home, when she was 15! The statement 'I'd say well I'd come but I'll stay by here⁶ behind' is not quite rational, suggesting some complex ideas at work. 'I would come but I will stay by here behind'. Are there two 'I's' here, one who would stride out but another (who eventually overrides the first) who remains invisible, so the 'difference between us' refers not to the two sisters but the two I's? If so, then one 'I' desires to stride out, to have agency, while the other has no face and thus no agency. In other words, Julie's thesis is one where the person who has a face has agency—to be able to act in the world (in Butler's terms, to be human) requires having a face. This thesis is remarkably close to Butler's, save that Butler explores how it is that a person can be denied a face by others, whereas Julie locates the responsibility in her own person. Crucially, Julie also shows the desire of the effaced person to have a face, to be 'by there in front'. Butler's work has throughout shown that the demonstration of such negative feelings about the self arise from discourses that inform selves which cannot live up to cultural norms and therefore have a denigrated status. So, Julie's thesis allows us to see what otherwise remains hidden: the face that is rendered invisible, the suffering that follows, and thus the impact of being rendered faceless. Julie labours but does not work: as labourer she has no face, and therefore she cannot be recognised—and so she cannot enter into that agonistic encounter between master and slave that gives identity.

Julie's account is a theory of the distinction between labour and work. This is: Julie labours, so has little opportunity to work on the self; she is therefore hidden, out of sight and faceless. Her sister who is in a professional career that allows opportunities to work (on the self) faces outwards, where she is recognisable to the world, which grants her recognition. In other words, work constitutes recognition (literally, one has a face to which a name can be put); labour negates the face, and one has no chance of recognition and therefore no identity.

However, Julie blames herself for her invisibility and her abject position, whereas Butler argues that some faces are facilitated in their visibility, while others are denied that opportunity. Butler calls the process by which this happens 'framing'. This allows further interpretation of the labourer as having no face and therefore being denied identity and the status of the human.

FRAMING

It is in *Frames of War*, and specifically in its concluding chapter, that Butler develops the claim of the need for the 'face' so that its claims can be heard and an ethical response given. This replicates Julie's thesis—without a face, there is no recognition, no possibility of being a subject to whom an ethical response is due.

Butler writes that the response to any claim 'has everything to do with how the claim is formed and framed, but also with the disposition of the senses, or the conditions of receptivity itself' (165), for the respondent is 'crafted forcibly by norms that often do a certain kind of violence as well' (ibid.). So the conditions of receptivity to being called into being as a subject (here she alludes to Althusser's thesis on interpellation) mean that the subject who is called 'is in the process of avowing its own social ontology'. In Julie's terms, the subject who is forced to hide her face has no such ontology; can she exist therefore as a social subject? Butler emphasises the interdependence of each with all others and the struggle for an individuality that is inevitably socially achieved, for I cannot be an 'I' without others to affirm me in my difference from them. In Butler's words, the

> singular 'one' arises through social determination, while the social is based on the presumption of 'singularization'—'who we "are" involves an invariable and reiterated struggle of dependency and separation. . . . That is the dehiscence at the basis of the "we", the condition under which we are passionately bound together: ragefully, desirously, murderously, lovingly'. (FW:183)

This leads to a non-moralised ethical responsibility to safeguard the life of the other by protecting that other from one's own potential for destruction. It is the self's desire to destroy the other, an other upon whom one is dependent if one is to be a self, that brings with it the responsibility to protect that other. Always there is this ambivalence, this desire to be unique, alone, an individual, that rests within a need to be part of the social. And so if 'the claim of the other upon me is to reach me, it must be mediated in some way, which means that our very capacity to respond with non-violence . . . depends upon the frames by which the world is given and by which the domain of appearance is circumscribed' (FW:180).

In other words, our capacity to respond with care depends upon the means by which we are encouraged and allowed to 'see' the world and our fellow human subjects. We do not enter the stage of recognition without power already having worked on us, telling us not only who we are but also who are our others, and power will have crafted the ways in which we identify others, as enemies or friends, as subjects or objects, as human or nonhuman. Faces may be the primary aspect in identification, but we may not look at faces innocently, untouched by power: our looking at faces, including our own, may be skewed by the power that shapes the prism of the lens through which we look. When Julie looks in the mirror, she sees an abject self that has not had an opportunity to work on its self, hence her desire for a haircut, new clothes, and so on. That is, she sees a *representation* of an image rather than the face of a human subject. What we see is influenced by 'framing'. In Chapter Two we will see how the manager 'frames' staff so that s/he sees them as zombie-machines who desire no existence except that of the worker. There is no human behind that representation. Butler argues that we need to be able to see beyond the representations of others to the human that lies behind the representations. For this purpose, she continues, 'we do not need to know in advance what "a life" will be, but only to find and support those modes of representation and appearance that allow the claim of life to be made and heard (in this way, media and survival are linked)' (FW:181). Ethics follow from 'being addressed and addressable in sustainable ways', which requires that there be a 'you' who can be heard and seen. This means we must interrogate the conditions by which persons can be seen and heard, or in Butler's terms how they come or fail to come to be framed. We can see that Julie, as labourer, can be neither seen nor heard, because she is representable only as an abject labourer, isolated from the work that would give her identity. In Chapter Three we will see that Shakeel, a manual worker, is regarded by management only as a pair of hands to be ordered to do specific jobs: he has been 'framed' in such a way that any other identity has been denied him. Importantly, we will see how he evades this imposition of the requirement that he labour but not work.

Framing, for Butler, is an epistemological problem, concerned with how we develop the politically saturated 'frames through which we apprehend or, indeed, fail to apprehend the lives of others as lost or injured (lose-able or injurable' (FW:1). This involves a consideration of ways in which suffering is presented to us and how our response is predicated upon the presentation (FW:63), for the form of presentation will define some as human and some as unnameable or non-regardable as human—as a figure of the nonhuman that 'negatively determines and potentially unsettles the recognizably human' (64). The 'frames' that work to differentiate the lives we can apprehend from those we cannot (or that produce lives across a continuum of life) not only organize visual experience but also generate specific ontologies of the subject.

When discussing the Abu Ghraib and Guantanamo Bay photographs which shocked the world in their portrayal of US soldiers raping, torturing and abusing prisoners of war, Butler defines a frame as 'active, as both jettisoning [that which the viewer should not see] and presenting [what it is wished that the viewer should see], and as doing both at once, in silence, without any visible sign of its operation. What emerges under these conditions is a viewer who assumes him- or herself to be in an immediate (and incontestable) visual relation to reality' (FW:73). This operation of the frame is 'not normally representable', that is, we do not know how the framing itself is carried out—who is the photographer, and what rules was that photographer following? What did s/he wish to show? How did the photographer choose what to include and what to exclude? There is thus a 'nonthematized background' within an unmarked, delimited field.

The framing of the frame generally remains out of sight. However, what is shown is governed by norms, and at the same time it enacts norms (FW:75), for photographs structure how they may be interpreted: they omit some things, include others, limiting at the same time as expanding our field of vision. Viewers are encouraged to believe they are seeing an unmediated reality. It becomes necessary therefore to consider the forms of power 'embedded' in the frame (FW:72).

Thus the decision (or nondecision) about whose photos should be exhibited on departmental and organizational websites is an act of framing that has political consequences. The head-and-shoulder photographs of academics suggest a transcendence of the body, in de Beauvoir's (1953/2007) terms, so all that is made visible is the head—the seat of the brain and, in Western thought, of the mind. The only work that is done here, the photographs say, is that of the mind. In a distinction that reverberates in our interpretations of ancient Greece and Rome, there is a sharp division between the *polis* and those who do the work. Only those who are members of the *polis* may vote and thus speak. All others are labourers—they ensure that the community can actually function, but their work is that of the body and is denigrated. I am not saying that this distinction has reached us directly from ancient Greece and Rome (although see Steiner, 1986), but our continued fascination with those civilisations may rest in part in our projecting onto them unregarded parts of our 20th- and 21st-century cultures. Those whose photos are not placed on websites, in this reading, become the invisible labourers who keep things going—they labour, but their labours are not involved in constructions of selves, only with getting tasks done.

In other words, the presence or absence of a photograph is a designator of the difference between 'work' and 'labour' or, in Butler's terms, of who it is that is human and who it is that is not.[7] The labourer, since Taylor (1911/2003) is a 'hand' and thus devoid of a face and incapable of being recognised (as human).

CONCLUSION: DISTINGUISHING BETWEEN LABOUR (DOING) AND WORK (BECOMING)

In this chapter I have interwoven an account of two sisters' working lives within and through Judith Butler's thesis in *Frames of War*. Butler's work, inspired by 21st-century warfare, has provided concepts I have adopted and adapted for thinking through what makes us recognizable and how (as I will argue in later chapters) we may reproduce ourselves through feeling and acting as subjects in the social realm of work, when under an imperative that we become zombie-machines whose working lives are not lived by ourselves.

I have used my sister's lay theory of who she is and why we live such different lives to argue the case for a distinction to be drawn between work and labour in an era when the self has become an ongoing project that must be worked on. To labour, I have suggested, is to do the physical and mental tasks required of us by those by whom one is employed and because of which one's time is so taken up that there is neither opportunity to nor resources for work(ing) on the self. To labour is therefore to be a life, but not a human life. To be a human requires that one can work on the self: to work is to be able to constitute identity or selfhood as part of the processes involved in our jobs. To labour is to occupy the subject position of a faceless zombie-machine; to work is to have a face and thus to have recognition of one's self as human. To labour is therefore to do; to work is to become. To labour is to be not recognised, to have recognition withheld. For those of us in privileged positions—as professionals, managers, academics, perhaps—at least some aspects of our work allow us to work (on the self) and to constitute an identity.

In later chapters I will show how management imposes the requirement that staff labour but not work and how staff evade that demand by looking elsewhere for the recognition that accords them status of the human. For now I will conclude by returning to the issue of the face. The face is inevitably part of the materiality of the body. Let us conceive of the self as being/having/doing (Turner, 2008) two bodies while at work: there is the body I have given over to the organization for the duration of the working day, that body often denied a face, and there is the body I call 'mine', the one whose reflection I see when I look in the mirror. The one I have given over to the organization is to a certain extent outside my control: it has to do what the employer requires that it do. The body I retain, which I call my own, is the body I can work on as part of the presentation and achievement of the 21st-century 'me', a body that is always social, always given over to others (Butler, 2009), for it is the body I present to the other in the scene of recognition. The first body is the material body of traditional capitalism: the body that exists only to labour and whose labour power is what is sought by the organization. This is the body still desired by organizations—it is a zombie-machine there to do physical, mental or aesthetic tasks—but always a body that should show no desire other than to work. This is a body that has life but is not alive because it is not human. Denied recognition, it is a deadened body in a deadened/deadening organization. The second body is the body caught up in the production of the I, always social, always outside itself, always contributing to the I's participation in being human. The first is the body that labours; the second is the body that works. The first is the body that is rendered faceless and denied recognition. The second is the body that has a face that looks out to others for recognition.

POSTSCRIPT

But there is one further issue that needs discussion. Throughout this chapter I have offered an uncritical perspective on academic work, with only minor asides referring to some of its frustrations and the dangers some commentators identify that academics are being reduced to labourers as higher education becomes managerialised. In that way, I adopted Julie's perspective on my job: it is she who frames it as glamorous and exciting (which it is in many ways). But if we reflect on academic working days (and nights), we know that we too are often positioned as zombie-machines, albeit with many more privileges than my sister would dream of. We are productive paper-writing, lecture-giving, administration-doing, exam-marking, conference-attending zombie-machines. Therefore I must qualify somewhat the allusions to the photographs of faculty that appear on websites. Although they accord us recognition, when we look at them we see reflected back a labourer, even though we might frame ourselves in such a way that we refuse that aspect of the self. I see very little resistance to the denigration of our work as it becomes a production line off which plops, spasmodically, another paper or, more regularly, another graduate. Indeed, tomorrow I will see my head of department for my annual performance review: have I been a good girl this year? I will answer yes, and the evidence is there in papers accepted for publication as listed on the forms I filled in. A complex working life is thereby reduced to a number of boxes ticked on a form.

This gives another reason, following those outlined in the Introduction, for looking not at resistance towards management but at other ways of being at work, because, although 'the management' reduces me to a series of numbers and I seem to offer no resistance to that demand, in other ways I evade their judgements and work on the self. This book, indeed, is a small act of resistance (to the preference in business schools for journal papers), but in the light of the dreams I had when I first became an academic, of the thoughts I would think, the books I would read and those I would write, it is a paltry souvenir of the me I had hoped to be. This book is therefore also a work that is thinking through, tangentially and opaquely, what it is to be an academic in the 21st century. The tension I note in my own work, of moving between zombie-machine and human, will be evident throughout many of the chapters of this book, save in the one which follows, in which, despite looking actively for it, I could not find in a manager's account of his working life any hint that he tried to evade the imperative to be a zombie-machine.

2 The Master's Tale

I was browsing in Leeds University's bookshop a long time ago and picked up a book, *The Psychic Life of Power* (PLP, 1997), by an author then unknown to me, Judith Butler. The opening paragraph was enthralling:

> As a form of power, subjection is paradoxical. To be dominated by a power external to oneself is a familiar and agonizing form power takes. To find, however, that what 'one' is, one's very formation as a subject, is in some sense dependent upon that very power is quite another. We are used to thinking of power as what presses on the subject from the outside, as what subordinates, sets underneath, and relegates to a lower order. This is surely a fair description of part of what power does. But if, following Foucault, we understand power as forming the subject as well, as providing the very condition of its existence and the trajectory of its desire, then power is not simply what we oppose but also, in a strong sense, what we depend on for our existence and what we harbour and preserve in the beings that we are. (1–2).

I was captivated (and confused—what did it mean?). I bought the book and then spent six years and three attempts at reading it before I could say that I understood at least some of its arguments. Reading it for the fourth time while writing this book, I became intrigued by how Butler's elaboration of Hegel's master/slave or lord/bondsman dialectic, referred to briefly in Chapter One, might be applied to interpreting accounts of working lives. This chapter is an exercise in doing that. Its aim is to develop a theory of the subjectivity of 'the boss', or how someone is subjected and subjectified by being called 'manager' or 'boss'.

Throughout this book I am referring to a management which requires that staff become zombie-machines. I am eager to maintain a distinction between managers, that is, the people who carry out the tasks of management, and management, that is, the profession, practice (Parker, 2002), discourse and subject position. Managers (people) are located within managerial subject positions, and it is important to remember Butler's point (PLP:10) that individuals are not reducible to subjects. Subjects are constituted through webs of discourse, psyches, bodies, cultures, history, in interaction with others and so on; they are 'a linguistic category, a placeholder, a subject in formation' (ibid.), so the subject position of 'the manager' influences how individuals (while) in that position constitute a sense of self in relation to others (see Harding, 2003, for a sustained exploration of this). However, it is on the body of 'the boss' or 'the manager' that capitalism is inscribed, and it is through the boss/manager that capitalism speaks. Who, then, is this person, the manager/boss? And what is the manager/boss's desire in regard to staff?

Despite the ubiquity of managers in management and organization studies, we know surprisingly little about the persons, subjectivities or identities of the individuals who labour under that job title (Hales, 1999). There is, arguably, an absence of curiosity about managers as people in 'mainstream' organization research which focuses on performativity (Fournier and Grey, 2000) and, through a preference for quantitative research methods, limits the possibilities for understanding subjectivities. There is a fantasy of managers in such work—they are creatures that are totally devoted to their work, and are rational and logical (Reed, 1989; Townley, 2008; Cabantous, Gond and Johnson-Cramer, 2010; Cabantous and Gond, 2011), even though more recently they are required to be reflexive, emotionally intelligent and self-aware (see, for example, Bass and Steidlmeier, 1999; Singh, 2006). They are leaders whose charisma is presumed to ensure that staff will follow them unquestioningly (see Harding et al., 2011, for a discussion). Such managers should have none of the usual human idiosyncrasies or failings, and within such a perspective there is room for neither subjectivity nor identity, save for the singular prescription of 'rational man'. That some managers fall from grace is increasingly acknowledged, but researchers then turn their minds to finding out how to ensure that the original state of perfection is restored (Sinha et al., 2012; Hochwarter and Thompson, 2012).

When we are analysing managers, a problem arises from the term's encompassing a diverse range of organizational actors. Middle managers are seen as a form of knowledge worker (Delmestri and Walgenbach, 2012) that has in some ways become disposable. They suffer from career insecurity (Rabin, 1999), routinization of their work (Redman et al., 1997), subjection to surveillance and direct and indirect forms of control (Ogbonna and Wilkinson, 2003), perhaps even proletarianization (Scarbrough and Burrell, 1996). There is concern about middle managers' work/life balance (Ford and Collinson, 2011), in a context in which organizations 'increasingly colonize . . . all the spaces in the manager's life with identity as partner and parent subsumed under the "greedy" discourses of management and organization' (Thomas and Linstead, 2002:88). This is a far cry from the managerial elites that hold power over the lives of those who work for them (Zald and Lounsbury, 2010; Reed, 2012)—it seems ridiculous to categorise them under the same label as middle managers.

Another issue is the generally low regard in which managers are held in Western Europe in the opening years of the 21st century. Handy (2002, in Clegg, Kornberger and Rhodes, 2007) cites statistics which state that 90 percent of Americans do not trust managers to look after employees' interests, and only 18 percent agree that they look after shareholders' interests. Brocklehurst, Grey and Sturdy's (2009) study of the subjective experience of being a manager shows a reluctance on the part of managers to designate themselves using that term, 'manager'. The 'image and ideal of management has become tarnished' (15). It now signifies very little, and what it does signify is undesirable in that it denotes inflexibility, a brake on productivity and thus the opposite of what it meant in the second half of the 20th century. People find it difficult to equate management, and thus managers, with goodness (Kociatkiewicz and Kostera, 2012), thus contradicting arguments about ways of constituting the ethical managerial self as one responsible to others (Clegg, Kornberger and Rhodes, 2007). If people do not identify themselves as managers, how then can we study them as managers? Notwithstanding this point, it is still the case that organizations are hierarchical, and the majority of people are governed by a 'boss', managed by managers, and perhaps led by leaders.

The more sociologically oriented studies of managers are not as informative as might be hoped in telling us about who it is that is 'the manager' or, more colloquially, 'the boss'. We presume that managers are possessors of competencies (e.g. Gilley et al., 2010), reflect upon themselves (e.g. Roan and Rooney, 2006) and have long been known to spend their working days in activities that differ radically from those that they should, in theory, be undertaking (Stewart, 1967; Mintzberg, 1980). They spend much of their time talking, and we know something about what they say and how that talk constitutes both 'the organization' (Ford and Harding, 2004; Spee and Jarzabkowski, 2011) and 'the manager' (Iedema et al., 2003; Watson, 2008). Studies of managerial identity work (Sveningsson and Alvesson, 2003; Watson, 2008) go some way towards illuminating the person who is (always-becoming) the manager, because they focus on the questions of 'who am I' (or 'who are we') and 'what do I (we) stand for?' (Sveningsson and Alvesson, 2003:1164). These studies, heavily influenced by Foucault, focus on the place of discourse in constituting identities. For example, Sveningsson and Alvesson (2003) argue that 'individuals create several more or less contradictory and often changing managerial identities (identity positions) rather than one stable, continuous and secure, manager identity' (1165). They analyse one manager and her positioning within 'a complex of discourses and roles' in which her identity work is located and argue that managerial and identity work 'mutually define each other'; that is, what the manager does is constitutive of her identity/ies, and her identity/ies constitute what she does. Similarly, Clarke et al. (2009) have studied how antagonistic discourses are 'drawn on' in constructions of versions of the self. Others use narratives rather than discourses for their analysis of identity formation (cf. Sims, 2008). However, a shortcoming of discourse- and narrative-based identity research for those following a Hegelian-influenced path is that such research analyses participants only in interaction with discourses. There is little about how interactions with other subjects and objects serve in the constitution of managerial subjectivities; the manager appears to exist in isolation from the social world.

We therefore know little about managers' 'subjective views and attitudes' (Pendleton, 2003:91) and even less about how managerial subjects are, in Butler's (1997) terms, subjected and subjectified, that is constituted as subjects within relationships of power.

This chapter's aim is to develop a theory of managerial subjectivity that explains the desire of the boss that the people s/he governs be reduced to zombie-machines. It is modelled on Butler's *Psychic Life of Power* (1997), as this is the text that, arguably, develops the most insightful explorations of subjectivity. *The Psychic Life of Power* is an exegesis and development of Hegel's master/slave or lord/bondsman dialectic. Its first substantive chapter analyses the dialectic itself, and its successive chapters expand on each of its major aspects. This chapter replicates that structure, but, as throughout this book, I am not concerned with an exposition or critique of Butler's work. Rather, I use Butler's insights firstly to rewrite the master/slave dialectic by inserting a manager between the master and slave. This gives the bare bones of a theory of managerial subjectivities. I will then draw on the theoretical elaborations she pursues to develop four propositions about managerial subjectivities.

The structure of the chapter is as follows. I firstly introduce Frank, the person on whose account of his working life I am building here, and then summarise Butler's interpretation of the master/slave or lord/bondsman dialectic. That summary takes us away from management and organization studies for a while, but it provides the background to the experiment in writing a master/manager/slave dialectic that follows. This has four major points, which I then develop in the form of four propositions that together add up to the theory that is the chapter's conclusion. The propositions are: (i) bad conscience propels the boss to be a zombie-machine; (ii) the boss is seduced by an erotics of power; (iii) subjection as 'the boss' requires that s/he work harder and harder; and (iv) managerial melancholy arises from grieving the loss of pleasure. The conclusion is that managerial identity, or the recognition of the self as manager when in the managerial subject position, requires that one work as hard as one possibly can, that is, as a zombie-machine. To be a manager, to have identity as 'the boss', is therefore to be a zombie-machine whose success is dependent upon driving all pleasure and joy out of (conscious) working life, so that staff likewise should be zombie-machines.

I am drawing on an interview with a man who, together with his wife, started a successful company after working for 30 years as a manager in the leisure industry. I am a family friend and know him as a humorous and generous person (even though his political views are very different from mine). I will call him Frank. I was initially struck by how he changed when being interviewed. Since I have known him, conversations with both him and his wife have always turned to their problems with staff and the eccentricities of customers. However, while the tape recorder was running, he spoke very differently: he has few problems with staff, and customers' feedback is what motivates him most. It is this change in his narrative that initially intrigued me. I had not seen such a marked difference when talking about their working lives with the other people who feature in this book. Why, then, did Frank speak very differently about staff and customers when being interviewed? I suggest that possibilities for speaking and being recognised change between subject positions. When I am a 'friend' and he is 'off duty', the recognition we seek from each other is as people able to share a joke, maintain a conversation and actively listen to what each other is saying. However, when I am a professor of management doing research and he is speaking as 'the boss', we have someone who is supposedly an expert in management able to pass judgement on whether the other speaker deserves the status of 'the boss'. This change arising from our different subject positions does not weaken the discussion, I suggest, but can be used fruitfully when exploring the manager's desire for recognition.

It is time to introduce Frank.

FRANK

In his mid-50s at the time of the interview, Frank had been born in a very tough, working-class neighbourhood in one of Britain's industrial cities. His father was an alcoholic who was violent to Frank's mother. His childhood was a repetitive cycle of his parents separating from each other and then getting back together. His mother would refuse to put up with the violence, take the children with her to live elsewhere, then relent and return home. When Frank was 15 and old enough to leave school, he gave his mother the ultimatum that it was either his violent father or him, after which his father was evicted permanently from the family home. Frank found a job as an apprentice for a national company, using his wages to help support his mother and three siblings. He finished his apprenticeship but realised he was more interested in management and persuaded the company to send him on its management training course. His subsequent rise through the company was, to use the old metaphor, meteoric. He was given his first general manager position at 22, breaking a company rule that managers had to be at least 27 years old before becoming general managers. As a 22-year-old manager, half the age of most staff in the branch of the organization he now managed, he instigated performance appraisals, consultation exercises and multiskilling, and within two years he had increased profits by 100 percent and won the title 'manager of the year'. He moved to a bigger branch of the organization, where, within 18 months, he won a major award for the company, after which they asked him to take on one of their more prestigious subsidiaries. His speciality became that of 'troubleshooter', taking over company branches that were in difficulty and turning them around. Eventually, after Frank went to work for a different organization that insisted on centralised policies that would not allow him the autonomy he needed to be a successful manager, he and his wife set up their own company. Within 10 years they had turned a mediocre business into a very successful one.

There seems little that relates Frank to the lord and bondsman in Hegel's master/slave dialectic, but through introducing them to each other I aim to establish a fruitful relationship.

REREADING BUTLER REREADING HEGEL: INSERTING THE MANAGER INTO THE MASTER/SLAVE DIALECTIC

In this chapter I restage Hegel's master/slave dialectic for the conditions of 20th- and 21st-century capitalism through inserting a manager between the lord and the bondsman. Since Taylor advocated the separation of the organization of work from its undertaking and argued that managers knew better how to do the work than did staff, managers have become a ubiquitous presence in organizations. They have to look at both the lord (their boss) and the bondsman (their staff). Does the peculiar position of this intermediary change the terms of the dialectic, and can it explain managerial subjectivities? Answers to these questions require first an analysis of the dialectic itself as interpreted by Butler, and this requires a deviation from management and organization studies for a while.

Hegel's master/slave dialectic, outlined in *The Phenomenology of Spirit*, is a mythical scene which encapsulates the conditions by which European subjectivities are constituted. It has been much analysed and is very influential in numerous theorists' work, although Butler points out that an important section has been virtually ignored. Her task in *The Psychic Life of Power* is to introduce this ignored section and develop its insights by drawing on Foucault, Nietzsche, Althusser and Freud. Throughout she 'let[s] the bondsman occupy the site of presumptive masculinity' (38), that is, she uses the masculine pronoun. For ease of explication I will follow her practice in much of this chapter.

This is the scene that Hegel described and Butler (1997) expands upon.

There is a master and a slave, each of whom cannot exist as social beings (become self-conscious) without recognition from the other, but the seeking of recognition is dangerous, so they are caught on the horns of a dilemma. To be subjects, they need to be recognised, but in reaching out to be recognised they could be annihilated. That is, they turn to each other for recognition but have to go through negation, or the individual consciousness has to get out of itself (negate itself) to meet the other consciousness, an other that is threatening and can undo or disavow the self (Benjamin, 1988). Each reaches out to this dangerous other, so each risks life/identity because only one of the parties can win and earn recognition from the other. Gurevitch (2001) illustrates this through a discussion where individual voices struggle to be heard but only one person can speak at any one time if anyone is to be heard. The silenced party is not recognised. This is a struggle in which there is a desire to eliminate the other (Benjamin, 1988), but, by finding ways of remaining in a relationship of interdependency, albeit one based on inequality, both parties survive and possess a sense of self (as self-consciousness) (Cole, 2004), although survival means one is superior and the other submissive. The slave, forced to produce goods for the master, eventually sees himself reflected in the products he has created for the master and realises he has produced the world; through this he comes to self-consciousness. The master, however, is dependent only on the lesser form of life, the slave, for recognition, and as the recognition from such an inferior form of life cannot be counted as recognition, the master cannot attain self-consciousness. Jean Hyppolite suggests this shows that 'the truth of the master reveals that he is the slave, and that the slave is revealed to be the master of the master' (Hyppolite, in Cole, 2004:579).

Butler shows how the lord 'postures as a disembodied desire for self-reflection' who desires that the bondsman be the lord's body (PLP:35). The master's wish requires that the bondsman become complicit with his ruse, so the imperative placed upon the bondsman is 'you be my body for me, but do not let me know that the body you are is my body' (35). This has fundamental implications for the bondsman: the very body that allows him to make the objects that enable him to recognise himself as a subject freed of the need for recognition from the master is the very body that, he realises, is destined to die. As an embodied being his life is transitory, and this awareness brings with it a recognition of his own inevitable death. His newfound freedom therefore brings with it terror (who am I? how will I survive?).

In desperation, he turns for reassurance to anyone who can help him cope with the fear of his own mortality. Religion offers that reassurance, but religion brings with it norms of behaviour that must be followed if life after death is to be achieved. The bondsman now judges himself against these principles and finds himself wanting. He constantly judges and berates himself because of his weaknesses. He thus moves from unhappy servitude to an unhappy consciousness.

Moreover, the freedom from the master is illusory, because the bondsman's psyche is split into two parts, 'a lordship and a bondage internal to a single consciousness' (PLP:42).

Hegel's conclusion is that redemption is eventually found through membership in a religious community. This contradicts his earlier arguments and Butler is unhappy with it. She turns to Nietzsche and Freud to argue instead (PLP:57):

If the suppression of [what we might loosely call] the body is itself an instrumental movement of and by the body, then the body is inadvertently preserved in and by the instrument of its suppression. The self-defeating effort of such suppression, however, not only leads to its opposite—a self-congratulatory or self-aggrandizing assertion of desire, will, the body—in more contemporary formulations it leads to the elaboration of an institution of the subject which exceeds the dialectical frame by which it is spawned.

What does she mean by this? Her discussion at this point revolves around how the act of negation or repression actually constitutes that which is negated or repressed. So the act of refusing identification with a body whose animal functions shame us actually constitutes the body as such, that is, as a shameful animal. This is a 'dialectical reversal' whereby what is censored by the law actually sustains that law (PLP, 58) and is Foucault's repressive hypothesis—that repression does not act on pre-given fields of pleasure and desire but constitutes the fields that are to be regulated and, as such, expands and proliferates them. In Freud, as well as in Foucault and Hegel, 'the instrument of suppression becomes the new structure and aim of desire' (PLP:60). But, Butler goes on to argue, the regulatory regime that produces desire is itself produced by attachment to the rule of subjection (60). If so (and here she returns to Hegel), then subjects will 'attach to pain' when regulatory regimes ensure that it is only painful sites that are available for attachment (61).

We therefore have a further stage in the lord/bondsman dialectic, one that is the thesis of *The Psychic Life of Power*: to become a subject requires that one absorb and enact requirements that can cause one pain. In short, if one is to be a subject and have a liveable life, one requires recognition from an other, including an internalised other, who not only establishes the laws one must obey if one is to be a subject but judges one's performance in obeying those laws and often (always?) finds one wanting. Despite this 'unhappy consciousness', we cling to the recognition that is offered, because without that recognition we cannot become subjects.

To 20th- and 21st-century organization theorists, there is something missing from this account: there is need for a manager to be inserted between lord and bondsman if the mythical scene is to hold good for analysing organizational encounters. In pursuit of understanding managerial subjectivities, I will therefore, perhaps wildly and unwisely, reimagine the scene, but I will insert Frank between the bondsman and the lord. In such a position, he looks both ways, to the lord and to the bondsman. Indeed, Butler's observation that the lord 'postures as a disembodied desire for self-reflection' who wants the bondsman to be the lord's body (35) suggests that for 'lord' we could read 'organization', whose metaphysical presence is inscribed on the bodies of its managers whose task is to articulate its desires (as if 'it', the organization, has an ontological reality that can have desires).

In what follows, I will reenact each stage of the master-slave dialectic identified by Butler. This is therefore an experiment in staging a master/manager/slave dialectic as a scene that has four acts.

ACT ONE

The bondsman, forced to produce goods for the master, eventually sees himself reflected in the products he has created for the master, realises he has produced the world and through this comes to self-consciousness. The master is dependent only on the lesser form of life, the slave, for recognition and therefore cannot attain self-consciousness.

Frank became a successful manager at a very young age, increasing profits and winning industry awards while still in his 20s. His working week was six days and more, and his off-duty hours were (and still are) very few. In those early years, everything he touched seemed to turn to gold. In his account of this time Frank, as the manager, mediated between the organization and the staff, but, although he refers to senior managers by name, there is very little reference to staff save when he is recounting a few difficulties that, he says, he easily overcame by introducing good management practices (e.g. performance appraisals). In those early years Frank therefore sought recognition from the lord/organization of himself as a manager, and it appeared to be freely forthcoming. In recompense for his hard work he was moved from one challenge to another. At this stage, we could say that he has an identity (the manager) but not subjectivity, because he is in thrall to the lord/organization, working hard to produce the goods that it will appropriate as its own.

However, Frank eventually met his nemesis in the form of promotion to a branch that required a great deal of refurbishment. Despite promises that money for the necessary investment would be available it was not forthcoming. Frank therefore refused to take that job further as he knew he could not succeed at that particular task without sufficient funding. He was then moved back to a branch of the organization near where he had started. Although he was to manage several prestigious subsidiaries, he was never to rise above the rank of branch manager.

There is in Frank's account therefore a story of a manager who is also a 'bondsman' who keeps working and working and working in order to obtain recognition from the lord. His staff, just like the slave to the original lord, cannot seem to give him the recognition he seeks. To achieve recognition from the organization, he works seven days a week, 52 weeks a year, trying to fulfil what he imagines is the master's desire. Staff, in this account, are not so much slaves as the objects on which the manager must work if he is to obtain the recognition he craves from the lord. The harder he works, the harder the organization makes him work—the only recognition it gives is of the managerial self as a hard worker (and therefore award winner). When he fails to achieve what the organization desires, that is, to turn around a failing branch without any funds for investment, they withhold recognition of any status above that which he has already achieved. The result is that he carries on working extremely hard, perhaps trying to reverse that decision, but doing the only thing he knows that could accord him recognition, that is, constant hard work.

At this point, the dialectic seems to hit irresolvable buffers: the manager just keeps on working as hard as possible to achieve a recognition that does not arrive, so he does not attain subjectivity. He will never be seized with terror at the recognition of his own freedom and will never engage in 'the simultaneous fabrication of ethical norms and the beratement of the bodily condition of his own life' (PLP:32). Although the organization may be inscribed on his body, it would appear not to be in his psyche. However, there is something else happening: the organization allowed Frank to feel as if he was free. His talk about this stage of his career is littered with references to the autonomy that he desired and was apparently given. The organization had a policy:

> *You're the general manager, you run the operation, um, [pause] and we'll have regular meetings, and providing, you know, everything is going well that's it.*

This organization was then sold to another company, and the new owner

> *believed the general manager should run the [branch], as had [the first company]. [They said] 'If you operate it and you meet your budget you don't get a lot of interference'. So that was fine. That went on for a few years.*

However, things were to change:

> *Unfortunately [the owner] had overstretched himself and had to sell the company. They brought in a guy called Smith. 'I think all the general managers should be known by their Christian names, you know, we're a friendly [cough]'. Being a suspicious [person], I thought uh uh this is going to be fun. The problem with him was that yes he was very friendly, but he wasn't going to consult, he was going to do it his way. Um. [Pause.] That's when I decided it was time to move on.*

Frank does not break free of the master/lord/organization until he realises that his autonomy is a sham. He had thought he was free but became aware that he had been deluded when he became subject to a centralised system of control. Within the terms of the dialectic, it is only at this point that Frank, the manager, attains subjectivity. He went through a difficult period when he became more and more aware of how limited was his freedom to act and then handed in his notice:

I was offered a position in a [big-city establishment]. There you are responsible, but you have no authority. Very much like that. You know. You are totally going to be responsible for everything in this place, but you can't make any decisions without asking. Dreadful. So I went through, opened the [branch], got through the Millenium, and then phoned [my wife] one day and says 'look, this is not on'. Er, and that's we looked at 30 establishments up and down the country, er . . .

He left the company he had worked for for most of his adult life to set up his own business. So Frank had thought he was free, and only when that felt freedom was taken away did he realise he had never been free. In Hegel's terms, he attained that freedom which leads to subjectivity only after he had left the lord/organization that had governed the first 30 years of his working life. However, we will see that, as Butler points out, the lord/organization is incorporated into the psyche of the freed manager/slave, so freedom continues to be illusionary.

ACT TWO

With freedom comes the recognition of one's mortality and a fear of death that invokes an ethical norm linked to the desire for eternal life. This can harden into a domineering religious stance—the subject has to fulfil certain laws if s/he is to earn a place in the next life.

We have seen that the manager is able to feel that s/he is free, but this is an illusionary freedom. Frank, who here stands in for all managers, feels that he has autonomy, but this is strictly circumscribed within limits set by the organization: it is not therefore autonomy but the opposite, the doing of the organization's will.

The fear of death engendered under illusionary freedom is, I suggest, that of the death not of the self but of the organization/lord. So long as the manager represents the organization, so long as the organization is inscribed on his/her body, then the manager has no identity of his/her own, no self that can die, but only identification with an organization whose death therefore is greatly feared (if the organization dies, the managerial self dies). Indeed, the business pages of newspapers and management journals, as well as academic texts and courses, repeat this message of the imminent death of the organization (Grey, 2009) and how it can be staved off only if the manager is sufficiently clever, resourceful and hardworking. This suggests that fear of the death of the organization imposes a dominant imperative towards maintaining the life of the organization.

The manager's task is therefore that of working as hard as possible to ensure that the organization does not fail. The need to work hard, cleverly, and resourcefully and indeed to find ways of manipulating staff identities, motivations, feelings and psyches (Hochschild, 1983; Alvesson and Willmott, 2002) means that managers must work ever harder. Hard work therefore becomes understood to be an ethical demand, because hard work comes to equal the staving off of (organizational) death. So we have a curious reversal when we insert a manager into the master/slave dialectic: the *organization* comes to have an identity that, mediated through the manager, requires that managers and staff work as hard as possible in order to stave off the organization's death.

However, Frank's working life changed very little after he had set up his own business. Asked what was the difference between running a large company and the much smaller one that he owned, he replied:

> *We probably do the same job, but it's done on a more informal basis. Where with a large company everything has to, you know, i's dotted and t's crossed, you know. A lot of what we do here. We have had various er appraisals on the place and they say, 'God, it's still got the discipline of a large business, but it's but it's done, you know'. I don't think in a place like this you can sit down with a part-time member of staff and say, 'right, you fill out that three-page appraisal. Tell me what you think and then come back to me, and I'll spend an hour going through it with you'. Where you will sit down and say, 'look, you are really doing well and but however if you just look at this and look at that', so it tends to be done less formally, but it's still being done.*

The distinction between 'manager' and 'boss', if there ever were one, disappears. Frank has learned one way of running a business, and he has taken that method into his new company. There is no freedom from the relentless hours he must work if he is to stave off the death of that organization, which, although he owns it, is his master. Although he may think he is free, because he has no boss to whom he must report, this freedom is the freedom to work as hard as ever: it is still illusionary freedom, as he is the slave of his own company.

ACT THREE

> *With ethical norms comes a realisation of the difficulties in living up to them. This invokes an unhappy consciousness that constantly judges and berates itself. Self-beratement evolves into self-mortification, in which the 'continuing inadequacy of the self in relation to its transcendent measure' is painfully acknowledged. The wretch seeks ways out of his predicament.*

Hegel's argument is that through various stages, the unhappy consciousness of the freed bondsman becomes a consciousness that constantly judges and berates itself for its contradictoriness. The lord is internalised within the psyche, from where it continues as the conscience of the freed slave and, it follows, uses the criteria set by the master in its judgement of itself. The wretch comes to rely on a mediator (such as a priest) to relieve the abject consciousness of responsibility for its own actions (PLP:51), resulting in rituals (such as fasting and mortification) designed to cleanse the body. Now, the manager must look in two directions at once for recognition: just like the bondsman, s/he desires recognition from the lord/organization for identity, and, just like the lord, s/he must desire the recognition of the bondsman/worker. What does the lord want of the manager, and what does the bondsman want of the manager, if they are to accord him/her recognition? The manager cannot know the answers: all s/he can do is guess. In relation to the master, s/he guesses that what is desired if s/he is to be accorded recognition is that s/he work extremely hard, and so we see that Frank works extremely hard. With regard to what the bondsman would require for recognition to be given, Frank's account suggests he imagines that staff judge him by the criteria he sets himself, that is, the criteria set by the organization/lord—that they will judge him on how hard he works, on his always being there and always being in charge:

> *We probably [emphasis] because it is our own business, we are reluctant to [have a break]. Um. Unfortunately on the few occasions we have tried [laughs], it hasn't been too successful. It would be nice, we were talking the other night and saying, it would be nice just to go and, forget two weeks holiday, but maybe three or four weekends away, um [long pause] and that's ideally what we would like. . . . But it's just that [exasperated sound] in a place like this the customers get used to seeing you and even if you have a night away there'll be something that's said when you come back. That in itself isn't a problem, but it's probably because of the level of staff that we have, um, because you don't have the formal duty managers and the heads of department, when you go away they they they tend to rely on you to guide them. Um. And in theory they should be able to do it, but in practice they just seem to kinda lose the plot somehow.*

Frank is still judging himself in the same way as he did when employed by a big corporation: he cannot take any time off because if he does, then he is not devoting himself 100 percent to the organization. Indeed, he can justify this on the grounds that staff are incapable of taking his place, but we must pose the question whether any member of staff would ever be good enough: does not Frank need them to be 'poor' so that he can justify to himself his continuous presence in the organization? Again we see that the freedom the bondsman earned is beyond his grasp: all he has is a simulacrum of freedom.

But there is another twist here: note how staff are seen to 'kinda lose the plot'. I asked if Frank ever saw people who, at 22, showed the promise he had shown:

> *Er [pause], here, no, when I was in the corporate [business] yes. . . . They were really ready to develop, but there was a process and that. Because we have a lot of part-time staff, some are second jobs, some, they don't, I mean, recently I've sat some of them down and said look, what about training courses, you know, but it's a part-time job to them and it's not a not a career . . . we have tried to run various courses but you know [sound of moaning].*

Frank made few references to staff during the interview, but when I meet him as a friend the topic of conversation always turns, almost obsessively, to the problems he and his wife have with their staff and the idiosyncrasies of their customers. Formally, on tape, none of those complaints were forthcoming. The quotation just presented is as near as he came to voicing his thoughts about staff. There is therefore a disjuncture here: when we talk as friends, he gives one version of his life, but when he talked to me in the formal position of academic researcher/interviewee, he gave another account. One aspect of this, I have suggested, is that when I was in the formal position of 'academic' I was ostensibly in a position to recognise Frank as a 'good manager'. It follows that when he discusses himself formally and on record as a manager or business owner with someone whose formal position is that of a business school academic and therefore supposedly with expertise in management, he has to present himself as having ideal staff, because the ideal manager would have only ideal staff, that is, people he has successfully developed, motivated and rewarded and now successfully leads. In other words, Frank the zombie-machine requires that his staff become zombie-machines if he is to be known as 'the boss'. That is, a sign of the success of the manager is his/her ability to reduce staff to the status of zombie-machines.

However, there are other explanations, and one of these is to be found in 'the plot' that the staff are losing. They have lost the script of the play they are supposed to be enacting, but what is this play? It would seem that it is a play about emulating the example of the boss in working hard and that the lost plot arises from failing to do that. Frank's account suggests that he sees himself as the ideal manager: utterly devoted to the job, working very long hours, implementing policies and practices designed to motivate staff and ensure that everything works extremely well. His personal and family life is bound up in the business: he and his wife work together, and many of their friends work in the same field. In other words, Frank is a zombie-machine that eats, sleeps and dreams the business. It is his major focus, he rarely takes time off from it, and he is good at it. This is how he wants his staff to be, that is, versions of himself, and these are the criteria by which he assesses them. But they have lost the stage directions and do not, it seems, know how to do that.

ACT FOUR

> *To become a subject requires that one absorb and enact requirements*
> *that can cause one pain.*

There are two constant themes throughout Frank's theory about what drives him; one is the need to do hard work, and the other is freedom. We have seen that the freedom he thinks he has is illusory. First, as a manager working in a big organization, he thought he had freedom to be an autonomous manager, making his own decisions. However, those decisions had already been taken elsewhere. Second, Frank desired recognition as a successful manager, and this required that he work very hard, efficiently and effectively, within limits imposed by the organization/lord's desire. Now, as a business owner, he finds his freedom is as illusory as when he worked for a large corporation: he is tied to the business, working just as hard as previously, but now he is his own judge, as he said himself, when asked about the difference between being the owner and being a manager.

> *Eh, well, you as an owner you don't, you you you put the pressure on*
> *yourself. Um. If if if you think about it, if you if you work for a for a*
> *corporate [company], you'll have an area manager, you'll have directors*
> *and various specialist departments. They will dictate things like pur-*
> *chasing policy, they will dictate things like um marketing policy, well,*
> *when you're an owner that's all down to you. The only, as I always say,*
> *the only person I have to convince once a year is the bank manager, you*
> *know, as long as he's happy, that's it.*

However, there is a chink in Frank's self-image: the body is mortified in that it becomes tired out. There are nascent plans for Frank and his wife to sell the business. I asked why. Frank almost shouted as he said 'probably'

> *Probably, [long pause] the hours you work. You're you're you're then*
> *beginning, you're beginning at the end of the night to feel it, you know,*
> *you kind of say, well, wait a minute. The other thing is when you see*
> *your friends getting ill and dying round about you. . . . I think it's now*
> *time we have got to think that's it, we've done our, because I've done*
> *40 [years] . . . and at the end of the day you want to enjoy yourself*
> *a bit.*

Note how the long hours and the hard work are seen as part of a judgement: how much should people work before they can be deemed to have made a fair contribution? His statement is redolent of a prison sentence. In many ways, we are seeing in Frank's account Weber's 'Protestant ethic' (1930/2001), an injunction that one must work as hard as possible in order to secure a place in heaven. The catch, however, is that one cannot know if one is one of those chosen from the hard workers until after one's death.

The imperative is therefore to devote oneself to one's work in the hope of being one of the chosen ones. Frank's closing words suggest that the work has not been enjoyable—pleasure will come when Frank is freed from the constant responsibilities and pressures of the manager/boss.

Therefore, becoming managerial subjects requires that people attach themselves to an identity that causes them to suffer: they must become zombie-machines, be judged as such, and judge others as such. There is a 'dialectical reversal' (PLP:58) here in that the requirement to work very hard and with total devotion to the business becomes something that is not imposed but is desired. 'The instrument of suppression becomes the new structure and aim of desire' (PLP:60).

SUMMARY: THE MASTER/MANAGER/SLAVE DIALECTIC

By inserting the manager into the master/slave dialectic, we have moved away somewhat from Hegel's mythical scene of encounter, but a theory of why managers require staff to be reduced to the zombie-machine, the non-human, is starting to emerge. The account so far is this:

- Thesis: inserted between the master and the slave, the manager thinks s/he is free but this is an illusion of freedom;
- Anti-thesis: deludedly thinking that s/he is free, the manager works extremely hard to achieve recognition from the lord, under the imperative of an ethical norm which requires that managers be utterly devoted to their work and that they prove their worthiness as managers by managing staff who they ensure work just as hard and efficiently as the managers do. The manager must therefore become a zombie-machine that works extremely hard at turning staff into zombie-machines;
- Synthesis: the requirement to work hard becomes a (managerial) desire to work hard. I work hard therefore I am (a manager).

To be a manager, to have identity, requires that the manager attach him/herself to this subject position of something that is less than, or beyond, the human, and thus be subjected and subjectified as zombie-machine.

In *The Psychic Life of Power* (1997), Butler progressively develops her understanding of each aspect of the lord/bondsman dialectic. I will now follow the twists and turns of her arguments, expanding upon this initial conclusion of managers as subjected and subjectified as zombie-machines, requiring that staff emulate their performance. However, some of the interpretations that follow may be speculative leaps triggered by thinking through ways in which Butler's arguments in relation to sex and gender can be applied to developing a theory of managerial subjectivities. I will therefore label the conclusions to each section as propositions. These are not propositions designed to be tested but are the building blocks of theory

(Sedgwick, 1991). Each one arises from interpretations Butler offers as she expands, chapter by chapter, upon Hegel's thesis of the master/slave or lord/ bondsman dialectic.

PROPOSITION ONE: BAD CONSCIENCE PROPELS THE BOSS TO BE A ZOMBIE-MACHINE

How does bad conscience (which is a turning on the self) serve the social regulation of the subject (PLP:66)? This is the question Butler next explores so as to better understand the formation of the subject within a mandatory passionate attachment to subjection, where a repeated self-beratement functions as that person's 'conscience' (67). Drawing on both Nietzsche and Freud, she argues that conscience is self-derived, that it arises not from external punishment but from the venting of one's aggression internally, that is, against oneself. From Nietzsche (72) she can argue that man is a promising being who establishes a continuity between a statement and an act—what he says he will do he will do. This 'protracted will, which is self-identical through time and which establishes its own time, constitutes the man of conscience.' However, there can be no 'I' without a moral labouring on the self: the 'I' takes itself as its own object, and it is this reflexive turning on the self that produces 'the metaphorics of psychic life' (76).

Bad conscience is the perverse joy taken in persecuting oneself in the service of, in the name of, morality. This arises from a prohibition against desire and that desire's turning back upon itself. This turning back upon itself becomes the very inception, the very action of what is rendered entitative through the term 'conscience'. We can imagine this as a scene. There is a desire for something, but, as the desirer reaches out towards what it wants, it realises that it is in danger of breaking the norms of its culture and therefore of losing the love of others, so it turns back on itself reflexively and chastises itself for wanting what it should not want. Eventually, what it desires is this self-chastising, because, according to Freud, prohibition reproduces the prohibited desire, preserves and reasserts it in the very structure of renunciation (81). Conscience is then figured 'as a body which takes itself as its object, forced into a permanent posture of negative narcissism or, more precisely, a narcissistically nourished self-beratement' (82).

There was no talk of desire for anything when Frank recounted his life working for big corporations, but when he discussed his current position, a desire for time away from the company, a weekend break, was articulated, as we saw earlier. Briefly, he said that 'it would be nice just to go and—forget two weeks holiday—but maybe three or four weekends away . . . and that's ideally what we would like'. Here, the desire, the turning outwards, is for time away, to be off duty, to be someone other than the boss. But he then represents customers as a cause that prevents his having a short break. If he is using the (imagined) responses of customers to articulate his own concerns about being away from the business, then we have this scene:

It is my desire to have time away from the business. But, as I reach outwards to fulfil that desire, I am pushed back against myself. I am a business owner, and if I am not there then the business cannot function, or perhaps even I myself cannot function. That could lead to the death of the business. I therefore cannot leave it for even a short time as that would be to break the law that the business must survive. Because I have to be physically present, then I know that I am the boss, and I am certain in that identity.

My first proposition therefore is that the bad conscience of the boss or the manager (this applies equally to those who work for others as managers and those who run their own businesses) is the feeling that one is not doing one's duty if one is not physically there, running the business. In Freudian terms, there must be a certain libidinal joy in this feeling—the boss both wants to be there and does not want to be there, but his/her identification with the business is such that s/he gets a thrill from being so attached to something that any time away from it would be a source of guilt. This is understood more clearly through the quote from Foucault which opens Butler's next chapter (p. 83): 'My problem is essentially the definition of the implicit systems in which we find ourselves prisoners; what I would like to grasp is the system of limits and exclusion which we practice without knowing it; I would like to make the cultural unconscious apparent'. The boss, it seems, is a prisoner within his/her own identity.

PROPOSITION TWO: THE MANAGER IS SEDUCED BY AN EROTICS OF POWER

From Foucault's *Discipline and Punish*, Butler writes, we get the understanding that we can become autonomous only by becoming subjected to a power and thus radically dependent on that power. Foucault saw subjectivation taking place through the body (and we saw with Frank how he felt the need to be *physically* present in the workplace). Butler interweaves Foucault's ideas with those of Freud and Lacan to expand upon Foucault's arguments about the prison:

There is no prison prior to its materialization; its materialization is coextensive with its investiture with power relations; and materiality is the effect and gauge of this investment. The prison comes to be only within the field of power relations, more specifically, only to the extent that it is saturated with such relations and that such a saturation is formative of its very being'. (PLP:91)

As with the prison, then so with the organization: it is saturated with power relations, as is the body of the boss, the materialization of which, just like that of the prisoner, is co-extensive with that of the materialization and investiture of the organization. Where Butler asks about resistance to the disciplinary apparatus of the modern state (101), I ask about the disciplinary apparatus of the organization. This leads to the question of how managers turn the disciplinary apparatus of the organization to their own ends, to achieving their will to power or what I suggest is an erotics of power over others. Managers have the whole panoply of organizational law (Harding, 2003) to assist them: they can discipline those who fail to achieve their objectives or break any organizational rules and regulations. They have brute, direct power over others.

This power, I suggest, has a libidinal energy arising from managerial power to require others in the organization to do one's bidding. Such power can substitute for Butler's discussion of sexuality in *The Psychic Life of Power*. That is, where Butler suggests that there is something about the relationship of sexuality to power that conditions and makes possible resistance (101), I suggest the fruitfulness of thinking about the boss's equally strong libidinal investment in power over others. We could call this an erotics of power.

Proposition Two is that there is an erotics of power within organizations, which is a power that seduces managers but to which they are also subjected, because they too have to do the bidding (of the organization). That power which managers desire therefore is the very means of controlling and subjecting managers; the boss desires that power over others to which s/he is him/herself subjected.

This leads us back to Butler's main thesis in *The Psychic Life of Power*— 'how are we to understand the disciplinary cultivation of an attachment to subjection?' (102). She answers this by drawing on Freud's argument of the subject emerging through its formation of attachment to prohibition and Foucault's analysis of the formation of a (sexual) subject through regimes of power that both prohibit desire and at the same time form and sustain that very (prohibited) desire. That is, in order to be, to have identity, to be a subject, we are passionately attached to subjection, to the name we are called and through which identity is granted. Althusser's thesis on interpellation helps understand the mechanisms in operation here.

PROPOSITION THREE: SUBJECTION THROUGH INTERPELLATION REQUIRES THAT THE BOSS WORK HARDER AND HARDER *TO BE* A BOSS

Althusser's theory of interpellation is influential throughout much of Butler's work, and it is in *The Psychic Life of Power* that she develops his thesis in some depth. Althusser, like Hegel, illuminates his arguments through the use of a mythical scene: a police officer calls out to a passer-by 'Hey you'. The passer-by turns in response to that hail and, in turning, takes on an identity, that of the criminal.

Butler points out (106–7) that this exemplary allegory literalizes the process of subjectification: it encapsulates a demand that one must align oneself with the law (that is, a generalized rather than state law) if one is to be an 'I'. In replying 'Here I am' to that call, one becomes a guilt-ridden subject able to reflect on its self. That is, Butler takes further the concept of conscience in the constitution of the self: to be a subject, that is, to be subjected and subjectified, requires that one have a conscience, defined as 'the psychic operation of a regulatory norm' (5) or, more colloquially, an internal voice with which one berates oneself. The law which governs the manager, as seen in Frank's account, is that of a demand to work hard. The manager, it follows, is defined by this law and is dependent on it for his/her existence: the person who does not work hard is not a manager. Thus, the manager's social existence or existence as a subject, in Butler's terms, is located in a reprimand that establishes subordination as the price of subjectivation (112). Existence as a subject 'can be purchased only through a guilty embrace of the law, where guilt guarantees the intervention of the law and, hence the continuation of the subject's existence'. In Frank's case, perhaps it is a customer who climbs onto the police officer's podium and shouts out, 'Hey you, why were you away from your work this weekend?' Indeed, Frank himself notes that when he returns after a rare weekend away, 'things are said' by customers. Frank turns, and in turning he becomes guilty of the crime of forgetting his managerial responsibilities.

It follows that there is a need to prove one's innocence, and Althusser argues that this is done through labour. As Butler interprets his arguments, 'To acquit oneself "conscientiously" is . . . to construe labor as a confession of innocence, a display or proof of guiltlessness in the face of the demand for confession implied by an insistent accusation' (118). Frank, the boss, claims innocence through working hard: I work hard; therefore I am a boss. To become a subject therefore involves: accusation; necessity to provide proof of innocence (through one's labour); execution of that proof (labouring); and subjectification within and through the terms of the law. 'To become a "subject" is thus to have been presumed guilty, then tried and declared innocent' (188). Importantly, because this declaration is not a single act but a status incessantly reproduced, to become a 'subject' is to be continuously in the process of acquitting oneself of a crime which, in Frank's case, is idleness.

There is here 'a lived simultaneity of submission and mastery' (117) which I interpret as meaning that one becomes a master at achieving one's own submission, in each of the incessantly repeated acts of turning towards what Butler argues is a voice that need not be present, need not indeed be articulated, but is there within the norms and laws of a culture. One becomes a subject through mastery of the skills of submission which requires not simply acting according to a set of rules, but also embodying and reproducing those rules as rituals in one's actions (119). Through such rituals a 'belief is spawned which is then incorporated into the performance in its subsequent operations' (ibid.). There is in all this a compulsion to 'acquit oneself', so the subjectified subject is an anxious subject.

Frank recounts an incident in his early career that can now be seen to inaugurate him as 'the boss'. He had then been an under-manager for about 18 months:

> *After about a year and a half, this is very interesting, um, [my boss] called me into the office and said, 'it's time you moved on'. I said, 'sorry'. He said, 'it's time you moved on'. He says, 'If I've been off duty and I come back and you've done everything then I worry about my position so it's time you moved'. [Laughter] Which I thought was a very nice way of putting it.*

We have here the following 'very interesting' scene:

- The voice of authority shouts out, 'hey you, come into my office—it's time you moved on';
- The passer-by turns round, feeling guilty. Is he being given the sack? Will he lose his job? He asks a question that is also an apology for the crime he is being accused of: 'Sorry?';
- But he is proven innocent because of his labours (he has done everything the manager should do), and he is therefore equipped to be a manager.

I suggest that this is the scene of inauguration of the manager, one in which the difference between 'manager' and 'worker' is achieved. To be called 'the manager' is to always have to prove oneself as a manager, and this is done through constant work. But the first two propositions suggest that the name 'manager' also incorporates secret thrills and pleasures that will introduce guilt or bad conscience into the managerial identity. This is a deviation from what the identity of 'manager' should incorporate, and therefore even harder work must be undertaken to overcome the guilty pleasures. Proposition Three is therefore: to be proven innocent in the court of law of the boss's conscience requires ever-greater focus on working hard at fulfilling one's managerial duties.

PROPOSITION FOUR: MANAGERIAL MELANCHOLY ARISES FROM REFUSED SYBARITISM, OR GRIEVING FOR THE LOSS OF PLEASURE

The final, powerful chapters of *The Psychic Life of Power* form 'a certain cultural engagement with psychoanalytical theory that belongs neither to the fields of psychology nor to psychoanalysis, but which nevertheless seeks to establish an intellectual relationship to those enterprises' (138). In them Butler develops a thesis of the melancholy induced in the psyche through its having to give up potential sexed/gendered identities. I am not exploring sex/gender in this chapter, but Butler's arguments provoke the question of what is given up, what objects are lost, to the boss when s/he is under a compulsion to work, and work, and work. I suggest (perhaps because of my own desires) that what is given up, the opposite of hard work, is sybaritism. The term (according to Wikipedia [http://en.wikipedia.org/wiki/Sybaris, accessed 13 July 12]) is synonymous with pleasure and luxury, and originates in a Greek city, Sybaris, which in the sixth century BCE was so rich that it was widely envied and admired. This contrasts markedly with Christianity's imperatives, as discussed by Hegel, Althusser and Weber, echoes of the last of these resonating, I have suggested, through Frank's account. In other words, Christianity's influence on Western European subjectivities is that they emerge out of bad conscience; I am suggesting (and this is Proposition Four) that what is suppressed by the internalised judgemental eye is the wish for pleasure, laziness and self-indulgence.

The argument is this (and I paraphrase Butler for much of this argument). From Freud (PLP:134) comes the thesis that the lost object haunts the ego as one of its constitutive identifications. That is, what is given up does not disappear but is internalised, although the regret or grief over what has been lost means that this is a melancholic incorporation. For Butler, what is given up is the possibility of different gendered identities and different loves. For the boss, I am arguing that what is given up is indulgence, pleasure and enjoyment. The memory of these, of what might be, is, however, incorporated, and their loss is a melancholic loss.

Second, just as heterosexuality (and sexed identity) is cultivated through prohibitions such as restrictions on whom one can love, so managerial identities are cultivated through what cannot be done (stop working and start playing). This is because, just as becoming a man requires repudiating femininity (137), becoming a manager or a boss requires repudiating everything that is other to the requirement for hard work. One's secret, guilty desires, those which one cannot allow to be articulated, are, however, projected onto one's other. The male knows he is male (rational, logical, transcendent) because he is not woman (emotional, close to nature); the manager knows s/he is manager (disciplined zombie-machine) because s/he is not worker (undisciplined, self-indulgent, needing to be controlled). But

> One of the most anxious aims of his desire will be to elaborate the difference between him and her, and he will seek to discover and install proof of that difference. His wanting will be haunted by a dread of being what he wants, so that his wanting will also always be a kind of dread. (137)

That is, staff become for the boss the receptacle of his/her repudiated desires: the manager dreads giving in to his/her own desire for pleasure and indolence, cannot articulate that dread wish to be lazy, but installs proof of the difference between him/herself as manager and the not/manager, the staff, by seeing in staff those repudiated aspects of him/herself. Where s/he is hard-working, s/he sees staff as trying to avoid work; where s/he is competent, s/he sees them as incompetent; and so on. This puts the manager in a psychic quandary. If it is the mark of the good manager to lead, develop, train, control and motivate staff so that they work hard as zombie-machines but the manager also needs to see staff as poorly disciplined and slothful, then the manager is in a double bind. If his/her staff become controlled, highly motivated and hard-working, then they will not carry his/her repudiated desires and s/he will feel him/herself to be a failure for having to admit to that desire for pleasure. But so long as staff embody (in the manager's eyes) those despised aspects of the managerial self, they cannot be hard-working, and so s/he will have failed as a manager. All s/he can do to escape from this bind is to push him/herself to work ever harder.

However, Butler's argument is that such loss brings about a 'disavowed grief' (139), resulting in a melancholia for what cannot be grieved (in our case, freedom from the necessity of constant hard work). This melancholia, Butler argues, becomes part of the operation of regulatory power (143), because such a radical refusal suggests that an identification has, at some level, taken place, but the disavowal of that identification results in the over-determination of the identification (149). In other words, the boss recognises him/herself at some level as someone who desires to be lazy, indulgent and free from responsibilities, so, to disavow him/herself of that identification, works ever harder to prove that s/he is not that which s/he, at one level, desires to be.

Melancholia returns Butler (168) to the figure of the 'turn' as a founding trope in the discourse of the psyche, that is, the turning back on oneself and the berating of the self for its failure to achieve normative ideals. In Hegel, turning back upon oneself comes to signify the ascetic and sceptical modes of reflexivity that mark the unhappy consciousness; in Nietzsche, turning back on oneself suggests a retracting of what one has said or done or a recoiling in shame in the face of what one has done. In Althusser, the turn that the pedestrian makes towards the voice of the law is at once reflexive (the moment of becoming a subject whose self-consciousness is mediated by the law) and self-subjugating. For Freud, the ego turns back upon itself once love fails. But it is melancholia, Butler argues (191), that links the psyche to the norms of social regulation. This is because the power that is imposed on the self and animates its emergence as an 'I', that power which makes selfhood possible, at that very instant also imposes limits upon selfhood, so in order *to be* one must sacrifice possibilities for the self one could be, and what is sacrificed is grieved (198). Thus, the discourses of a culture that make possible 'the boss' or 'the manager' provide the motive power that constitutes the identity of 'the manager', but at the same time they impose norms of what the boss can or must do if s/he is to sustain that identity as the boss. To be a manager requires giving up possibilities for joy, leisure, self-indulgence, play and so on, and at the same time it requires that the manager bar staff from sybaritic pleasures.

The figure of the 'turn' in management thus becomes something like the following, not quite mythical scene:

A manager is walking down the corridors of an organization and sees a group of staff by the photocopier machine, conversing and laughing. S/he stops, desiring to join in the conversation and the pleasure in colleagues' company. 'Hey you, you human being', they seem to have been calling out, 'come and join us'. But they become silent and turn to getting the photocopying done. S/he realises s/he has misheard the voice: it had been drowned by his/her presence, which had said, 'hey you, get on with your work'. S/he sees him/herself reflected in the backs now turned towards him/her: his/her conscience is clear because staff are busily working; his/her conscience is not clear because the pleasure of genial company has been lost, and s/he is the cause of that loss.

Proposition Four is therefore: what is suppressed by the internalised judgemental eye is an injunction to enjoy and indulge oneself. To be a manager or a boss requires that one sacrifice possibilities for pleasure, self-indulgence, and so on. This is an ungrievable loss which must be guarded against, and it becomes projected onto the not-I, the worker. The manager must strive to ensure that staff do not enjoy themselves save when pleasure becomes a tool for control (Fleming, 2005), and this at the same time ensures that the boss is a melancholic subject.

CONCLUSION: TOWARDS A THEORY OF MANAGERIAL SUBJECTIVITIES

In this chapter I used the life story told me by a boss who had spent 30 years as a manager before setting up his own business, and I have read his account with, through and alongside Butler's *The Psychic Life of Power*. This has led to an outline of Hegel's master/slave dialectic in which I inserted the manager in between master and slave and to the development of four propositions designed to expand upon the stages within the dialectic. These together lead to the following theory of the subjectivity of the boss/manager and why the manager desires or requires that staff become zombie-machines and less than human.

Managers think they are free, but this is an illusory freedom. Even when they set up their own businesses, they are governed by cultural norms and discourses that both make the identity of manager possible and place limits upon what can be done if the attempt at the impossible identity of self as manager is to be sustained. Within those cultural norms is a requirement that managers work, and work, and work (that is, become zombie-machines). The person who does not work hard cannot be a manager. Hard work is therefore an ethical norm. Any desire for a break from work provokes feelings of guilt (bad conscience) and fear of the failure of the company. This drives the manager to work even harder. However, there is a thrill of pleasure in the knowledge that the boss appears to be indispensable, along with an erotic thrill of power over others. These contradict the definition of what it is to be a manager, to be called by that name, and they induce guilt (bad conscience). Managers therefore have to prove that they are not guilty of failing to fulfil the normative ideal of 'the manager', and to do this they have to work ever harder at fulfilling their managerial duties. However, this drive to refuse all sybaritic pleasures, to disown one's capacity for joy and pleasure in things other than work, produces the managerial self as a zombie-machine suffering an ungrievable loss, the loss of pleasure. Unable to indulge in pleasure at work, managers are driven to ensure that no one else can enjoy what they cannot themselves enjoy.

To be a good manager requires that staff work very hard, efficiently and with devotion to the business (staff must become zombie-machines): staff who do not do this testify to the manager's failure to motivate, lead, control or in other ways get them to perform. However, staff are receptacles of managers' repudiated selves, that is, their desire for sybaritic pleasures, and so managers have to seek to drive those pleasures out of staff. They are therefore in a double bind, because whichever of these tasks they fulfil negates the other. The only way out is to work harder, and thereby sustain the norm and the status quo. Management is therefore a melancholic function where the success that is desired by managerial subjects is impossible to attain but what is lost in the striving cannot be regained. The power that subjectifies the managerial subject, which facilities the identity of 'manager', thus subjects the manager within a melancholic subject position.

In terms of the distinction between labour and work introduced in Chapter One, there is no distinction for the manager. That is, to labour as a manager is to work on oneself as manager, and thus to be a manager is to work on oneself.

This is a theory of how the norms that govern managerial identities play out in practice. It is not necessarily a description of how all managers actually behave all of the time, and indeed Butler illuminates ways in which such normative requirements can be evaded or even fail in their enactment. There may be misrecognition in interpellation when the name is a social category such as 'manager', because it then is a signifier that can be interpreted in a number of ways (96). The strict connection between name and identity may also be derailed in the imaginary, which disorders and contests what is attempted in the symbolic. Indeed, she suggests that identity always fails. Further, Foucault's thesis on resistance as an effect of the very power that it is said to oppose is important (PLP:98). There is the dual possibility of being both constituted by the law and an effect of resistance to the law. For Foucault, the symbolic produces the possibility of its own subversions, and these subversions are unanticipated effects of symbolic interpellations (99). The iterability of the performativity of the subject allows a 'nonplace' for subversion, where the reembodying of the subjectivating norm can redirect its normativity (99). Butler suggests (100) that the strategic question for Foucault is: how can we work the power relations by which we are worked, and in what direction? Finally, a failure of interpellation may mark the path towards 'a more open, even more ethical, kind of being, one of or for the future' (131). There are therefore possibilities for change.

What I have aimed to do in this chapter is not to demonise the manager but to try to understand the imperatives that constitute managerial subject positions and impose limitations on what managers can do if they are to sustain that identity of manager. In Chapters Three and Four I will show how people evade or sidestep requirements about how they should act as zombie-machines and, in so doing, constitute the self as human. I have not done that with the manager. Partly this is because Frank's account is one of relentless hard work, and numerous statistics show that he is not alone: the length of managers' working weeks is a cause for concern (Ford and Collinson, 2011). But also there is within his account a sense that this person is a good man. He rescued his mother from a violent husband, rose out of the slums to become a successful businessman and enjoys the generosity that comes from running a successful business. My concern is how that person is, when in the subject position of the manager, so driven, and driven to drive others. If we are to move towards 21st-century organizations in which domination, exploitation, aggressive control over people's lives and the reduction of working selves to disposable pieces of furniture are to be challenged, we need to find ways of including managers within the category 'human'. Indeed, it will be impossible to change the terms within which working lives are lived without doing so. This chapter therefore finishes with a question that cannot be answered here: how do we change the norms within and through which managerial identities are constituted and managerial self-making occurs?

3   The Bondsman's Tale

In Chapter One I drew a distinction between labour and work: the former involves undertaking the tasks required to fulfil the terms of the job and is undertaken by a zombie-machine; the latter is concerned with constituting selfhood in which the status of the self as human is claimed. Chapter Two introduced the boss my sister Julie might meet if she found paid employment. I argued that bosses are melancholic subjects who, seeking recognition and identity, are driven to work themselves harder and harder and harder. It is imperative for them, in their quest for managerial selfhood, that staff do likewise. In this chapter I explore the encounter between manager/lord/master and worker/bondsman/slave from the latter's perspective. The person whose working-life story informs this chapter is not and has never been one of Frank's staff, and rather than delving further into *The Psychic Life of Power* I am now drawing for inspiration on Butler's *Antigone's Claim* (2000), a book that also informs the next chapter. *Antigone's Claim* explores another mythical encounter, but it focuses in some depth on the person who faces the lord/master rather than the lord/master him- (or increasingly) herself. It is a scene in which recognition is refused and carnage follows. The greater part of this chapter focuses on *The Antigone* and how Butler's reading can illuminate a person's account of his/her working life; it then returns to the scene of recognition.

Antigone's Claim is an analysis of Sophocles's ancient tragedy *The Antigone*. It may seem peculiar to turn to an ancient Greek tragedy to understand 21st-century organizations, but I suggest that there is much to be learned from them that management and organization theorists have not yet touched on. Ancient Greek philosophers such as Plato and Aristotle are referenced by management theorists, especially in discussions of business ethics (for example, Parker, 2003; Rämo, 2004; ten Bos, 2003), but their near-contemporaries, the dramatists Sophocles, Aeschylus and Euripides, are rarely so. There are a few references by organizational analysts to the gods who inform the works of these earliest playwrights, including Cummings (1996), Handy (1995), who developed a typology based loosely on Greek gods, and Gabriel (2003), who looked to Homer's *Odyssey* for illumination. But, apart from a tangential recourse to Oedipus by means of the Oedipal complex (Stein, 2007), the tragedies remain largely unexplored by organization researchers. In this we differ markedly from many disciplines, for philosophers, cultural theorists, psychoanalytical theory, feminist theory, political science and film and theatre studies have found in ancient Greek tragedies a fecundity of thought that, though 2,500 years old, assists the development of important insights into contemporary issues. I therefore start this chapter's discussion by outlining the influence of ancient Greek tragedy in the contemporary academy. I then introduce Shakeel, whose story becomes the bondsman's response to the boss's desire that he, feckless being that the manager thinks he is, work and work and work, like a zombie-machine. An outline of *The Antigone* is included as a short appendix for those unfamiliar with the tragedy. The play has three acts, a structure mimicked in the main part of this chapter. The theory which emerges suggests that employees do not require recognition from the manager if they are to have selfhood, although the manager, as we have seen, requires recognition from staff. Staff seek recognition elsewhere.

But first, I justify the reasons for turning to Greek tragedy for understanding contemporary organizations.

THE INFLUENCE OF ANCIENT GREEK DRAMA IN THE CONTEMPORARY ACADEMY

Anyone who has eaten popcorn and sipped a cola (or, in this grannie's case, drunk a cup of tea) at the cinema with young relatives watching *Percy Jackson, Lightning Thief* or *Clash* (then *Wrath*) *of the Titans* will have seen Greek dramas and mythologies re-presented to 21st-century audiences, so will have witnessed the continuing circulation of these ancient stories. A more intellectual reading was offered by Freud (1915–17/1973), who, of course, recognised in the Oedipus tragedy an issue he thought fundamental to the entry of every (male) child into the social world. Other psychoanalytic theorists, of the stature of Lacan (2002) and Irigaray (1985), have followed his lead and turned to ancient Greece for inspiration and understanding. More recently, Mitchell (2000) drew on the Medusa to fill in a major gap in Freudian thinking.

Philosophers turn in a major way to the Greek tragedies: Most influential of all, perhaps, is Hegel's interpretation of *The Antigone*. He draws on the play, albeit without referring to it by its name, in the section of *Phenomenology of Spirit* (1977) entitled 'The Ethical Order', in a discussion entitled 'Ethical Action. Human and Divine Knowledge. Guilt and Destiny'. His analysis revolves around the distinction between divine and human law: the former is that of the family, the household gods and the female; the latter that of the public realm, of rationality, objectivity and masculinity. He writes (1977, para. 475, p. 287) that 'Human law in its universal existence is the community, in its activity in general is the manhood of the community, in its real and effective activity is the government'. This law is dependent upon the Family, which is 'presided over by womankind' (1977, para. 475, p. 288), and Antigone, it is clear, becomes his model for womankind. Womankind threatens 'the earnest wisdom of mature age' that is 'indifferent to purely private pleasures and enjoyments' (ibid.) and thinks only of the community. The confrontation between King Creon and his niece, Antigone, therefore marks for Hegel the emergence of the distinctive realms of the public and private. Creon insists that his loyalty to his kin should be subordinated to his loyalty to the state; if not, he takes the denigrated female position. Antigone, the female, represents the family, its role being to provide sons who will support the state while keeping the female safely outside the public realm (a position Antigone notably refuses). Hegel thus interpreted Sophocles as articulating the emergence of, and the difference between, the public realm of the state and the private realm of the family, issues that continue to perplex 21st-century societies (Stroud, 2005) and that would seem applicable to organizations as public realms.

The Antigone proved similarly influential in the works of Fichte, Holderlin and Kierkegaard (Steiner, 1984). In the wonderfully titled *On Germans and Other Greeks*, Schmidt (2001) explores the influence of Greek tragedy in the work not only of Hegel and Holderlin but also of Nietzsche and Heidegger. For Schmidt (2001), the importance of the tragedies lies in the assumption, derived from Plato and Aristotle, that tragic art informs the development of ethical and political thought.

Feminist theorists find emancipatory potential in the tragedies. Kristeva (1982) argued that Sophocles was representing the death of matriarchal culture following its overthrow by patriarchy, demonstrating that the current gender order is not immutable. Jacobs (2006), inspired by *The Oresteia*, identifies in Athena's mother, Metis, swallowed by Zeus after he had raped her, a symbol that contributes to development of a feminist agenda for the 21st century. Scott (2005) has a similar intention: she also turns to the *Oresteia*, and specifically to the matricidal Electra, to achieve her aim.

Butler and other feminist thinkers ask, in reference to Freud's choice of Oedipus rather than Antigone as his archetype for the psyche, what is foreclosed by 'rendering one imaginative device and narrative an authoritative canon' (Pollock, 2006:89) and what would be made possible using different imaginative devices. The artist Bracha Ettinger's response (in Pollock, 2006), arising from her interpretation of *The Antigone*, is a matrixial border space, where matrix, or womb, countermands phallic imaginaries. That is, 'the condition of being humanly generated and born is an ethical ground *ab initio*, a form of linking . . . that appears transgressive to a phallic autism when its archaic foundations are activated and invoked politically, ethically, aesthetically, symbolically as the basis for human thought and action' (Pollock, 2006:104). In other words, rather than psychoanalytical theory's isolated ego, the matrixial border space emphasises the co-emergence of subjectivity and thus connectedness and, it follows, a responsibility towards the other and possibilities of a new organizational ethics.

Pointers towards such an ethics are given by Chanter (2010), who suggests that tragedy can be used to bring about an epistemic shift through identifying and registering how regimes of suffering render some forms of pain meaningless: we need new ways of understanding what suffering means. Sjöholm (2010) looks to *The Antigone* and to Sappho for an alternative to Foucault's history of Eros. Her argument is that we should distinguish between active/passive, rather than male/female, and imagine an erotics that goes beyond sex, a suggestion I drew on in the previous chapter to argue about an erotics of power. In the same volume, Bernstein's (2010) sympathetic rereading of Hegel's account of *The Antigone* provides a recognition of an absence in Greek ethical life not only of any concept of a self independent of its roles but also an absence of knowledge of any self expressing a singularizing 'who' through its actions. Bernstein argues that it is the woman, Antigone, who carries for Hegel the task of instigating the 'I' or the 'me', separate from a collectivity of roles.

Through popular culture, as noted earlier, we are invited, again and again, to explore ancient Greek myths. The focus of this chapter, *The Antigone*, has been used by dramatists such as Bertolt Brecht (1984) and Jean Anouilh (1951/2000) to help explain the incomprehensible in the 20th century. For artists, as the frontispiece of Seamus Heaney's (2004) verse translation explains, the play explores how 'language speaks truth to power, then and now'. Theatres regularly hold performances of the plays: in the north of England, where I live, I was able to see the *Oresteia* one month and in the next watch a live transmission into cinemas of London's National Theatre's staging of *Phèdre*.

The reasons for the continued circulation of these ancient texts have been debated. McCarthy (2003) argues that social scientists in Europe peer at the world through a Greek lens, whether they know it or not, for Marx, Weber and Durkheim were all heavily influenced by their studies of the dramatists and philosophers of ancient Greece and absorbed those ideas into their own theories. Steiner (1984), meanwhile, suggests not only that their continuing resonance lies in their having articulated nearly all of the major problems that continue to bedevil Western nations but also that, in that articulation, they entered these problems into the syntax and semantics of European languages. Foley (1995), however, is adamant that the continuing relevance of the Greek tragedies to ways of thinking through intractable problems of the modern, industrialised and postindustrialised world lies in the way they break free of the linearity of writing and thought. They offer 'multiple codes' that educate us in appreciating ambiguity and 'refusal of easy closure' (Foley, 1995:131).

Greek dramas 'work' because they focus on families and their members: they propel us into identification with individuals thrown into the most appalling of circumstances. Our response, if the actors are skilful, is visceral.

After Medea has murdered her children in an act of desperate revenge on her unfaithful husband or Queen Agavë has ripped the heart from the chest of her son in *The Bacchae*, one leaves the theatre with the breath punched out of one. Philosophers, meanwhile, or, more precisely, those rare 'master readers' (Steiner, 1984:291) who bring together 'text and consciousness' offer inspired interpretations of the plays, casting light on current dilemmas and, in their own way, take away the breath with the brilliance of their analyses. They offer different, insightful ways for understanding organizations and working lives in the 21st century. As Foucault suggested when looking at other aspects of ancient Greek culture, they allow us to 'think differently than one thinks, and perceive differently than one sees', and this is 'absolutely necessary if one is to go on looking and reflecting at all' (Foucault, 1985:8).

INTRODUCING SHAKEEL AND ANTIGONE

I am not suggesting that Shakeel's life is in any way a tragedy, although it is in many ways an account of triumph over adversity. Rather, I want to place him analogously opposite Frank, to explore how the slave might respond in the conditions of 21st-century working lives to the boss's desire for recognition. The story of a working life that Shakeel tells us was of himself, age 30, then working in a mail-sorting office (he has since emigrated to Canada). Originally from Pakistan, he had come to Britain four years previously. He was employed doing manual work in a mail-sorting office but has a master's degree in the sciences. He is a gay man working in a still-homophobic working environment. His ethnicity, education and sexuality would seem to place him multiply 'outside'. His account, read through a Sophoclean lens, suggests something very different. It shows that Shakeel the worker speaks in the idiom of management, that he weaves his way in and through spaces and places in which managers are intruders and spaces and places of which management are unaware. He refuses to conform to the position of the bondsman/slave, as he demands recognition of himself as separate and distinct from the manager/master/lord. He refuses recognition to the manager.

Butler (2000) uses *The Antigone* and influential commentaries by Hegel and Lacan to analyse issues surrounding 'gay marriage', thus putting into question laws concerning kinship (a topic I will return to in the next chapter). In so doing, she shows that it is not the state that is the maker of the law about who can and cannot marry; rather, it is the law that informs Lacan's and Hegel's analyses, an unwritten general law, the law of the Other, operating at the level of the psyche and perpetuated through philosophical and psychoanalytical works. Although Butler's focus is upon kinship, the questions she asks of the play are questions that can be fruitfully applied to studies of workplaces. This again involves not giving an exposition of her account but, rather, drawing on it to delve more deeply into the interpellative scene in which manager and worker emerge. For example, Butler asks (2000:5) two questions. The first is: can there be kinship without the support and mediation of the state, and can there be a state without the family as its support and mediation? The second is: can the terms sustain their independence from each other? Her answers are that state and kinship are in a chiasmic relationship; neither can exist without the other, whilst, at the same time, state and kinship are articulated through the law of the Father. This analysis is what renders Butler's Sophoclean thesis so useful for organization theory, for it allows us to think of managers and staff experiencing a similar mutual dependence but within cultural laws that prescribe and proscribe possibilities of being, doing, thinking and, it follows, giving recognition.

Scene One: The Encounter

Creon, King of Thebes, has issued a decree that the body of his nephew, Polyneices, son of the incestuous relationship between Oedipus and Jocasta, shall remain unburied following an act of treachery against the state. Twice, the guards report, someone has broken that law, and they have now dragged the lawbreaker before the king. The criminal is his niece Antigone, sister of Polyneices. The penalty for breaking this law is death by stoning: Creon appears caught on the cusp between family and state—is his loyalty to his kingship or his kin? Antigone has no such quandaries:

> Antigone: Would you do more than simply take and kill me?
>
> Creon: I will have nothing more, and nothing less.
>
> Antigone: Then why delay? To me no word of yours
> Is pleasing—God forbid it should be so! –
> And everything in me displeases you.
> Yet what could I have done to win renown
> More glorious than giving burial
> To my own brother? These men too would say it,
> Except that terror cows them into silence.
> A king has many a privilege: the greatest,
> That he can say and do all that he will.
>
> Creon: You are the only one in Thebes to think it!
>
> Antigone: These think as I do—but they dare not speak.
>
> Creon: Have you no shame, not to conform with others?
>
> Antigone: To reverence a brother is no shame.
>
> (Sophocles, 2008, p. 18, lines 499–511)

Butler's aim in her reading of *The Antigone* is to generate a 'productive crisis' (Butler, 2000:29) between Hegel's and Lacan's readings, and it is this 'crisis' that facilitates our using *The Antigone* for theorising organizations. Rather than state and families, our reading is of organizations and the people who work in them. In this reading, organizations are analogous to the state, as are managers to Creon and staff to Antigone. However, we rarely see in organizations such direct encounters between a defiant individual and a manager as that which we see between Antigone and Creon. Such a direct encounter may be missing from Shakeel's account, but the organization is a scene of repeated encounters in which master and bondsman face each other, either directly or obliquely.

I had asked Shakeel to describe the previous week's work. It was the end of November and the start of the Christmas rush period, when work intensifies as the volume of mail posted increases.

> *Well, we had an extraordinarily busy week last week . . . and the managers were falling [over] themselves to get the work through because, well I think there is a tension building . . . in the workforce and the management. Management is under pressure to cut down costs and so they are trying to get through as maximum amount of work as possible . . . with less number of people, so they are trying to utilise . . . the available people and they didn't [ask for extra staff as is normal at this time of year]. So we are under pressure to get the work through. . . . It's difficult because when you are receiving an extra volume of work you aren't gonna get through at the finishing time. So everybody is strained and you can feel it, and . . . there is tension that is bound to build up between the workforce and managers.*

This tension is not articulated through encounters between managers and staff, so we do not apparently see replicated here that encounter between Creon and Antigone that has influenced so many scholars. For Butler, however, Creon and Antigone are mirroring rather than opposing each other, because, in one representing kinship and the other the state, 'they can perform this representation only by each becoming implicated in the idiom of the other' (Butler, 2000:10). The state cannot be represented separately from kinship, and kinship achieves its identity through the state. Similarly, we see deployed in Shakeel's account a managerial idiom, for he is concerned that managerial aims are instigating the problems that will prevent achievement of those aims. This is emphasised in the following description of how the tension was exacerbated by overcrowding and managers' constant presence:

> *There are certain areas which become the centre of the attention of managers, or that area takes precedence over other areas, so they will pull people from other areas and bring them here. [This] makes it crowded, and then people who don't work usually with you in that area*

they don't know the codes of how to work or what to do . . . and you
feel like you've been encroached . . . we are like well, you shouldn't do
that, and why is he throwing a package in my . . . container because
if he keeps throwing[them] in my container [then it] will be full before
I've checked it.

Shakeel represents himself as a worker *within and through a managerial*
idiom of getting the work done: he is critical not of the job that is to be done
but of the inefficiency that arises from management tactics. Indeed, as his
description of his working week continues, he develops a theory of managers encroaching on staff territory, that such encroachment demotivates staff
and reduces their willingness to perform their work, and that his role is
therefore one of undoing the damage done by managers. I will illustrate this
by juxtaposing two accounts from Shakeel's narrative, one of being watched
by managers and another of escaping from their gaze.

Of one particular manager, he says his

entire body language is so full of malignance and malign, he's so vicious
in his posture. People hate him when he's stood [behind] their back,
and he likes to be where he shouldn't be. . . . So this sort of character or
attitude draws some ire and people don't feel comfortable, because why
is he here, why is he looking at us, like we owe something to him?

However, Shakeel escapes from this oversight:

I am not a robot. . . . I would wilt and wither if I don't talk to people . . .
so . . . I would find the time even after 5 o'clock when we're so busy
to wheel round containers [and] stop by let's say for 30 seconds to say
'hello' or 'how are they doing', also sometimes [say] something funny
you know and they will burst out into a fit of laughter and you know
my job done, and then move on to other people. . . . But for me it's im-
portant that people are smiling and laughing and so that's a typical day.

'Job done'—Shakeel's job, as defined by himself, involves ensuring that
other people are absorbed into the social whirl of the place of work. He is
enacting much of the advice given since Douglas McGregor's (1989) influential work, that those who would be good managers should interact with
staff so as to motivate them. What could be interpreted as resistance or
disobedience (Shakeel leaves his workplace) is, from Shakeel's perspective,
a critique of managers' ability to motivate staff. Shakeel implies that he not
only knows how to keep the work flowing but knows better than managers
how to do so.

There are marked similarities here with empirical studies of managers that
show they spend the vast proportion of their working day communicating

with others (Stewart, 1967; Mintzberg, 1973): not only is talking their major form of doing, but it is advocated as a way of practising excellent leadership (Kotter, 1990). Shakeel sometimes appears to be rebelling against managerial rule and escaping managers' gaze. Indeed, he says at one point, '*sometimes I do wonder you know . . . how I can get away with it the way I do*'. But what he is 'getting away with' is motivating his colleagues—his job is done if he can make people enjoy their work. He thus appropriates from managers what is claimed to be one of their major functions—motivation—and he does it through the very act that managers are supposed to use to fulfil that function: talking.

In terms of the master/slave dialectic, not only is there no recognition forthcoming from Shakeel for the manager; there is, rather, an active denial of recognition. Shakeel does not see in the manager someone working as hard as possible to ensure the continued success of the organization; he instead gazes on someone who, from his perspective, is inefficient and an impediment to effective working. I suggest that what we see in Shakeel at this point is the first act of the master/slave dialectic, in which the bondsman comes to self-consciousness. He has recognised his own worth through the work he does but is frustrated at the master's continuing imposition of his will. Further, there is in Shakeel's account no evidence of a recognition of mortality and fear of death (Act Two of the dialectic) or of an unhappy consciousness that constantly judges and berates itself (Act Three). There is, rather, the final act of the dialectic, in which the bondsman has absorbed the master into his own psyche. The recognition his labours bestow on him are given in the master's voice: he has internalised the law that is management into the ways in which he speaks, and he judges managers using the very criteria they adopt to judge him and his colleagues.

This can be understood by following Butler's distinction between Antigone's two deeds: the doing of the act of scattering dust over her brother's cadaver and her use of language to claim that deed. The description of what she has done thus becomes an act in itself, and actions can be reported or understood only within language: embodied actions become meaningful only through language. Shakeel's work can similarly be seen as having two parts: that recognised as legal by the organization and that as illegal, the latter taking him away from his post and enacted through his verbal interactions with colleagues. However, the acts the organization regards as illegal Shakeel articulates through the language of the organization/master. Antigone's act can be performed only through 'embodying the norms of the power she opposes' (Butler, 2000:10), for the power of her verbal acts lies in 'the normative operation of power that they embody without quite becoming' (ibid.). Shakeel opposes management, as we have seen, but his opposition arises from his critique of managerial abilities—he does not question the organizational norms of efficiency and effectiveness. The person who appears to be a rebel, a transgressor of organizational laws, is, rather, someone who upholds those laws.

Butler, in arguing forcefully that it is through language that Antigone acts, shows that it is the language of the 'authoritative voice of the one she resists' (2000:11). In appropriating the other's voice, she gains her autonomy, but this appropriation 'has within it traces of a simultaneous refusal and assimilation of that very authority' (ibid.). Creon and Antigone, state and kinship, are thus chiasmic (chiasmus: a repetition of ideas in inverted order; http://humanities.byu.edu/rhetoric/Figures/C/Chiasmus.html, accessed 9 November 2012); what is of the one is also of the other. It is not just that a subject knows itself through not being its inferior other but that the subject defines itself through appropriating and inverting the language and actions of the other. Shakeel's verbal acts reverse the normative operation of power; he uses a managerial idiom and takes on the position of the (good) manager, even as he defies managerial rules by wandering away from his work station. The result is that which Butler observes in Antigone: acts performed in the name of one principle, if taking place in the idiom of the other, 'bring into crisis the stability of the conceptual distinction between them' (10–11). Who is the manager and who the worker? What recognition is given by whom and to whom, and what possibilities for selfhood emerge? These are the questions this account of one working life, read alongside *The Antigone*, leads us to ask.

In Shakeel's account we have therefore a curious reversal: the manager is granted recognition *qua* manager when s/he is physically present, as staff bend to doing the job in the way the manager requires. That is, staff give the impression of recognising the manager's status, but this is a recognition given only under the duress of the manager's power to require that staff conform to his/her orders. There is no erotic charge to this power from the staff's perspective: it is felt as heavy and oppressive. Staff, meanwhile, do not recognise managerial expertise and authority but find managers inefficient and intrusive.

At this stage of the encounter, therefore, we could say that Frank (the boss) requires Shakeel (the worker) to carry out workplace tasks, and he desires that Shakeel become a zombie-machine. Shakeel gives the impression of conforming to this requirement while Frank is present, but he does this because he is forced to and not out of respect for Frank, or because of his leadership skills or abilities to motivate staff. In fact, his opinions about Frank are diametrically opposed to what Frank expects them to be. Shakeel has no need for Frank at all: he has secured his own identity. There is no hint of an unhappy consciousness or of bad conscience in his account. Rather, there is a bad presence (Frank's), which forces Shakeel to enact the role of zombie-machine, an illusion he disallows at every opportunity, as the next Scene will show.

Scene Two: The Organization in Question

The laws of the gods do not allow Creon to condemn Antigone to death by stoning, so he sentences her to be walled up in a cave, for by such means he will not be directly responsible for her death. Despite the pleadings of his son, Haemon, who is betrothed to Antigone, Creon will not revoke the sentence. We see Antigone one last time before she is led away to the cave. She is in dialogue with the Chorus.

Chorus:

> There was one in days of old who was imprisoned
> In a chamber like a grave, within a tower;
> Fair Danaë, who in darkness was held, and never saw the pure daylight,
> Yet she too, O my child, was of an ancient line,
> Entrusted with divine seed that had come in shower of gold.
> Mysterious, overmastering, is the power of Fate.
> From this, nor wealth nor force of arms
> Nor strong encircling city-walls
> Nor storm-tossed ship can give deliverance.
>
> (Sophocles, 2008, p. 33, lines 944–950)

The Chorus warns that, even when entombed in a cave a person may engage in activities unbeknownst to and so beyond the knowledge of those who have entombed them. I turn now to Butler's reading of the state in *Antigone's Claim*, in which she aims to bring about a crisis in its legitimation (Lloyd, 2005). Using her arguments to analyse Shakeel's description of his working week brings about what could be called a crisis of legitimation of management, for, as well as speaking in the idiom of management while doing some part of his work and thus putting into crisis the question of who is the manager, he also constitutes other spaces and places within the organization that are inaccessible to the manager/master/lord.

Butler's reading of the State in *Antigone's Claim* is located within her demand for 'a rearticulation of the structuralist presuppositions of psychoanalysis and, hence, of contemporary gender and sexual theory' (2000:19). The state thus figures not as an overarching national organizational function represented by government, the judiciary, the police, and so on, but as the law of the Father. In challenging psychoanalysis, Butler therefore challenges conceptions of 'the state'. In this, her arguments echo those challenges found in poststructuralist theories of organization to any overarching presence of 'an organization' (Burrell, 1988a; 1988b; Chia, 1994; 1995; 2000; Cooper and Burrell, 1988; 1989).

Butler argues that when her critics object that she is challenging the law, their utterance that 'It is the law' becomes the 'utterance that performatively attributes the very force to the law that the law itself is said to exercise' (2009:21). The state, and it follows for this book, organizations, can thus also be challenged as laws that are performatively achieved. It is through acknowledging their powers that we retroactively bring those very powers into being. In doing this, theorists elevate those 'things' we call organizations to 'the status of a certain order of linguistic position without which no signification could proceed, no intelligibility could be possible' (2009:20), and so they become one of the 'elementary structures of intelligibility' (ibid.). I have substituted organizations here for kinship, for Butler's arguments on kinship are equally applicable to organizations: we cannot, it seems, think of how to do work without thinking of 'organization'.

If this is so, then we must interrogate the performativity of the term 'organization'. Poststructural theories of the becomingness of organization/selves (Burrell and Cooper, 1988a; 1988b) dismiss the idea that organizations could either be separate from organizational subjects or enjoy a superordinate position 'over' those who work 'in' them. However, the word 'organization' continues to circulate. In previous work, Jackie Ford and I (2004) showed that organizations appear as only metaphysical presences for the nonmanagerial staff who work 'in' them. In a reanalysis for this chapter of a random sample of the interview transcripts from that study, I found that eight managers used the word 'organization' a total of 192 times while eight members of the nonmanagerial staff used the word only seven times between them. Shakeel, like the nurses and doctors in that earlier study, never uses the word 'organization'. In a transcript that is 8,700 words long, he uses the name of the company ten times but uses the word 'company' only four times, three of which are in its meaning of being in the presence of others. The fourth use of the word 'company' is ambivalent. He says 'we are all working in the same company', which can be read as meaning 'the same organization' or 'the company of the people brought together to work in this place', an ambiguity that is potentially highly productive. It thus seems that people are introduced to the word 'organization' when they work in managerial positions or study management degrees.

In light of what Butler argues, this presence in managerial narratives and absence from staff narratives of the word 'organization' is significant, for managers, it would appear, work 'in' organizations that become endowed with a presence (the 'rational' organization) that is very different from the territory occupied by nonmanagerial staff. Staff do not utter the word 'organization', so for them there can be no performatively enacted law of the organization. They would occupy spaces (not places) (Lefebvre, 1991) very different from those occupied by those who would otherwise appear to be co-occupants, managers. In Shakeel's account, this distinction is material as well as discursive. The place in which he works is big and noisy, as huge machines are used to sort the mail. Managers occupy a physically different place, and they do not seem to enter the noisy shop floor: so invisible are they that Shakeel is not sure whether or not they work a five-day week:

> *We have a three-storey building in the first part and a small administration block, so all the office management, like the human resource department, and accounts and the rest of it, they are there so you don't see, we don't see as many people on Fridays as we see during the week, so probably I don't know if they're working Monday to Thursday or what.*

Managers do appear to watch over the work, and indeed each section of the shop floor has a line manager but

> *his duties will take him somewhere else, you know, so now he's here, now he's not here*

The appearance of other managers is treated with suspicion:

> *the numbers of managers has gone up in the last couple of years . . . the higher management wants to recruit more managers and then if the workforce go on strike . . . they can utilise the managers to get the work through . . . and so that is why they encourage the managers to work with us so at least they know . . . how we are working, how the work is done.*

There is in this account a description of a working space in which managers, normally absent, are seen as intruders into the territory of staff. Managers are resented and distrusted; they interfere with the smooth operation of the production process. There is no respect shown to them; they are not accorded any status other than that of inefficient intruders. The master might look to this bondsman for recognition but gets no more than a workforce that *seemingly* fulfils the management's wishes; when the manager's back is turned they themselves determine how the work shall be done.

However, Shakeel has no language in which to articulate the intrusion of managers into his working territory. Butler points out (2000:39) that Hegel interprets Antigone as acting at the intersection of two opposed laws: that of the state and that of the gods, with the latter being unrepresentable. She shows that Hegel attends to Antigone's act but not to her speech, perhaps because her speech would be impossible were she to represent this other, unrepresentable, law. If, Butler writes (ibid.), what Antigone represents 'is precisely what remains unconscious within public law, then she exists for Hegel at the limit of the publicly knowable and codifiable'. This law, she goes on to say, 'leaves only an incommunicable trace, an enigma of another possible order' (ibid.), for the law that Antigone is representing is that of alternative models of kinship, of a type that is inaccessible within (Western) culture. It is important to remember, from Butler's reading of Lacan in *Antigone's Claim*, that when something appears to hold true universally, it is not that it does so but that it *appears* to do so. As such, 'organizations' become 'contingent social norms' (30) which work on the psyche and give rise to permissible forms of being that prevent the conception or articulation of other ways of organizing work.

Or at least that is the case for those who use the word 'organization'. Shakeel does not. Rather, the space(s) he occupies is/are on the 'horizon of the zone of intelligibility' (Butler, 2000:22) to those of us who conceive of 'organizations'. The representative function of the word is cast into doubt, so much so that it is difficult to talk of the place Shakeel occupies in language.

There are organizations run by managers and organizations researched and pondered by academics. The 'bondsman' (a term it seems we must refuse because the master/slave dialectic has failed because of Shakeel's disinterest in recognition from the master) seems to work elsewhere, in some other space. In Shakeel's account, there is a sense of other spaces and places in which staff meet and work. They are spaces that are perhaps coterminous with management space but that are constituted very differently by its occupants. These are spaces not governed by managers, who organize everyone else's work and ensure it is carried out effectively. Rather, these are spaces in which work is done but in which managers are intruders who disrupt the efficient flow of work. This is 'organization' turned on its head, one almost unrepresentable in language. Managers here are not rational and organized pursuers of efficiency and effectiveness, not *organizers*, illegitimate usurpers of other's territory.

The word 'organization' thus fails to encompass lived, working spaces. It figures managers' working spaces in which staff must become zombie-machines but does not figure other working places that are beyond the purview of managers, in which work (that very same work the manager desires be done) is done by people who are not reduced to zombie-machines.

Just as Antigone's possibilities of selfhood were foreclosed by a political power that enforces rigid rules over what sort of lives can be lived, Shakeel cannot represent the shop floor as 'his' territory, even though, in the absence of managers and in his own account, he and his colleagues govern it. There is no language in which he can discuss this. In the absence of the word 'organization', there is a discursive space, one that is lived but within which there is a lack of a language to report on the deed of enacting it. It is, as Butler suggests of Antigone (2000:52), following but critical of Lacan, a place that is on the threshold of the symbolic and the social and thus is a place that cannot become assimilated to a symbolic order and so remains on the side of the incommunicable sign. Shakeel cannot turn to managers and show them how the work should be organized, for organizational language does not allow that. There is thus a foreclosure of the possibilities of speaking about work and the lives that are lived on the shop floor, save in the language of management theory. However, there is not a foreclosure in *doing*—he can do the deeds he feels are necessary for getting the work done.

I have shown that Shakeel, when speaking about work, speaks in the idiom of management. But we can also now see that what he *does* is outside that idiom. He walks around, talking to and laughing with people. As he does his rounds, he has a different topic of conversation to suit each group: with some, he talks about '*what we watched the previous night on TV or some music or some important political event*'; with some women, he talks about fashion and '*will point out some nice-looking man over there and we'll laugh*'. He will move on to another group of women who '*are talking about work and talking about management you know how cunning and how vicious they are, so I'll drip some vitriol into the conversation*'.

Where Butler shows that it is words that compel Antigone, it is deeds that compel Shakeel. Antigone's words are her deeds; Shakeel's deeds are his words. As he takes his container and moves from one work group to another, talking in the idiom of management even as he undermines managers, his deeds trace a place that is different from 'the organization'. Here is a company, that is, a place in which people spend time together. Acts, and not just those concerned with output, are performed. Friendships are made, collusion against managers forged and the exercise of the self as an autonomous person, separate and distinct from both organization and management, is put into process. There is no language in which to describe these acts, for they break the laws of organizational hierarchy.

The scene of recognition between master and slave cannot take place in such unrepresentable space. Rather, it would seem that recognition is accorded by staff to other staff (such as when Shakeel joins in the anti-management conversations), and managers are excluded.

So, interpreting Shakeel's account of his workplace through Butler's interrogation of *The Antigone* allows us to speak about different scenes of recognition, *where the scene itself must be recognised*. Within the physical places of work, those who appear to share the same physical place may actually be occupying different spaces. To Frank, the manager, there is one organizational space, that which he occupies and where staff follow his orders—this is the space of labour undertaken by zombie-machines. To Shakeel, there are at least two organizational spaces. One, the place of work, is devoted to getting the work done while enjoying the company of colleagues and having fun as the work gets done and in which a sense of self (as a social creature who has fun with friends and colleagues but is opposed to management) is constituted. The other space he occupies is that of the labouring zombie-machine, in which all pleasure is expunged because it is governed by the manager's intrusive and disruptive presence. It follows that the scene of recognition differs, something that needs teasing out.

Scene 3: in the (Organizational) Cave

The tragedy reaches its climax in the absence of Antigone, after she has been led away to be entombed in the cave. Her final words are spoken at line 908, and we hear no more from her, even though the play is only two-thirds through. All we know is that at some point between her being walled up alive and the cave being opened, she has hung herself, with tragic consequences for Creon and his family. The Chorus has the last words:

> The proud man may pretend
> In his arrogance to despise
> Everything but himself. In the end
> The gods will bring him to grief.
> Today it has happened here. With our own eyes
> We have seen an old man, through suffering, become wise.

> (Sophocles, 1988, p. 188)

The gods are unseen but govern the fate of individuals. In 21st-century organizational terms, there is much beyond immediate understanding that prevents organizations from being managed in the rational, logical way in which management theory dreams it should be. Here the arguments seem to end. It is only the encounter between Creon and Antigone that has been much analysed, so it is only their words that have seemed to need analysis. But theorising about organizations brings a different curiosity to bear: I wonder what went on in that cave? That is, what if we conflate organization and cave as a way of attempting to gain a better understanding of the curious spaces that Shakeel occupies but that are outside vocabulary? This chapter continues with another imaginary scene, or rather three scenes, in which Antigone and Shakeel enter the cave/organization together.

MOMENTS IN/OF THE CAVE

Most of us have to go to work: we have no choice if we are to acquire the means of sustenance, make that contribution which is demanded of us as members of our societies and, as this book argues, engage in processes of self-making. This is a Creonic decree we cannot gainsay. As we arrive at the office, shop, factory, farm, mine, sailing ship, restaurant, call centre, lecture theatre or wherever, we engage in the master/slave dialectic in some way, seeking recognition so that we can exist as subjects. In this chapter, the Bondsman's Tale, we have seen that Shakeel does not turn to the manager for that recognition which is necessary to recognition and thus to selfhood. Shakeel constitutes a working space that is very different from that imagined by management, and he speaks in the idiom of management while regarding managers as intruders who disrupt the efficient working of his working space. He does not, it seems, concede recognition to managers.

If we ask Shakeel to shadow Antigone as she enters the cave/organization, we can tease out what this means in regard to the constitution of subjectivities and selves at the workplace. I have suggested above the need for exploring the scene of recognition. Butler suggests that the stage had already been set on which the master and bondsman faced each other. This book suggests the need to consider how power occludes other possible scenarios. There are at least three: different scenes of recognition, three different 'caves': that of the manager, that of the managed worker who conforms to the manager's presence and that of the insouciant worker who ignores management. Furthermore, we can imagine four 'moments' in the cave: as Antigone enters the cave, she is a living being but dead to the world; then she becomes the living dead, having taken the decision to end her life; then there is the time when she is dead but the world thinks she is still alive; and finally there is the moment when the cave is opened and the world knows she is dead.

In the Master's Cave

Let us start with the Master's Cave, that is, the organization as apprehended by managers, where staff appear to conform to the self as a zombie-machine.

As Antigone enters the cave, she is a living being but no longer in or of the world. This is both Creon's position in regard to Antigone and the work/life balance debate in relation to staff. As we cross the threshold at the start of our day's work, we traverse the hyphen/slash from 'life' to 'work'.

There is a moment next when Antigone perhaps is alive to herself, and she is undoubtedly alive so far as the audience and participants in the impending tragedy are concerned: in this time, Teirisias can give his warning and Haemon beg for his father's change of mind. Perhaps there was also a moment (we can only imagine it) when Antigone's will to life forced itself to the surface and she hoped to be saved. In our own case, as we clock in or register our presence at the start of the working day, we imagine ourselves to be alive. We are immersed in cultures which think of death largely in biological terms: social death, that death of identity I am discussing here, is not in our vocabulary. 'Social death' is a term used to describe both slavery (Patterson, 1982) and the condition of people who are terminally ill and who, in this transitional stage between life and death, become isolated and alienated *as if they were already dead* (Mulkay, 1993:49). That is, Western culture recognises conditions where the body lives but the person is dead, a knowledge lived out vicariously through watching films about zombies. At this moment of entering work, we become zombie-machine: we think we are alive, but our capacity for being human, for anticipating and fulfilling future selves, is dead.

In the next moments, Antigone becomes the living dead—she has decided to kill herself, so at this time she will be dead to herself although her body still lives and goes about its task of preparing to hang itself. But is this suicide, or is it murder? Although she has hastened her own death, her own hand is nothing but the tool used by the state. Her death sentence means she has been murdered by a state that cannot allow her that expression of individuality which signals the birth of the Western ego and its distinctiveness from its role. The worker's position in the master's cave echoes this: we are reduced to nothing but role, all individuality lost. In Shakeel's case, as a manual worker, he is a 'pair of hands'. Neither brain nor heart is located in the hands: all they have is motor power that allows them to do activities. Similarly, for those of us who are knowledge workers, we are reduced to brains that work for the organization, while those of us who are in the caring or service professions become bodies that are designed to do nothing more than offer care or provide services. We become task-doing mechanisms whose thoughts and feelings must be limited to those required for this doing. That is, we become zombie-machines.

And then comes the time when Antigone has hanged herself and her body is lifeless. However, Haemon (and others) believe she is alive. This is the point where the worker has succumbed to the master's demand that he work and work and work. There is nothing alive but the body bent to its tasks. Shakeel sorting the mail became an extension of a machine, a pair of hands attached to a body that is devoid of that which would make it human, where the human has memories of its past and visions of its future self, the me it anticipates it may be. He has not killed himself, save through the necessary activity of going to earn his living, an activity without which he cannot live. Therefore, the very act of clocking on for his job is a form of suicide: he has to give up all that is Shakeel in order to carry out this workplace role, subsume himself within a body that works but a mind that is denied the possibility of activity. At this point I suggest we see the archetypal management textbook position—working out how best to use the 'hands' (or brains, emotions or beauty) but unaware of the impact of those recommendations on anything but profits.

Finally, Antigone is physically dead, and, the cave being opened, the world knows she is dead. For centuries, people have puzzled over why she refuses the possibility of being a wife or mother, why she sees these future roles as secondary to her relationship to her unburied, dead male sibling (although not to her living, female sibling). The symbolism in terms of the arguments of this book is, I suggest, profound, because with Antigone's death dies her line: fecundity and the future are sacrificed, and the past is worshipped. I suggest that this is analogous with organizations—what Taylor laid down a century ago, in very different cultural, social and economic conditions, prevents ways of thinking different futures of organizations. Staff should be treated as if they have few powers of judgement of their own and must be constantly watched over by managers or other supervisors. This is a very different sentiment from the concept of the human in the 21st century, one in which individuals claim their rights for recognition.

The master's cave is therefore a place where staff are voided of any identity beyond that of the zombie-machine. As such they cannot give recognition to the manager: all they can do is give the impression of conforming, and thus the manager can feel confident in his/her identity as manager because staff appear to be obeying him/her. That is, the recognition of the self as a manager requires that staff appear to be zombie-machines, or as if they are dead. The master/manager *knows* s/he is a manager if staff cease to live for the duration of the working day. We will see next that in the managerial interpretation of the organizational cave, although staff do not recognize managers, their very presence allows managers to see a reflection of the self that provides recognition and thus selfhood and thus identity.

The Seemingly Submissive Worker's Cave

Let us now follow Antigone into the self-same cave, but now a cave that represents the workplace as seen by staff members when the manager is present. From Shakeel's account we know that staff may be bent to their tasks, but their subjective experience is very different from that imagined by the manager.

As Antigone enters this cave, she is a living being who, although dead to the world, is alive to herself. As she passes into the cave and hears the rocks being piled up over its entrance, she no doubt feels a turmoil of emotions. Such fears and grief are not ordinarily the lot of those going to work, who as they enter this cave/organization are similarly fully alive to themselves as human.

However, Antigone next becomes the living dead, having taken the decision to end her life. She has one form of agency (she can kill herself) but few other possibilities (she has been walled up alive by those who enact the powers of the state). For Shakeel, this is the point where the manager appears on the shop floor. Shakeel must immediately look as if he is working hard and obediently. But subjectively, he has told us, there is much going on that the manager cannot see.

So, that next moment, when Antigone is biologically dead but the world thinks she is still alive, represents for Shakeel/the worker the time when the manager thinks the worker is alive and working hard but the worker is dead to him/herself, just a set of body parts that work. Although for Hegel it was the bondsman's production of goods that eventually allowed him subjectivity, Marx retorted that the goods were taken away by the master, so the bondsman could not possess them as his/her own and so could not have subjectivity. This is what we see in Shakeel's case: when the manager is present, all that he does must be done as if he were an attachment to a machine, with no possibility for demur or active contribution. He exists not as an individual, merely as a cog in an organizational machine. The master knows that s/he is master through seeing that the bondsman has bowed to his/her will and, as we saw in Frank's case, seeing this as a sign of his/her own abilities.

Finally, there is the moment when the cave is opened and the world knows Antigone is dead. In this cave, the cave of the seemingly submissive worker, this would appear to be the moment when work ceases for the day and the staff are free to go home, crossing over the threshold in the opposite direction to the start of the shift, returning to 'life' from work.

In this 'cave', therefore, we see a much more nuanced sense of a working self, one that moves in and out of agentive positions. When the worker is apparently bent to undertaking tasks in the manner of the zombie-machine, her/his mind may insist on its freedom to escape from the confines of the cave, even as the body is bent to the task. There is therefore subjectivity and sense of self here, although sometimes there will be lapses into the unthinking body that goes about doing workplace tasks. The worker gives the appearance of being a zombie-machine but is never fully incorporated into that role.

In the Insouciant Worker's Cave

Shakeel has told us that as soon as managers have left the shop floor or even under their gaze if he is clever enough, a different organizational world is constituted, one in which work is carried out more efficiently and with fun and laughter.

As Antigone enters this cave, we can imagine her feeling that she is free at last. All the terrible responsibilities she has borne are now behind her. She is out of sight of Creon and therefore free to do whatever she wishes, although she is under the dire restrictions of the confines of the cave. This is the insouciant worker's position: there are managers somewhere, but, for the moment, while they are somewhere else, there is the freedom of concentrating on the task in hand and doing it as they feel most fit, and there are options for doing other things. The freedom is highly bounded (by the walls of the cave), but still there are possibilities for agency unrestricted by managerial diktat.

Becoming the living dead, having taken the decision to end her life, must also now be rethought. What life is it that must be ended? In this space where there is fun to be had and pleasure to be wrought from doing the work and socialising with colleagues, the life that is refused is that of the zombie-machine. Shakeel insists on agency, the capacity to circumvent management and spend his working days within conditions of limited autonomy. He can act, albeit not within conditions of his own choosing.

Finally, the moment when the insouciant worker's cave is opened and the world knows s/he is dead must also be read differently. I have suggested above that Shakeel occupies space that is on the threshold of comprehension: we do not have the words through which to describe it. This is the moment in the cave when we again encounter that threshold: as we (that is, we the organization theorists or managers) peek into the cave as it is opened, we see what we expect to see: a cave occupied by a young woman in the case of *The Antigone* or a workplace where staff work diligently when managers are present in the case of Shakeel. However, what Shakeel and others see is very different—they may see the young woman lying there, but they know that, just out of the onlooker's sight, something else is going on.

The scene of recognition between master and bondsman is thus seen to be far more complicated and tentative than anticipated. We have a bondsman who does not require recognition from the master, because the master is someone s/he despises. Thus, the terms of the original master/slave dialectic are reversed; Hegel thought the slave not worthy enough to grant recognition to the master, but here we see the master is thought not worthy enough by the worker for recognition to be granted. In Chapter Two we saw that the manager requires that staff become zombie-machines in order for the master to be secure in his/her identity as master. We can now restage the master/slave dialectic in the form of the following scenes, in each of which the master requires that the bondsman become a zombie-machine so that the manager knows him/herself as master:

(a) The bondsman acquiesces because of the power of the boss. Such a recognition can be no more than tentative, always liable to being withdrawn should the balance of power change;

(b) The bondsman appears to acquiesce but nurtures some resistance within him/herself, notably a critique of the managerial abilities of the boss and a belief that s/he can do the job of the manager far better than can the manager him/herself, so that although the worker's body may appear to conform, his/her mind does not. If the master senses this, then s/he will be engulfed in an existential crisis, not knowing whether s/he is or is not the boss and therefore uncertain about the extent to which s/he can demand that the worker become a zombie-machine;

(c) The scene of recognition is a charade: the bondsman gives recognition only grudgingly and withdraws it as soon as possible.

(d) The scene of recognition is a fantasy, borne of the managers' or organization theorists' theory of what exists. Just out of sight, just round the corner, just in another construction, another scene is occurring.

And so the scene of recognition breaks down, or perhaps there never was a scene of recognition between manager and staff member. Each party may look elsewhere for recognition, for the achievement of selfhood.

CONCLUSION

This is the theory that is now developing: in Chapter Two I argued that the manager is driven by hard work, which becomes an ethical norm to which the manager must conform if s/he is to be recognised as a manager, so the manager him/herself must become a zombie-machine. This zombie-machine is dependent for its identity as manager on staff's conforming to the requirement that they too labour as zombie-machines. From the master's/boss's perspective, there can be no pleasure at work, nothing other than the duty to work extremely hard, although there is a guilty, erotic pleasure in the power over others. This chapter uses another interview, with a manual worker, and another scene of encounter, that between King Creon and his niece Antigone as interpreted by Butler. This suggests that staff do not provide recognition to the manager, save grudgingly and tentatively. Staff themselves do not require recognition from the manager: they achieve it elsewhere. Rather, they go through the motions of conforming to the manager's requirements but experience the manager as a bad presence, one that inhibits the efficient accomplishment of work. It is not that staff do not want to work or prefer, in Taylor's terms, to 'soldier'; it is rather that they have different ideas about how the work should be done, and so they speak the idiom of managers even though they cannot be recognised as managers. They must conform to management's requirements about how to do their work when the manager is present, but when the manager is out of sight they take charge of the working space, transforming it into a different type of space in which much more takes place than the mere doing of workplace tasks. However, that which is done is always restricted by the limitations imposed by management—there is no freedom of choice of task or means to its accomplishment. The possibilities for being therefore appear very limited.

In Hegel's outlining of the lord/bondsman dialectic, the slave eventually achieves identity through producing the world, while the master does not attain identity and so the roles are reversed. The theory I developed through building on Frank's thesis of his working life is that the manager/boss strives for recognition through evidence of his/her extremely hard work, but in this chapter we have seen that Shakeel, as worker, withholds recognition from the manager. What the manager regards as extremely hard work the worker regards as inefficient intrusion into working space. The manager must therefore look elsewhere for recognition, and we saw in Frank's case that this elsewhere is 'the organization' which demands that s/he work and work and work, with the evidence of his/her abilities *qua* managers resting on his/her ability to make staff into zombie-machines that work and work and work.

Shakeel has shown us that although managerial power means that staff must appear to conform to the requirement to be a zombie-machine when under the gaze of the manager, staff evade that identity. The worker becomes alive, becomes human, when out of the direct control of the manager. This does not mean that the worker can produce 'the world', because what can be produced, what work on the self can be undertaken, is always limited in some ways by what the organization deems permissible. Shakeel, for example, must sort the mail, and even though he carries out the tasks of management he is not recognised or recognisable as doing so. Limited in the work s/he can do, existing in the eyes of managers only as a zombie-machine, still the bondsman achieves recognition of the self as a living human subject. It is in the social life of the workplace, that which Shakeel constitutes when he evades managerial oversight, that he would appear to gain such recognition of the self. How this occurs will become clearer in the next chapter.

4   Becoming Human

Julie's story (Chapter One) introduced a distinction between labour (the doing of tasks by the zombie-machine) and work (through which one constitutes one's identity and the self as human), arising from her dreams of what she could become if she found paid employment after years as an 'informal' carer. Frank (Chapter Two) acquainted us with the boss as a zombie-machine who needs staff to become zombie-machines if the boss or manager is to have the identity of manager. Meanwhile, Shakeel (Chapter Three) showed the extent of the gulf between managers and staff and how the boss's need is denied: staff become zombie-machines while under the watchful eye of the manager, but this is only a temporary subject position, one that is moved into and out of. At other times, in other subject positions, staff insist on becoming human. They do not respect managers or managerial knowledge, feel they know better how the workplace should be organized and find ways to escape from the manager's watching eye so as to get the work done. In these and other ways they insist on their status as more than zombie-machine, as subjects constituting self-hood while at the workplace. At the same time, staff are severely constrained in what they can do.

This chapter develops the distinction between labour and work, between the zombie-machine and the human. It follows one person through a working week and takes us deeper into the territory alluded to by Shakeel. I am calling her Alex. Her work is short term, physically hard, uncomfortable and low-paid. Staff move from one temporary job to another, with periods of unemployment in between. They often have to live far from home, sharing inadequate accommodation with strangers. They labour largely outdoors; their tasks involve much shifting of soil and mud and the day may finish with the worker wet through, freezing cold or sunburned (according to the season) and exhausted. Yet this is work that is regarded by its participants as high status and rewarding. Alex is not a fruit or potato picker, moving from farm to farm, but an archaeologist moving from dig to dig. Although there are major similarities between the physical work of potato pickers on farms and archaeologists on excavations, their status is remarkably different. The distinction between labour (here digging) and work (constitution of the self that occurs despite rather than because of the actual labouring carried out) becomes clearer. My particular focus here is on what it is, over and above the physical doing of a job, that facilitates self-making, the making of the me, in which one's status as human is constituted and recognised. Alex's account leads me to explore work-based friendships as fundamental to such recognition.

What struck me as I read and reread the record of our discussion was a number of what Critchley (2012:22), referring to Althusser and in the context of an analysis of Rousseau's *Rights of Man*, calls 'décalages, displacements or dislocations'. These are contradictions in meaning or arguments whose sense is questionable. There are three of these in Alex's account. The first is the nature of the job itself: it requires hard physical labour in often-difficult conditions, yet is a high-status profession. The second is Alex's induction into excavation as a university student. It was horrendous, and she felt put off for life; however, she underwent what could be described as a neo-Damascene conversion during a temporary job after graduation. Finally, running through Alex's account is the importance of the bonds of friendship within archaeology. Her contrasting account of interactions in the administrative roles she takes between digs tells us a great deal about her archaeological self-making, and it is the account of friendship that allows us to make sense of how Alex becomes, constitutes herself as, an archaeologist. Friendship is a little-studied area within management and organization studies, yet Alex's account shows that workplace friendships are fundamental to recognition of the self as human rather than zombie-machine. Analysis of these three displacements leads to a thesis of the importance of workplace friendships in the recognition and affirmation of the self as human.

I draw on two aspects of Butler's work to analyse the three displacements in Alex's account: her development of Althusser's theory of interpellation (already discussed in Chapter Two) and further aspects of her reading of Sophocles's tragedy *The Antigone* in *Antigone's Claim* (2002) (already discussed in Chapter Three). It was Butler's *Antigone's Claim* that led me to wonder about workplace relationships because it is in this book that Butler challenges the heteronormative presumptions that define our understanding of kinship. Alex is the partner of an old friend. I visited her at their home, where we sat down with mugs of tea and the tape recorder running. Our discussion of her working-life story lasted two hours. As with records of all the people who have discussed their working lives with me for this book, I have not 'subjected' the transcript to an intense analysis but have read it alongside the works of Judith Butler as if they were the works of another philosopher that I am now interpreting with and through Butler's work. In Alex's case, her account of an archaeological dig brought to mind Butler's analysis of Sophocles's tragedy *The Antigone* because Antigone attempted to bury her dead brother's body by throwing earth over it. Alex does the opposite—she attempts to uncover what has been buried by taking away the earth that has covered it. The metaphors of burying and uncovering informed how I read Alex's account: what has been buried in our understanding of organizations that Alex uncovers in her description? That led to identification and interpretation of the three disjunctures.

DISPLACEMENT ONE: LABOUR AND WORK—THE ARCHAEOLOGIST IN THE TRENCH

Archaeologists, in Alex's account, are peripatetic workers hired on short-term contracts. In eight years she had worked for 27 different companies in the UK, for many of them more than once, and she had worked on several excavations outside the UK. This is how she described a typical week's work.

The working week starts on Sunday afternoon, when she packs her equipment and work clothes, which include waterproof clothing, a steel hardhat, and a flash jacket, because often she will be working on construction sites cataloguing evidence of past histories before they are buried beneath layers of 21st-century concrete. If the dig is far from home, she drives there late on Sunday night or early on Monday morning to get to the accommodation, usually a rented holiday cottage, which she shares with five or six people who may never have met before they were hired for this excavation. It involves sharing a twin bedroom, perhaps with a stranger. The day starts at 6 a.m., and work starts at 7 a.m. She takes a packed lunch and 'quite large volumes of food' because the work is 'quite physically demanding' but 'in the middle of nowhere', so all provisions have to be obtained beforehand. If there are no facilities for boiling water for drinks on site, she takes a flask of hot water, but 'if you are lucky they might boil a site kettle, but if you're quite far away from the site there might not even be time to do that'. It 'would be a dreadful catastrophe if you forgot your flask because you're outside'.

At the site, the workers put on their protective clothing, and the site supervisor

> *would either give you your tasks not finished off on Friday, or perhaps explain to you the next section of work that he wants to do, um, and on most sites you have a rough idea of what you are expecting from either a geophysics survey done previously or a desktop study where they look at records of what's previously been found, so you would know perhaps that we're on a mediaeval site and we're expecting to find lots of rubbish pits, so someone might set to and go to that section and dig out half of it and then draw the cross-section and plan them.*

She takes her equipment, including lamp, spade and drawing equipment, to the site where she will be working. If it is a 'large feature', she may

> *work in a pair. Alternatively I work by myself with some other people a few metres away from me, doing individual work, and there'd be a*

supervisor probably for every 10 to 15 people who would come across and check our work. . . . But for the most part I would be expected to go onto site, select my own order of work for the day, and study the different features, remove all the soil and take it away, and do the drawings.

There are standardised recording sheets to be completed, and 'If we have found any artefacts then we might bind those up separately' and number them. They usually have two or three breaks in a day: a 15-minute break in the morning, a 30-minute lunch break and a 15-minute tea break. There is little socialising during the working day, and much of the work is done in isolation and in silence:

Someone might call and ask your opinion over what you think, but if you're seen just talking the supervisor might glare at you or come across and shout, but it's usually the young ones who've just started who do stuff like that.

The terms and conditions of employment are not good: 'It's standard practice to lay people off at Christmas and the New Year' and to be on fixed-term contracts: 'I know someone who had a two week contract . . . which of course is illegal now'. Many employers, Alex thought, try to circumvent employment laws. The longest contract she has been on was '11 months and 2 weeks because they laid me off a few weeks before I got any employment rights'. This she regards as 'typical', but she sees no point in protesting because 'getting a reputation as a troublemaker would effectively blacklist your career, that's something you don't tend to do'. Further,

Career progression is very difficult, and I certainly have been up to four or five grades above a basic figure and then gone right the way back to the bottom again on the next position simply because I would rather stay in work rather than worry too much about pay and progression.

In many ways, then, Alex's account is of an exploited workforce. Archaeologists' work has similarities with that of 'precarious workers' (Anderson, 2010) such as migrant workers recruited to work on temporary contracts in factories and farms all over Europe (MacKenzie and Forde, 2009). They engage in hard, manual labour in often-appalling working conditions, have no security of employment, move from one job to another, and cannot organize or complain for fear of not getting the next job. The first thesis of this book, discussed in Chapter One, is that labour and work should be distinguished from each other: labour involves the tasks we do, and work is the processes of self-making over and above the mere doing of tasks. In relation to Alex's work, archaeologists' *labour* involves tasks that largely exclude anything other than the construction of abject selves.

However, many archaeologists, Alex said, are from rich backgrounds (Alex is an exception), and entry is to a profession (rather than an ordinary job) via a university degree. There is therefore much about the job that elevates the labour into work that allows construction of a (professional) self. Alex loves her work and self-consciously revels in the identity of 'archaeologist'. She described advertising for someone to share a flat with her:

> A: *I put 'female archaeologist, 24, seeks flat mate' and I looked at it and I thought well, [pause] that's what I think of myself, I don't think, you know, Aquarian, or, you know, I don't think female rugby lover, I think female archaeologist, that's what I've always identified myself as.*
> N: *So you define yourself by your job?*
> A: *Pretty much, yeah.*
> N: *And your gender.*
> A: *But I think I had to tack the female on because I had a few mixed-sex flat shares and wasn't too happy about them . . . but I think I also thought that being an archaeologist, people see you as an interesting person and that I might get someone like-minded to share with if I sort of emphasised that part of my personality.*
> N: *So why do you think of the archaeologist as interesting?*
> A: *[Long pause] Certainly a lot of archaeologists are considerably better travelled than people in more conventional jobs. . . . And again [raising voice], it does tend to be called a glamorous job, which it isn't in the slightest, it's a very wet, cold, miserable job.*

Earlier, when talking about why she had chosen to pursue an archaeology degree, Alex had said, 'I just wanted to do something more interesting and more unusual, I didn't want to do what everybody else expected', so she chose a career that she understood to be different from other careers and, she understands (hence the raised voice when referring to a general other that calls the job glamorous), one with a reputation for glamour.

So, Alex knows the physical reality of the job ('very wet, cold, miserable'), but she also engages with a fantasy of it as 'glamorous'. She engages in a fantasy in which material experience is subordinated to an image of the job. I suggested in Chapter One that fantasy is important in the distinction between labour and work, between the doing of tasks and work on the construction of the self who does those tasks. In this chapter we delve into a shared fantasy, in which the camaraderie of the dig is the site of self-making, of mutual recognition of the archaeologist self. Fantasies about work facilitate my development of the me I aspire to be; in Alex's case, this is a me who does glamorous, exciting work and who is therefore a glamorous and exciting person.

There is an analogy here with *The Antigone*, because Alex is burying an unpalatable issue. I do not want to stretch that analogy too far, but there is further inspiration to be found in the pages of *Antigone's Claim* (2000). Although I was intrigued initially by the analogy between soil and burying/disinterring when I heard Alex's account of her work, it was the importance of friendships within that telling of the archaeologists' world that first took me back to *Antigone's Claim*, whose main thesis concerns kinship, for a more meaningful way of understanding Alex's working life.

Reading the First Displacement through *Antigone's Claim*

Butler's interpretation of *The Antigone* facilitates her critique of the limitations psychoanalysis places upon who can be classified as kin. I will draw directly on that argument later; at this point I am using only a small part of her analysis of Antigone's encounter with Creon to pursue Alex's experience of the *labouring* involved in her *job*. This contradicts the fantasy of the *work* that she does, that is, constituting a professional identity as 'the archaeologist'. Butler's interpretation of that seminal encounter, transferred to an understanding of Alex's account, establishes that for labour to become work requires that recognition be afforded. That is, Antigone's deed of carrying out the funerary right of scattering soil over her brother's body is not what turns her into a lawbreaker. The fact that she has done what she sees as her duty to her dead brother becomes a fact only when she is hauled before Creon and other witnesses and affirms what she did: it is the act of speaking about the deed, rather than the doing of it without witnesses, that is the deed itself. In other words, I am developing further the distinction between labour and work and between the zombie-machine and the human by exploring the importance of speech rather than labour for recognition.

Alex illuminates the distinction between labour (the work that is done by the zombie-machine) and work, wherein the self is constituted as human. The crucial statement here is Alex's definition of what makes her, as an archaeologist, interesting and glamorous:

> *it does tend to be called a glamorous job, which it isn't in the slightest, it's a very wet, cold, miserable job.*

The important reference here is to what the job is 'called', that is, how it is articulated in language. Butler (2002) draws out the distinction between Antigone's two deeds: the doing of the act of scattering dust over her brother's cadaver and her use of language to claim that deed. In Alex's account, we have a similar distinction between the act itself (digging in the dirt of the archaeological excavation) and her describing it to me. Butler argues that Antigone's *description* of what she has done is an act in itself, for actions can be reported or understood only within language, so embodied actions become meaningful only through language. It is when affirming her act in language that Antigone becomes criminalised; prior to that moment she was, it could be argued, doing nothing other than performing the required funerary rights for a dead brother (Blundell, 1995). The same act could be interpreted in very different ways. It is in her speaking about it and her refusal to deny that she had done this deed that, Butler argues, renders Antigone a criminal.

I suggest that in Alex's account, the mechanisms are similar, but the outcome is very different: that is, through affirming her act in language, she transforms mundane labour into glamorous work. That is, it is the act of talking which performatively constitutes archaeological labour as that which is done by exciting and glamorous professional staff.

Antigone's act can be performed only through 'embodying the norms of the power she opposes' (Butler, 2000:10), for the power of her verbal acts lies in 'the normative operation of power that they embody without quite becoming' (ibid.). We saw earlier how Shakeel, a sorting-office labourer, embodies managerial norms even as he appears to resist them. Alex, however, does not oppose the power of the employer but instead uses the normative operation of power of the professions (Friedson, 1986; McMurray, 2011) to claim a professional identity. She refuses to acknowledge that the messy, dirty labour is merely digging in the dirt. The scraping away of soil and the poor working conditions are described as something that is palpably different from how we must imagine the material reality and thus Alex, through the words that are her deeds, can transform labour into work on the self.

In other words, Alex can speak from the position of archaeologist only if she accedes to that prior claim that archaeology is a glamorous, exciting *profession*. To be an archaeologist rather than a labourer requires that she talk about glamour and excitement and about being a member of the profession. In her speech, she must refuse her work's mundane everyday characteristics even as she acknowledges them. Through defining the profession as exciting and glamorous she upholds the law of the language of the profession of archaeology, a language that belies, at the same time as it redefines, its material practices.

DISPLACEMENT TWO: BECOMING AN ARCHAEOLOGIST—FROM HATRED TO LOVE

Alex's words are her constitutive deeds: through speaking, she becomes archaeologist.

The second major contradiction in Alex's account concerned how she was converted from hating excavations to loving the experience of them. Analysis of this second displacement shows the importance of witnesses to speech acts.

Students of archaeology at the university where Alex studied went on their first excavation at the end of their first year. She hated the experience. Looking back at it, she said, the archaeology was 'the best archaeology I've ever seen'. She 'made some really good friends when I was there, but the weather was abysmal and there was a lot of very hard physical labour that I wasn't used to and I hated it'. She said that

> *we weren't really in any way trained to dig, and so you were almost thrown in at the deep end and that combined with . . . really poor weather made it six weeks of hell for me.*

She therefore decided to focus on working in museums. However, forced to take the first job that came her way after graduating, she found herself working as an archaeologist at an excavation that involved teaching students. She did not have a car at that time, so the journey to this first dig involved a daily four-hour commute, but:

> *it was AMAZING. . . . I spent a lot of time hiding behind a Land Rover reading the manual to work out what skills I was supposed to be teaching, and then I'd sort of read this secretively and then walk round the Land Rover and tell everybody what they were supposed to be doing. It was an Iron Age excavation, and it was one of those golden summers. It was beautiful weather, the people were really nice, both professionals [and mature students], and they were the most amazing bunch of really dedicated people who were really passionate about it. And the site was really interesting, and good fun. Suddenly all the problems that I'd had long ago [on the students' dig] didn't seem to matter. I realised it was just that place at that time that I didn't enjoy.*

There are many similarities between the two occasions: in each, Alex felt underprepared for the tasks she had to do, but she reports that the archaeology itself was interesting at both sites. She had made really good friends on the student dig and enjoyed the company of the people on the second excavation. The weather was very different, but she has subsequently come to take it for granted that the weather will generally be awful—surely one 'golden summer' could not have accustomed her to the physical experiences of her many later digs? We saw earlier that Alex is able to hold comfortably two contradictory perspectives of her profession, that it is hard, dirty work and that it is glamorous. I will suggest that her first experience of a dig, at the end of the first year of a degree that she thought would prepare her for a glamorous profession, revealed its physical reality to her and shattered her original fantasy. However, her second experience was as a graduate who could now call herself 'an archaeologist', and I will argue that the experience of being an archaeologist required that the fantasy be restored. This is because of the performativity of the identity 'archaeologist'.

There are two scenes of encounter in Alex's story of a neo-Damascene conversion from hating archaeological digs to loving them. In the first, Alex is a student in company with fellow students being taught by archaeologists; in the second, she is an archaeologist who is teaching students and working alongside fellow archaeologists. At this point, what is important is the performativity of the terms 'student' and 'archaeologist', so Butler's development of Althusser's theory of interpellation offers most help in exploring the scenes in which Alex is interpellated first as 'student' and second as 'archaeologist'.

Butler on Interpellation

Butler challenges ontologies: rather than there being preexisting domains, domains are materialized through discursive, material practices. There is thus, Butler told us in her early work (1990; 1993) no gender prior to its citation: no male or female preexists the discursive, material practices which bring about their masculinity or femininity. Butler (1993:7) eliminates causality: there is neither precedence nor succession, but,

> Subjected to gender, but subjectivated by gender, the 'I' neither precedes nor follows the process of this gendering but emerges only within and as the matrix of gender relations themselves'. (Butler, 1993:7)

The materiality of the body, its sex and gender, the 'I' that locates the body as the site of its emergence, are all thus performatively achieved through a constantly reiterated process of becoming. Applied to Alex, this means there is not a 'student' or 'archaeologist' who precedes the identity but one that comes into being, is constituted within and through the terms of these appellations. The 'student' and the 'archaeologist' are sites in which identities are constituted through reiteration, reestablishment and sedimentation of discourses, materialities, psyches and affect, with the terms themselves acting in, through and upon the materiality of (performatively achieved) bodies and, in so doing, constituting subjects and subjectivities.

Most fundamental, perhaps, the 'I' depends upon recognition that it is a human subject, a recognition given through language and interaction:

> We have a primary dependence upon language because it is through language that we are constituted. Language, and the address of the Other, is what makes us recognisable, and therefore gives us both identity and a place in the community. (Butler, 1997:5)

The subject is constituted by, within and through language, so language is 'the condition of possibility for the speaking subject' (Butler, 1997:28). We have already seen that in Alex's case, it is the speaking about archaeology as an exciting and glamorous profession that facilitates the constituting of the archaeological self. That speech acts 'constantly renew' sets of relations and practices which traverse human and nonhuman domains (Butler, 2010:150) means that the very use of the terms 'student' and 'archaeologist' re-cites a history which, without needing conscious articulation, speaks of expectations of how tasks shall be undertaken, hierarchies maintained and economic and social practices sustained. Further, Butler (1997) shows how power, in the ways in which it works on and through the psyche, both subjects and subjectifies. Power makes identity possible but at the same time constrains and subordinates subjects' possibilities for existence. The subject must conform to cultural norms that work in and through the psyche if it is to be recognized and thus be able to be. All of this takes place within a scene of recognition (Butler, 1997). Butler builds on Althusser's model of interpellation to explain how language constitutes the self. Briefly, as discussed in Chapter Two, Althusser famously outlines a scene in which a police officer hails the passer-by with "hey you". The passer-by, in turning to answer the call, comes into being (takes on an identity). Butler shows that the one who recognizes him/herself and turns around to answer the police officer's call does not, strictly speaking, preexist that call. The act of recognition is thus an act of constitution: the address animates the subject into existence and provides identity (1997:108).

This takes us back to Alex and the two contrasting scenes of recognition.

Imagine ourselves for a moment with Alex in that first summer on a dig. We are trudging through mud, are cold from the wind and the rain, and are scrabbling to remove soil, no doubt encountering worms and creepy-crawlies, seeking to find anything that might tell us about the earlier occupants of the site. We are students: that we do not know much about what we are doing and have to turn to lecturers for advice about every little aspect of the work means we are interpellated, at each of those turns for advice, as 'student'. The history of the term carries with it a baggage of meaning that involves study, revelry, rebellion, and initiation into adulthood. There is within this history of the term 'student' no hint whatsoever of working outdoors in mud, wind and rain. In the subject position of 'student', Alex saw what she was doing through the lens of the student, and she saw not glamour but drudgery. The physical reality proved much different from the fantasy of glamour and excitement that, for her, was part of the 'inherited set of voices' about archaeology. Hailed 'Hey you, student' she turned and slipped in the mud.

Move forward now to the second excavation. Alex has graduated and is an archaeologist, although she has not yet done anything other than voluntary work in a museum. At the dig, she works with fellow archaeologists and teaches students about archaeology. The terms through which she is interpellated, the possibilities for being, have changed dramatically. Now, when she is called, she hears 'Hey you, archaeologist', and she turns in response to a name that carries with it a history of glamour, excitement and professionalism. To be that person, the archaeologist, requires that she see what she is doing through a different lens: rather than mud and dirt, she will now see ancient historical sites that are in danger of disappearing forever if she is not there to catalogue them. The mud and the dirt are regarded from this subject position not as the cause of personal discomfort and unhappiness but as the sediment of centuries that has kept safe the artefacts she will disinter. Her whole physical experience changes because, *qua* archaeologist, she undertakes her work from within a different subject position: she is a member of an exciting, important profession, and every movement of her body constitutes that archaeological self. She must guard herself against the worst predations of the weather and equip herself with the wherewithal to withstand its discomforts, but those acts are now part of the performativity through which 'the archaeologist' is constituted. Removing the soil becomes not drudgery but an act through which, reiterated time and time again, she becomes 'archaeologist'; every little movement of fingers and bending of back repeated, over and over again, and (more important) every recounting of these experiences to the witnessing interviewer constitutes Alex 'the' 'archaeologist'.

Alex's conversion, in this reading, arises from her occupying different subject positions, in which the name that she is called facilitates different interpretations of exactly similar acts. Within the subject position of student she sees material surroundings and bodily acts very differently from how she sees them when in the subject position of archaeologist. In the first, the bending of the back and the digging away of the dirt, moment to moment to moment, carry with each movement a history that she refuses: that of toiling as a labourer in the soil, rather than achieving the intellectual distance of the student with her books. In the second, the bending of the back and the digging away of the dirt, moment to moment to moment, carry with each movement a history and an understanding that performatively constitutes the idea of 'archaeologist'. It is not merely the acts that are important but the very names, 'student' and 'archaeologist', which facilitate her interpretation of the acts. These names encapsulate the sedimented meanings and histories of the identities. They reverberate in the psyche, calling forth despair and loathing or joy and determination, according to subject position.

Further, Althusser's thesis on interpellation, as expanded by Butler, shows that it is not the person who calls out 'hey you' that is important but the identity or subject position of that person. It is only because the individual is in the subject position of police officer that I become a criminal in that moment of turning. Thus Alex *qua* student is constituted in that identity through fellow students and their teachers; Alex *qua* archaeologist is constituted through the conferring of recognition by fellow archaeologists and her students.

Alex's account shows that it is not the supervisor, manager or employing organization that accords her the identity of archaeologist (and thus of the human). The supervisor allocates responsibilities and ensures that everyone's attention is given to the tasks of the job: no talking is allowed on the dig save that which is directly concerned with progressing the excavation. In the sight of the supervisor, the people employed on the dig do nothing but labour. They scrape away soil, catalogue and record what they find and try to make sense of the history they are uncovering. They are digging/cataloguing/interpreting zombie-machines. How then do they become archaeologists, proud of their profession? Who interpellates them into that identity? In the two scenes examined here, it was the people with whom Alex had been working and sharing time, to which must be added the third scene, that of the interview, in which I addressed Alex as an archaeologist. The third displacement in Alex's account elucidates the crucial importance of friends in recognising the self as a human rather than a zombie-machine.

DISPLACEMENT THREE: WORKING AS AN ARCHAEOLOGIST: THE IMPORTANCE OF FRIENDSHIP

It is necessary to understand the contradictions in Alex's account, between the manual labour she does and the glamorous professional status she claims and her sudden conversion from hating to loving the labour, in order to comprehend the place of friendship in the transitions between labour (digging in the dirt and hating it) and work (regarding the self as a professional and loving it).

Displacement One showed that Alex's words are her constitutive deeds: through speaking, she becomes archaeologist. Displacement Two shows that the witness to her words, the witness that hears her speak and, in responding, confers recognition, must return her words to her if she is to be interpellated as human. The supervisor does not do this—his/her hail is to a digging machine. It is fellow archaeologists who call out 'hey you, archaeologist', and it is by responding to that call that Alex becomes archaeologist. The third displacement explores further who it is at the workplace that affords that recognition. The contradiction in Alex's account in this third displacement is her contrasting the friendships she has when working on a dig with the absence of friends when working temporarily in offices in between excavations. Whereas 'the organization' as embodied by the supervisor recognises only zombie-machines, Alex's account illuminates that workplace friendship does the work of identifying the self as human.

Alex alluded, in her description of her working week, to sharing a house with five or six strangers. As she expanded on her description, the importance of these people and the camaraderie of the work featured very strongly. Although much of the work is carried out in isolation and chatter is frowned upon, 'there's a big sense of camaraderie on site'. Alex gave a thick description of the establishment of the group of comrades:

> I think when you start a dig it's quite often almost there's a sensing out of the pecking order. . . . There's a lot of questioning, you know, have you worked a few years, are you friends with this person or that person. . . . It's quite a small profession, pretty much everyone knows each other or they know a friend of a friend, so you might have heard stories about the people who, or you might randomly bump into someone that you've done work with previously. Which sometimes is great and you bump into friends, sometimes it's dreadful when you bump

into ex-boyfriends or, um, people that you literally cannot stand or you think they are dreadful and they're childish, and so those first couple of days are always a lot of stories, setting out you know . . . who's better than me, who's worse than me, is there somebody who perhaps is very new to this and needs looking after, is there somebody who's lazy and needs a kick now and then, is there somebody who is a brilliant fount of all knowledge and a really, you know, somebody that you would want to pick their brains and learn from them.

There are opportunities for discussions during the dig:

People have to go back and forth to collect equipment and deposit records, and that takes place all the time, so quite often as they go past you they'll sort of stop and make a few comments or ask how your work is going, and that's accepted because somebody else might have a perspective on what you're doing. A lot of these things come down to interpretation, to what do you think is going on, . . . so it's quite important to have opportunities to speak to people working in the same area.

But it is the pleasure of the company outside the actual working hours that is very much valued:

Well, it's great. I've spent hours and hours with a radio next to me and been perfectly happy knowing that in two hours time I'm going to be in a small metal site hut with 20 people that are all laughing and joking and I'll go off by myself again tomorrow.

There are many opportunities for interactions away from the dig itself (where talking is not allowed):

You're with people 24/7, usually away from home, you work with them, live with them, you socialise with them.

There is time spent in the pub and time spent in the shared accommodation. Care is an important part of the time spent together:

I have REALLY good friends in my work. [They leave] cups of tea outside my bedroom door. I'd come home and someone would have been to the shop and bought a chocolate bar, you know, and it's thousands of times, you know. . . .

People help out with some

of the heavier or more brutal chores, removing spoil works. . . . It's those little kindnesses that make the site feel like a family.

Archaeology supervisors not only have a policing role—they inhibit talk on site—but also are described at one point as having an emotional role, as if they are an important part of this family: they

almost take on like an avuncular role. . . . They tend to look for the emotional well-being of their staff or the best supervisors do, as well as just the progress of the work.

Alex compares this with what happens in the offices she has worked in as an administrator between digs:

when I've done office work, temporary, in between digs, I've always been struck by how supervisors are there to concentrate on the work, and it's very [physically] close to people, but it's quite isolating, you don't end up in personal chitchat, you don't get to know these people, you just work with them. . . . I get the impression that people [in offices] go there and then they go home to their friends.

How Alex constitutes the role of the supervisor is important here. It was only when drawing a contrast between office work (denigrated) and archaeological work (lauded) that Alex introduced the idea that archaeology supervisors have an emotional (and therefore valuable) role that is absent from office supervisors' role, which she reduces to solely that of policing. In other words, Alex has to do repair work to her earlier statements in order to sustain her account of the differences between archaeological and administrative work.

I will argue later that this contrast with office work is informative: the people Alex works with as a temporary administrator cannot give her the recognition of herself as an archaeologist but recognize her only as an administrator, an identity she does not want.

Why is friendship so important? What is constituted within and through these interactions with workplace friends? I suggest that these encounters between workplace friends are not 'innocent' but are constitutive of workplace selves. It is in these moment-to-moment encounters that the self is interpellated, on each temporary stage where that self meets its other. During the interview, I was also witness to (and thus was able to re-cognise) Alex's constitution of herself as an archaeologist. In what follows, I will argue that each encounter between workplace friends does a similar service, over and over and over. It is they who give us recognition that we are human and who therefore help us refuse the identity of zombie-machine. First, I will stage Alex's encounters with supervisors, fellow archaeologists and office workers as scenes of recognition such as that between Creon and Antigone. This will lead into the final part of this chapter, where I will develop a theory of workplace friendship's place in the recognition and thus in the elevation of labour to work, or self-making, and in the movement from the zombie-machine to the human.

ALEX AND RECOGNITION

Butler's reading of *The Antigone* facilitates her critique of Western psy-choanalytical theory's perpetuation of the Oedipal triangle and thus the possibilities for kinship. That interpretation is vital for the theory I will develop in this chapter because it asks questions about whether or not 'blood' can be the sole arbiter of who it is that we are, can or should be close to. However, I am not interrogating that aspect of Butler's reading in this chapter, but rather keeping its query in mind as we explore what 'workplace friendship' may be. At this point, I want to continue to ex-plore interpellation within the scene of the encounter, and particularly the limitations on identity in the scene between Creon and Antigone: Creon can accord Antigone the identity of kin or tragic criminal; Antigone can accord him that of kin, king or tyrant. I am reading Creon as analogous to the organization and Antigone as analogous to a member of staff and, more specifically, to Alex. Creon/organization demands conformity to its power to state what can and what cannot be done. That is, it demands that the staff member become zombie-machine, and Antigone/employee must either bow down to that power and become zombie-machine or escape from the site of Creon/organization into spaces where friendships flourish and the self can become human. Alternatively she may do both, as we will see. At the same time, I want to keep in mind Bernstein's (2010) sympathetic rereading of Hegel's account of *The Antigone*. She teases out of his writing recognition of an absence in Greek ethical life both of any concept of a self independent of its roles and of knowledge of any self expressing a singularizing 'who' through its actions. It is the woman, Antigone, who carries for Hegel the task of instigating the 'I' or the 'me', separate from a collectivity of roles. In this scene of encounter between Creon/organization and Antigone/employee, we will therefore be explor-ing how the 'I' or the 'me' can constitute its self when the organization allows no such identity.

The First Encounter: Organization and Self

When Alex arrives at a dig, the supervisor allocates work for the day or the week and monitors the activity of each archaeologist. The supervisor prevents any socializing at the dig itself. Discussions, Alex points out, are limited to talking about the job they are doing:

> *People have to go back and forth to collect equipment and deposit re-cords, and that takes place all the time so quite often as they go past you they'll sort of stop and make a few comments or ask how your work is going. . . .*

But 'just talk' or non-work-related talk is a 'waste of time', and if the supervisor sees that happening, then

*the supervisor might glare at you or come across and shout, but it's usu-
ally the young ones who've just started who do stuff like that.'*

Alex will therefore spend 'hours and hours with a radio next to me'.

This first scene of encounter therefore involves supervisor/organization/
Creon, who demands that archaeologists be no more than digging/catalogu-
ing machines. Antigone disappears from this scene: she perhaps joins her
sister, Ismene, in the 'women's quarters', that place reserved for those who
are not allowed participation on the public stage. There is conformity to the
tyrant's rule, so only labour can be carried out. The work of self-making, of
becoming human, must go on elsewhere, in the spaces and places where the
acts of talking about the work are responded to by those with a different
power, that of interpellation into the human.

The Second Encounter: Friends and Self

We must therefore look to another scene of encounter, one that must per-
force take place away from the site in which labour is carried out. Alex
recounts numerous interactions between her and her fellow archaeologists
who spend every moment of their waking days in each other's company. In
these encounters, no Creon-like figure appears. Power is not evident, and in
its stead there is freely given recognition.

Archaeology is 'quite a small profession, pretty much everyone knows
each other or they know a friend of a friend', so when people arrive for
the first time at a new dig, they spend some time identifying who is who.
Alex's account gives precedence to the personal characteristics of the new
colleagues: is this a person that is liked or not? The ordering of a professional hierarchy comes next, with the self locating itself as an archaeologist
(who's better than me, who's worse than me). Finally, the self accords recognition to other archaeologists: should individuals be looked after, kicked or
approached as a brilliant fount of all knowledge? In the shared accommodation, participants are acknowledged as humans with professional skills.
The pleasure of the company of these people is very much valued. Alex is
perfectly happy to be isolated, 'knowing that in two hours time I'm going to
be in a small metal site hut with 20 people that are all laughing and joking'
and later sharing accommodation with really good friends who provide care
for each other (making tea, buying chocolate, helping with some of the more
difficult workplace tasks).

The recognition of the self as something different from zombie-machine
therefore takes place away from the watchful eye of the supervisor.

As soon as the physical labour stops socializing begins. The labourer puts
down her tools for the day and, walking away from the site, turns to talk
to friends and colleagues and, in so doing, becomes something more than a
labourer: she is transformed into archaeologist. This is a very different scene
of encounter, in a place or space where not only does the rule of Creon/or-
ganization have no sway but it is as if it does not exist.

Recognition as an archaeologist comes through interaction with other archaeologists—in the metal hut, the pub and the living accommodation—where the person is recognised as an archaeologist by fellow archaeologists who do not recognise themselves or their colleagues as digging machines. The limitations on recognition imposed by Creon/organization disappear. When archaeologists face each other in joking, laughing and socialising, they do so not as labourers but as fellow archaeologists in a 'glamorous and exciting' profession. They accord each other this identity but, in so doing, also recognise each other and are in turn recognised, as human. The act of talking about their labour, away from the site of that labour, resignifies that labour as work (on the self). It is in these encounters that the self, sharing with others its understanding of the profession, is called into its desired identity, that of (glamorous, exciting) archaeologist, and thus the fantasy of the selves they want to be informs the selves they constitute when in interaction with fellow archaeologists.

The recognition of the archaeological self as fully human and therefore with the weaknesses and need for care of the human is recorded in all the little kindnesses mentioned by Alex: the purchasing of bars of chocolate, the making of mugs of tea, the offering of help when a colleague is moving large amounts of soil. All these are done by the friends who work together and who provide recognition of the self as not a labourer but a worker who constitutes an identity or self beyond that of labourer.

The scene of recognition here is therefore, as Bernstein observes in Hegel's account, a separation of individual, or subject, from its role: the subject becomes distinguishable from its labour. However, what is not recorded in the Antigone is any account of friendship. There is family and there is the state, with nothing else between. *The Antigone* fails us at this point, albeit only temporarily.

The Third Encounter: Self and People Who Share a Work Space

Alex's reference to her experience of the temporary office work she carries out between digs shows that it is not just any colleague or friend who can accord recognition. The desired recognition can be constituted only through interaction with others occupying the desired subject position. I will repeat here what Alex says about temporary office work:

> *I've always been struck by how supervisors are there to concentrate on the work, and it's very [physically] close to people, but it's quite isolating, you don't end up in personal chitchat, you don't get to know these people, you just work with them. . . . I get the impression that people [in offices] go there and then they go home to their friends.*

Her description of what is happening here is in many ways similar to her description of a dig, where there is also no 'personal chitchat' on the job and where supervisors focus on keeping people working. What is different is that she does not develop friendships with other people in the offices in which she has worked. As a temporary worker, she remains something of an outsider, and it could be that she is not accorded recognition because she will be in that job for only a short time. However, this contradiction in her talk with regard to supervisors suggests something else. She has to correct herself in her account of archaeological supervisors after this point, describing them as 'avuncular', in order that her arguments do not contradict her stated dislike of what goes on in offices. That repair work not only hints at the work she has to do to maintain her story of archaeology and herself as archaeologist but also directs us to look more closely at this statement about office work. Where here is the scene of encounter?

There does not appear to be one. The work is 'isolating', and, as 'you just work with' people, there is no scene in which interpellation and recognition of the self can take place: Alex refuses to turn when called to be office worker. The self she desires to be, that of the exciting and glamorous archaeologist, cannot be constituted in the office. In other words, Alex refuses any working identity other than that of archaeologist, so she turns away from encounters that accord her anything other than her desired identity, of the me she wishes to be.

SUMMARY

An archaeologist's account of her working life contains three displacement, or points where there are contradictions or where the sense of what she is saying breaks down. Analysis of these three disjunctures leads to the thesis that it is through speaking about herself *qua* archaeologist that Alex constitutes her desired identity, of the me she wishes to be, which is that of a member of an exciting and glamorous profession. However, she requires witnesses to her words who go beyond the position of listener to that of active interpellator—for her to recognise herself as an archaeologist requires that fellow archaeologists recognise her as archaeologist. Without such recognition, she is someone whose work involves hard manual labour in poor and difficult conditions. The recognition that allows her to work on herself, as well as to labour in the dig, comes not from the organization but from her friends, fellow archaeologists/diggers in the dirt. Where witnesses are ignorant of her work or lack the power to re-cognise her, she does not turn to their call. When the witness is the supervisor or perhaps another representative of the employer, Alex is interpellated as a zombie-machine, a position in which she labours but does not work and where the power of speech is (literally) denied her. When the witness is a fellow archaeologist, recognition is given and received, and Alex can work on herself, constituting herself as an archaeologist which, in her fantasy of this self she desires to be, elevates her into the human. One role of friendship in the workplace is therefore highlighted. It is the friends with whom we work who have the power to interpellate or to recognise one as human, so it is our workplace friends and not the organization that facilitate our constitution, so far as is possible, of that aspired-to self, the me-I-desire-to-be. The organization demands that one labours and so become no more than a zombie-machine. Agency thus arises outside the place of labour and in the company of friends.

Workplace friendships are therefore vital in the becoming-human at work. However, workplace friendships are largely ignored in management and organization studies, as I will now show, and friendship is a topic that has been little studied in the social sciences more generally. Indeed, although Butler's *Antigone's Claim* is a critique of the narrow limits imposed upon kinship within Western cultures (that is, based on blood relationships within and around the heterosexual couple), she does not explore friendship per se. This chapter's next task therefore becomes that of outlining some steps towards a theory of workplace friendships. I will start with summarising what is currently known about friendship.

Friendship in Management and Organization Studies

Studies that look specifically at friendship in MOS are few and scattered. Although the term 'friendship' is often used in passing, its meaning is not explored. There are only a limited number of empirical studies but numerous conflations of friendship with managerialist terms such as 'networks'.

Gender, or the biological categories of male and female and the descriptors that are presumed to attach to those categories (see Chapter Five), informs some of the limited number of empirical studies of workplace friendships. For example, Elsesser and Peplau's (2006) US-based study found that professionals are inhibited in developing cross-sex friendships because of fear of negative third-party judgements (such as expectations that friends are in a sexual relationship). These studies are part of a wider tradition that presumes, first, that men's friendships are instrumental and much weaker than women's and, second, that women are more successful than men at friendships and value them more highly. Such essentializing and homogenizing of men and women is now widely criticised (Rumens, 2010), with norms governing the constructions of gender shown to precede rather than constitute friendship practices (Smart et al., 2012).

There is another tradition which presumes that workplace friendships are agentive and instrumental and should be contrasted with the presumed communal and intimate friendships of private life (see Rawlins, 1992). Not only has the drawing of such boundaries been criticised for its heterosexist and familistic presumptions (Siltanen and Stanworth, 1984), but Pettinger's (2005) study of female shop assistants in the UK proves the opposite. She found that friendships blur boundaries between work and non-work lives because socialising at and outside work is interrelated. She argues that friendship has instrumental purposes, in that it is important in the getting and keeping of a job and in the capacity for coping with a job's demands, but it also has emotional and social value, as workplace friendships may replace kin networks in an era of family breakdown.

A small body of work continues the agentive/instrumental perspective and argues the benefits to the firm of workplace friendships. For example, Riordan and Griffeth's (1995) survey of staff in one company explores the implications for management of their finding that friendships directly influence job involvement and job satisfaction and indirectly affect organizational commitment. A similar finding is reported by Dickie (2009), who assessed the viability of a Workplace Friendship Scale developed by Neilson et al. (2000). This instrumental view advocates that organizations actively encourage the development of workplace friendships, because it presumes direct links among good friendships, the happier working lives they engender and productivity. The instrumental view of friendship at the individual level is seen also in those accounts whereby friendship is regarded as useful in, for example, career development (Kram and Isabella, 1985); an inability to form friendships can be a 'career disadvantage' (Elsesser and Peplau, 2006:1078).

In total contrast to the instrumental perspective on workplace friendship, some studies show how organizations impede, if not damage, non-work-based friendships. Careers in accountancy, for example, require that trainees sacrifice non-work-related friendships (Anderson-Gough et al., 2000), and the film industry's pattern of intense immersion away from home in short-term contracts disrupts non-work friendships (Rowlands and Handy, 2012). Furthermore, in the film industry, intense relationships that flourish over the short course of a project are replaced by distance and competition (for further work) at its end, so that both workplace and private friendships are damaged.

On the other hand, Rumens' (2008; 2010) and Rumens and Kerfoot's (2009) exploration of gay men's workplace friendships shows the value of workplace friendships not only for support and pleasure but also as 'relational sites for interrogating heteronormative definitions of themselves as organizational Others' (Rumens 2010:1556). Friendship, in Rumens' studies, is therefore seen as a site of self-making.

Grey and Sturdy (2007:166), arguing for research into workplace friendships, conclude that 'it is increasingly clear that we cannot understand processes such as networking and knowledge management and transfer if we denude them of their emotional and experiential meaning and of friendship in particular, but also if we conceive of them solely in terms of their contribution to organizational or individual performance'. They allude here to the ways in which friendship haunts the margins of much writing in management and organization studies. There are numerous references in research papers to friends and friendship, but these tend to be made in passing, with the terms neither defined nor examined. For example, a study of workplace humour (Korczynski, 2011:1427), shows that, 'For many, the key redeeming factors in their working lives at MacTells were the friendships and community among their co-workers', where '[b]onds of togetherness and friendship ran deep on the factory floor'. Implicit but unexamined in Peirano-Vejo and Stablein's (2009:451) study of resistance to organizational change was fear of losing close friendship ties. Sometimes research participants use the terms 'friends' and 'friendship' only to have researchers relabel them. Vogl (2009), for example, subsumes under the term 'community' quotes from interviewees that are replete with references to 'friendships', 'mateship' (4.8) and 'your mates' (4.25). Korczynski and Ott (2005:721) similarly transliterate interviewees' use of "friends' and related terms such as 'mates' into 'trust-based networks'.

There are numerous studies of 'networks' which, in reference to 'weak and strong ties' that are 'at the core of the debate about network benefits' (Elfring and Hulsink, 2007:1849), imply the existence of friendships but leave the topic unexamined. This is seen in an early paper by Lincoln and Miller (1979) which conflates friendships and networks. A more recent example that refers in passing to friends is that of Kikjuit and van den Ende (2010:452), who explore networks of people involved in ideas generation and development. They argue that 'network relations with friends or good colleagues outside one's own subunit are particularly important for idea improvement and survival': the question of the distinction between 'friends' and 'good colleagues' is not posed. These authors advocate 'strong ties and dense networks', where network density refers 'to the degree to which actors within a network are tied to each other' (455), but what, we must ask, is the nature of these 'ties'? High density, they argue, includes development of a shared language, an increased willingness to help and the creation of trust, so where, then, is the dividing line between 'networks' and 'friends'? Strong ties combine 'time, emotional intensity, intimacy and reciprocal services', trust, psychological safety and mutual understanding (456), a list of characteristics that could equally well define friendship (see Grey and Sturdy's [2007] folk definition, later in this section). Other studies offer a range of terms that perhaps encompass friendship and further bedevil the distinction between friendship and other workplace relationships. One such term is 'embeddedness' (Mitsuhashi, 2003), that is, 'the process by which social relations shape economic action' (Uzzi, 1996, in Mitsuhashi, 2003:321). Others are 'community' and 'teamwork' (see Vogl, 2009): the distinction between 'community' or 'team member' and 'friend' are unclear: the terms need unpacking.

The explicit use of the word 'friend' may pose more questions than it answers. For example, Essers (2009) discusses how a relationship with a participant in her research study became a friendship, yet one always troubled by concerns over power and exploitation: was she using a friendship to elicit more interesting information? A friendship emerged gradually after the first interview, she said, through her stopping at the interviewee/friend's shop for a chat, a drink and discussions of 'all kind of things' (168). This poses the question of how the boundaries between the identities of 'interviewee' and 'acquaintance made through an interview' successively gave way and the identity of 'friend' emerged.

The absence, if not the impossibility, of definition confounds some research. Haythornthwaite and Wellman's (1998) exploration of the use of electronic media in a university research group distinguishes between 'work and friendship ties' (1102). It uses a 'social network approach' that examines patterns of ties among people, organizations and other institutions: 'ties are functions of pairs of actors' (1102). They distinguish between 'formally constituted work ties, actual work relations, and friendship relations' (1102). Work ties are defined as describing what there is, in practice, in contrast to work status, which describes what ought to be (1101). 'Informal' contacts characterise work ties—the example given is of faculty members who offer informal advice to students they are not supervising. Friendship ties are described rather than defined (1103)—'the intimacy of coworker's friendships can range from just working together, through acquaintanceship and friendship, to close friendship'. Intimacy seems to be here the term that distinguishes between friendship and what Allan (1979, in Silver, 1990, and referring to Adam Smith) calls 'strangership'. Haythornthwaite and Wellman's (1998) study shows more frequent interactions between those with intense work ties and intimate friendships, again leading to the question of what distinguishes the two, a question we can also ask of Rowlands and Handy (2012). Where is the boundary between friendship and colleagues in 'the intertwined social and professional networks that . . . enable [freelance workers] to secure future employment' (Rowlands and Handy, 2012:660), especially when they are members of 'closed' networks that 'comprise people who have worked together previously and actively seek to re-create themselves as project teams whenever possible' (ibid.)? These questions are difficult to answer, because often the division of subjects of research into networks, teams and other interpersonal relationships eliminate from analysis the embodied, breathing, emoting individuals who staff organizations: they are hidden behind such euphemisms as 'ties' and 'market actors' (Elfring and Hulsink, 2007).

The paucity of studies of workplace friendships has not gone unremarked. Grey and Sturdy's (2007) exploratory article suggests that this neglect is due in part to the subject's being relegated to the 'informal organization' where any deviations from the achievement of organizational goals are regarded as problematic. Second, the focus on the functioning of work groups, evident since the Hawthorn Studies of the 1930s, has subordinated friendship beneath the group. Friendship is therefore 'in some sense the "other" of formal organization' (160). Third, very long-standing traditions in sociology have maintained a dualism between work and friendship. Fourth, friendship may not be regarded as a proper or serious topic for study (162). Grey and Sturdy point out the difficulties of defining friendship and observe that most attempts at delineation 'rely on the drawing of three boundaries between friendship and, respectively, kinship, sexual relations, and paid work' (160). They argue that friendship should be regarded as a folk concept 'where what is emphasized is shared cultural and situational understandings of meaning' (158) and in which friendship is typically understood as meaning 'a relationship of relative and, typically, mutual affection, support, intimacy, and freedom that may be discursively, if not always experientially, distinguished from some familial and sexual relations on one hand and "casual acquaintances" and "just work colleagues" on the other' (163). It also involves trust.

Another paper that starts to theorise workplace friendship is that of Marks (1994), who, pointing to evidence that about one-half of American workers have close friendships with coworkers, argues that at workplaces 'intimacy appears to be a rather pervasive phenomenon' (853). He argues that human actors construct places of intimacy, 'new private niches', in whichever part of the organization their work takes them. Rather than dividing societies into sharply differentiated nuclear families, with intimacy found only within the family, he argues that 'institutional differentiation on the macrolevel, and individuation, dyadic intimacy, "self-disclosure", and privatisation of space and time on the microlevel march together, and these processes unfold in full force both inside and outside families and organizations' (1994:846). In Marks' (1994) study, friendship is defined as emerging from self-disclosure.

Although studies of workplace friendship are sparse, those which avoid an instrumental approach point towards some propositions of a theory of workplace friendship. That is, workplace friendships include emotional bonds and are aspects of self-making. Alex provides insights as to the processes through which self-making occurs. She referred often to the social bonds she shared with her archaeological friends, but she went further in describing the caring work they afforded each other and still further in illuminating how friends confer recognition of the self in its identity. We therefore have some emergent propositions for a theory of workplace friendships, which sociological research, as I will now discuss, can augment.

Sociology and Friendship

In sociology, as in management and organization studies, friendship has not been a major focus of study. However, recent empirical research suggests that boundaries between friendship and kinship are disintegrating.

The most sustained sociological research into friendship is perhaps that of Liz Spencer and Ray Pahl. Their recent empirical work in the United Kingdom (Spencer and Pahl, 2004; 2006) suggests that we bundle under the single label of 'friendship' a wide array of relationships. Participants, asked to outline their 'personal communities', described some friendships as very close and others as distant. They looked to some people for 'fun' and to others for nurturing, care and intimacy. Some friends and relatives were trusted with the most closely guarded secrets, whereas others were told only superficial details of thoughts and feelings. Some blood kin were close and described as friends; others were unimportant, even estranged, and friends provided the closeness that otherwise may have been missing from their lives. Friendships ranged from the superficial to 'soulmates', with some friends described as 'brothers' or 'sisters'. Close kin were described as if they were friends and best friends as if they were kin. Most people have in their personal communities a variety of close and distant friends and family members. It is personal communities, Spencer and Pahl suggest, that provide a sense of belonging and identity through 'biography and the active maintenance of longstanding relationships' (2006:210) and in which friendship and friend-like kin provide 'an important form of social glue'.

The workplace, Spencer and Pahl (2006) report in a frustratingly brief discussion, is an 'extremely important context in which friendships can be made' and where shared interests or beliefs can be 'a powerful basis for friendship' (96). However, the heterogeneity of forms of friendship is seen also in workplace friendships. Some are 'of the moment' and do not survive after people have changed their jobs; others continue and deepen over years. Some workplace friends do not socialise outside work, whilst others do. Workplace friendships suffer sometimes from strains of competitiveness or hierarchical status, but work often takes its toll on non-work friendships.

All this leads Spence and Pahl to conclude that there is a 'suffusion' between friends and family: the boundaries between the two have become blurred. There is no 'polar opposite' between them; rather, there is 'subtlety and complexity [in] people's micro-social worlds' where 'Not only can friends and family play overlapping roles, but kin and non-kin can occupy similar positions in terms of the degree of choice and commitment the relationship entails' (125).

Similar conclusions are reached in the work of Shelley Budgeon and Sasha Roseneil (Budgeon and Roseneil, 2004; Roseneil and Budgeon, 2004), who maintain that 'the category of the family is increasingly failing to contain the multiplicity of practices of intimacy and care which have traditionally been its prerogative and its raison d'etre' (Budgeon and Roseneil, 2004:127). Rather, relationships now cover a broad range, including household communities, non-coresidential intimate partnerships, friendships, and so on, which provide 'intimacy, care and companionship in an individualizing world' (128).

In their recounting of their empirical research, Roseneil and Budgeon (2004) begin by opposing 'family' and 'networks of friends' and end by collapsing the distinction between them. The family, they write, is an 'idea' which 'retains an almost unparalleled ability to move people, both emotionally and politically' (135), for this is where 'cultures of care' are presumed to be located. Networks of friends, meanwhile, are located in 'the burgeoning diversity of contemporary practices of intimacy and care' (136) which are hidden within a heteronormative sociological imaginary which inadequately analyses contemporary changes in cultures of care and valorises the heteronormative family. Friendship's importance is emphasised:

Across a range of lifestyles and sexualities, . . . friendship occupied a central place in the personal lives of our interviewees. There was a high degree of reliance on friends, as opposed to biological kin and sexual partners, particularly for the provision of care and support in everyday life, to the extent that it could be said that friendship operated as an ethical practice for many (Roseneil and Budgeon, 2004:146).

Importantly, 'care and support flow between individuals with no biological, legal or social recognized ties to each other' (Roseneil and Budgeon, 2004:153). Indeed, Smart et al. (2012) found depth and intensity of emotions between close friends. Friendships, they write (2012:99), 'can be ontologically unsettling. By this we mean that the more "complex" the friendship the more it engages the "self" and is part of a process of the formation of one's self-identity or sense of self'. Friendship is thus an intersubjective entanglement involving trust and self-questioning.

Workplace friendships may be one of those areas of understanding that are constantly visible yet whose very commonplaceness makes them invisible (Dollimore, 2001). Have they existed since the days of the first manufactories, ignored except by those involved in them? Before the industrial revolution, households consisted of people who were and were not related by blood. The emergence of a middle class able to invest in its own accommodation led to a movement out of a more generalised, shared household and into 'houses'. Now there emerged changes in the language, by means of which 'relation' and 'relative' were endowed with the property of kinship, in other words, being defined as related by blood and marriage (Strathern, 2005). Although we know that the home became the domain of private relationships, we do not know what forms of affective relationships flourished in the public space of manufactories. Did remnants of the relationships of the shared household inform how people adapted to each other as they began to learn to obey clock-time and the dictates of the supervisor? What we do know is that workplace friendships have been ignored in the context of a heteronormative matrix in which power dictates which relationships can and cannot be valorised (Borneman, 1996). Modern forms of marriage, Borneman (1996) argues, instigated a series of Derridean 'violent hierarchies' where the lesser (the non-married or those in different forms of affective relationship) are always the abjected supplement upon which the dominant relies for its completeness. Kinship has been regarded as superior to friendship (Schneider, 1984). Strathern (2005) writes that forms of kinship and selves that have held sway for two centuries may be malleable if 'the signs' are changed. It may be that other forms of affective relationships have flourished throughout the centuries since the industrial revolution but have remained largely unmarked and unremarked. Alex's experience shows that workplace friendships provide care, support and, most important, recognition. We know from anthropological research (Douglas, 1997) that the sharing of space and eating together, constitutive of kin relationships in some cultures, are also constitutive of close relationships in the West. When we share the space of the office or the factory floor and eat together over a snatched lunch, are we therefore constituting some form of relationship that is perhaps not kin but is important in the constitution of the self? We therefore need more understanding of workplace friendships. For now, I can only draw together the threads of this chapter to see how they contribute to a theory of workplace friendships. This theory is that it is through workplace friendships that recognition of the self as human and constitution of the self as a me that does more than labour are achieved.

TOWARDS A THEORY OF WORKPLACE FRIENDSHIPS

Alex's account of herself as an archaeologist has three curious contradictions or dislocations. She does hard, physical labour in poor conditions but regards herself as a member of a glamorous profession. She hated the labouring when she first tried it as a student but had a Damascene conversion during her first experience as a graduate archaeologist. Friendships are vitally important aspects of working as an archaeologist, but she does not seek them when working in other jobs. I have argued that it is the friends with whom she works, fellow archaeologists, who grant to one another recognition of themselves as professionals, a recognition that is not granted by employers. To the employer and the student, archaeological labour is hard, physical work carried out by people who must follow rules and regulations (that is, zombie-machines). To the archaeologists themselves, however, their labour is an aspect of the work involved as members of a glamorous profession, and it is the function of their fellow archaeologists to grant one another recognition of that identity and thus to turn their jobs into work. Friendship's role thus includes care and nurturing but extends further into recognition. Friendship's recognition of the other allows constitution of that archaeological subject that can be cared for and nurtured. The archaeologist is not cared for by colleagues but rather is constituted through the care they lavish on him/her. In the terms used in this book, friendship lifts one from zombie-machine and into the human.

However, friendship has been largely ignored by researchers in management and organization studies, perhaps indicating further the heteronormativity of much MOS research. Research confirms that social relationships in western Europe in the 21st century are in flux, and individuals are turning to friendships, including workplace friendships, for the physical and emotional sustenance that was previously presumed to exist in the domain of the family. This suggests that boundaries between work and non-work lives are now difficult to draw, as emotional and other needs are articulated and succoured in the workplace as well as in the home. Some research has shown how organizations try to exploit people's needs for the sort of security that friendship gives (Hochschild, 1997). Costas's (2012) important study of how management attempts to foster a friendship culture designed to achieve organizational ends shows that the results are ambiguous. The strategy's emphasis on choice, openness, egalitarianism and diversity actually propagated dependency, social exclusion, hierarchy, competition, ambiguity and inauthenticity. Friendship thus became a form of normative control, although one with unintended outcomes. This chapter's study is very different, as it explores friendship in a context where these relationships had little to do with management. They exist in those aspects of working lives into which management cannot reach, where there is rather than was not so much resistance to as insouciance towards management. We cannot *be* in isolation; we are always ek-static, outside ourselves, in the constitution of that which we call an I or a me (Butler, 2000), and so we turn to others, to friends, for the granting of recognition, as well as for care and support. At its most mundane level, this can be seen in Vogl's (2009:5.5) observation that 'Feeling connected and a sense of relatedness to others in the workplace was very important for the participants in this study. A general sense of community existed across all the workplaces [studied], despite attempts by management in some of the workplaces. . . . to undermine this community'. Workplaces are therefore important sites for the relatedness that is vital in the constitution of the self, and this relatedness is found in close workplace friendships.

Despite the pretence that organizations are governed by the imperatives of rationalism and logic (Townley, 2008), they are constituted through interactions between the people employed to work in them. People are complex *turmoils* of emotions, feelings, affect, needs, desires, psyches, sexualities, embodiedness and so forth (Bollas, 1993; 1995). Workplace friendships, I am suggesting, are sites of reassurance against the torments of the labour and the problems that accompany being with others in a place of work. At the same time, they are sites in which pleasure and joy found in the work and in the company of others can be experienced. They protect us against the worst that the organization can do and offer some of the best that being at work can provide. Workplace friendships therefore are sites of affect and intimacy in which members of our personal communities provide a sense of belonging (Spencer and Pahl, 2006). However, and this is the thesis I am developing here, they extend beyond non-work caring relationships, even though they are similar in so many ways, because of the ways in which they *confer identity*.

Alex's account shows that workplace friendships perform the function of recognition, allowing constitution of the self as human rather than zombie-machine. This is supported also by hints in other research, such as the observation that friends are 'two women who recognise each other (Kaplan and Rose, 1993, in Andrew and Montague, 1998:355), and friendships 'do indeed play a particularly important part in reflecting and maintaining identity' (Andrew and Montague, 1998:360). 'The organization' may refuse us recognition as selves, but we find it nevertheless in the social spaces and places beyond the purview of the management that allows recognition only as a labourer.

However, workplace friendships are not recognised by the organization, and so management can trample over them at will, breaking up groups of friends during restructuring, mergers and acquisitions or other processes of change. This is a form of violence because it inflicts emotional pain that is not recognised or even recognisable and thus cannot be articulated as 'real' pain. Where kinship is recognised in law and has certain rights, workplace friendships are unrecognised and have no rights. The harm that organizations can wreak on employees' lives includes the destruction of friendships and thus of identities. This needs to be challenged by making workplace friendships visible, giving recognition to their importance and ensuring that they become governed by a range of rights.

5 Becoming and Not Becoming Gendered

The category of women does not become useless through deconstruction, but becomes one whose uses are no longer reified as 'referents',
and which stand a chance of being opened up, indeed, of coming
to signify in ways that none of us can predict in advance. (Butler,
1993:29)

When I was seven or eight years old, I read an Enid Blyton story in which
the Famous Five went on holiday to Wales (I think it must have been *Five
Get into a Fix* [1958]). I remember that the farmer's wife who featured in
the story said 'look you' at the end of many of her sentences. I never used
that phrase, resulting in what I would now call an identity crisis: could I be
Welsh if I did not say 'look you'? If I wasn't Welsh, what, then, was I? Similar questions beset me as I read lists of the attributes of the male and female
culled from the literature cited in this chapter. The male is/must be rational,
non-emotional, strong and disembodied/close to culture, the female caring,
nurturing, emotional and embodied/close to nature. My body is biologically
female, and, after it has fallen out of bed each morning, I dress it up so that
it conforms to its biological identity (makeup, hair, nail varnish, clothes,
shoes); after 30 or 40 minutes' labour, I turn the requisite set of arms, legs,
torso, and the rest into a semblance of a woman. Much of this work is pleasurable; what can be painful is the outcome, which places me in a category
in which my career prospects may be limited by gender rather than capabil-
ity (Fotaki, 2011) and in which I may become invisible and silenced. When
one's ideas are dismissed not because of their content but because of the
body that articulates them, that body flinches and shrinks as it experiences
the insult as if it were an act of physical violence.

However, it takes just a few minutes' thought about norms to realise that
these basic distinctions between male and female/masculine and feminine
arise (in the first instance) from categorizations according to physically evident (albeit socially interpreted) characteristics: with/without breasts, vagina
and penis. To these are attached *normative* attributes, widely mistaken for
positive differences: rational/emotional; strong/weak; public/private; logi-
cal/caring. If one is to be a 'real' man, that is, if one does not have breasts or

a vagina but does have a penis, then one has to conform with the norms on the left side of each slash in this list. Those with or without the other requisite bodily protuberances and orifices must constitute themselves according to the appropriate set of norms. Failure to approximate sufficiently well these normative attributes jeopardises, if not makes impossible, recognition and therefore selfhood (Butler, 1990; 1993). This is despite their being culturally variable and arbitrarily, albeit historically, allocated. When I stumble across myself thinking or debating or working, in those times when I become consciously aware of both body and mind, it strikes me that I am not conforming neatly to gendered categories: although I am sometimes within them, at other times I straddle both sides of those boundary lines, and I am sometimes outside them altogether. What gender therefore is the (apparently female) me that is rationally and unemotionally (in an apparently masculine way) considering how it genders itself? More pertinent, what is this 'gender' that Butler has shown I am performatively achieving?

Much research contradicts the belief that sex/gender is a given and immutable biological category, that men are born men and women, women. If that were the case, there would be no need for a chapter on gender, unless it was to explore the continuing inferior position of women and women's jobs. However, that path is very well trodden and I would add little to it. Rather, it is the changes in occupations that intrigue me, notably in management and the professions into which women have made many incursions so that, at least at junior and middle levels, they are very visibly present.[1] This is very different from when I looked for my first job, at the age of 16, when clerical posts were advertised with two pay scales for the same post, one for men and a lower one for women.

Women today are in some ways very different from the matriarchs who crowded in on my mining community childhood a half-century ago. However, I look round at family gatherings and see how my own sisters have in their turn become matriarchs, provoking thoughts about the possibility of the influx of women into management and the professions constituting an organizational matriarchy. Such thoughts would be misplaced, because they imply in some ways a fixity to gender identities that contradicts four decades of feminist and gender studies that attempt to interpret what is going on 'out there', outside the concrete and glass towers of modern universities, and which try to understand what gender *is*. When gender theorists let down their hair and used it to climb out through the windows of the masculine ivory towers they had struggled so hard to enter, they escaped from huge numbers of studies, especially those carried out by psychologists, which regarded, as they still do, male and female as biologically given binary opposites. These studies are blind to feminists' counterargument that gender is a social construction built on biological organs and to poststructural gender theory, instigated by Butler, which argues that biology itself is not fixed and unchangeable but apprehended only within discourse. Indeed, Foucault shows that how we understand genitalia is itself a construction.

How does this relate to the well-established constructionist argument that organizations mandate gender identities, requiring that staff constitute gendered organizational selves in conformity with that requirement (Adler, Laney and Packer, 1993; Benn and Gaus, 1983; Benschop and Doorewaard, 1998; Cockburn, 1990; Duncan, 1996; Gherardi, 1995; Grant and Porter, 1996; Mills, 1992; Mills and Murgatroyd, 1991; Pateman, 1983; Trethewey, 1999)? Many jobs are gendered, with those more concerned with care, such as nursing, elder care and nursery teaching regarded as 'women's' and those requiring, say, heavy physical labour regarded as those of 'men' (Adler, Laney and Packer, 1993; Duncan, 1996; Lam, 2004; Gatrell and Swan, 2008). Organizations 'themselves' are gendered—they are masculine (Alvesson and du Billing, 1992; Calas and Smircich, 1991, 1992; Hearn, 1992; Collinson and Hearn, 1996). That is, they are detached, logical, unemotional places, banning any distractions beyond the work at hand; they are stable, powerful and authoritative (Hearn and Parkin, 1986; Hearn, 1992; Mills and Murgatroyd, 1991; Ross-Smith and Kornberger, 2004). As such, they are not caring, emotional, subjective places close to nature. That is, they are not feminine, not masculinity's inferior, polluting other (Gherardi, 1995; Da Cunha and e Cunha, 2002). The approach of these studies is constructionist. They leave unanswered the question of what gender *may be*, beyond the presumption that masculinity and femininity rely on each other for definition: I am female because I am not male, and vice versa.

To understand *being at work* in the 21st century, we therefore need to understand what gender 'is', how it is constituted, and how it shapes the self as zombie-machine or human. In Butlerian terms, this requires exploration of the performativity of gender in organizational public spaces that were previously the domain of men but now are occupied by both women and men. That is the aim of this chapter: an exploration of the performativity of gender so as to seek answers to the question of what 'is' workplace gender in the early 21st century. In the context of this book, the questions I am exploring include: what is gender in today's organizations? Does the distinction between labour and work hold good when discussing gender? Is the zombie-machine gendered, or the human, and where is gender in my aspirations for the me I desire to be(come) through/in work?

I interviewed two people for this part of the study, a woman and a man. They are academics, chosen because academia, traditionally a masculine profession and one dominated still by men, involves male and female staff carrying out the same tasks regardless of gender, so I anticipated that it would be a useful forum for exploring the performativity of gender: how do female and male academics constitute gendered identities and gendered bodies when undertaking similar tasks—what turns one into a man, and the other into a woman? Do they escape from these binary oppositions? But I also explore how cultural products are reflecting back to us changing gendered cultures of workplaces by discussing the hit science fiction television series *Battlestar Galactica*. The thesis I develop is that we lapse out of gendered identities but are surprised back into them. I use a vignette from the work of Patricia Yancy Martin to illustrate how this happens. But first, the literature review.

DECONSTRUCTING 'GENDER'? A POSTSTRUCTURAL PERSPECTIVE

The questions I am pursuing in this chapter arise from poststructuralist gender theory that challenges the stability, biological or constructed, of masculinity and femininity. It shows that what can seem utterly immutable at a particular point in time is subject to flux and change over a longer period. Those seemingly fixed identities, sex and sexuality, are two categories that have been shown by historians and cultural theorists to be fluid. The male and female, the hetero- and the homosexual, indeed, even the body in modern Western cultures are conceptions of the industrialised era (Foucault, 1979, 1986, 1992; Lacqueur, 1990). Until the industrial revolution, gender was on a continuum along which movement, regardless of embodied identity, was possible (Fletcher, 1995; Harrison and Hood-Williams, 2002). Bodies did not have necessarily determined sexual or gendered identities (Lacqueur, 1990), and the body itself was subject to very different interpretations of its materiality (Judovitz, 2001). It was in the last quarter of the 18th century that what had been a single continuum of gender froze into the binary structure which held sway until late in the 20th century (Fletcher, 1995). Only in the 19th century did the binary divide between hetero- and homosexuality emerge (Sedgwick, 1991). Indeed, it was in this era in the West that the interiorised ego evolved (Brennen, 1993; Taylor, 1992). Presumptions about the fixity of sex/gender are betrayed by contemporary scientific disciplines: research in embryology, endocrinology, urology, psychology, genetics, neurology and other fields shows a 'dizzying variety of sexes available to any human being' (Hester, 2004:218). Factors combine in organic, not mechanistic ways, so that 'variability, multiplicity and pluriformity are integral and necessary aspects of sexed morphologies, identities and sex-object desire' (ibid.), so that 'it is no small exaggeration to suggest that there are not two sexes, nor even five sexes . . . but literally hundreds of possible sexes that humans can inhabit' (219). These are compressed into two cultural codes (Foucault, 1966) that are used when making sense of gender in organizations (Ely and Meyerson, 2000; Kark and Waismel-Manor, 2005; Barry, Berg and Chandler, 2006).

Butler's early work in *Gender Trouble* (1990) and *Bodies That Matter* (1993) on how gendered bodies are performatively constituted is vitally important here. I will next lay out the theoretical framework for this chapter, which includes a summary of Butler's account of the performativity of gender alongside ideas from psychoanalytic theory. This not only illuminates further the ways in which bodies and gender are only arbitrarily related but also explores how gender can be oppressive and constraining. That will lead to the introduction of the people whose accounts will help develop the main thesis of this chapter, which is that work provides an opportunity to step outside the oppressions of gender until, that is, we are surprised back into gendered identities. The thesis that concludes this chapter is that labour requires that we conform to traditional gendered identities, while work allows us to experiment and play with our gendered identities and sometimes escape from their pains.

BUTLER AND THE PERFORMATIVITY OF GENDER

Butler (1990:8–9) states that there are discursive limits that both presuppose and preempt possibilities of gender configurations save those predicated on familiar binary structures: we have no language in which to imagine anything beyond the male/female binary. This is an important observation for this chapter, in which I will explore how an embodied gendered identity may have little relationship to a *subjective* experience that is, to all intents and purposes, outside gender. Although we will meet two people whom we would identify, on first meeting, one as a man and the other as a woman, we do this because of what we see before us: one is taller than the other, one has a lighter voice and so on. Butler, however, in the opening pages of *Gender Trouble*, unties sex and bodies:

> it does not follow that to be a given sex is to become a given gender; in other words, 'woman' need not be the cultural construction of the female body, and 'man' need not interpret male bodies. This radical formulation of the sex/gender distinction suggests that sexed bodies can be the occasion for a number of different genders and further, that gender itself need not be restricted to the usual two. . . . If gender is not tied to sex, either causally or expressively, then gender is a kind of action that can potentially proliferate beyond the binary limits imposed by the apparent binary of sex. (1990:111–112)

External genitalia, traditionally assumed to be the 'sure signs of sex' (1990:110), are part of a cultural discourse which requires that a subject be gendered if it is to be intelligible and have a livable life. The 'inner truth of gender is a fabrication' (1990:136), because gender 'is a fantasy instituted and inscribed on the surface of bodies' (ibid.).

The bodies that are discussed in this chapter are, in Butler's terms, performatively constituted. That is, each micromovement of the body, each tiny, repeated act, occurs within a set of meanings that allows us to constitute it as masculine or feminine. These meanings preexist us: we are born into them and learn how to move within them, to 'constitute the illusion of an abiding gendered self' (1990:140). Thus:

Where there is an 'I' who utters or speaks and thereby produces an effect in discourse, there is first a discourse which precedes and enables that 'I' and forms in language the constraining trajectory of its will. Thus there is no 'I' who stands *behind* discourse and executes its volition or will *through* discourse. On the contrary the 'I' only comes into being through being called, named, interpellated, to use the Althusserian term, and this discursive constitution takes place prior to the 'I'; it is the transitive invocation of the 'I'. Indeed, I can only say 'I' to the extent that I have first been addressed, and that address has mobilized my place in speech; paradoxically, the discursive condition of social recognition *precedes and conditions* the formation of the subject: recognition is not conferred on a subject, but forms that subject. (1993:225–226)

One can 'never be' a gender because the normative assumptions of each of the familiar genders are impossible to achieve and because the process of becoming gendered never ends but is repeated moment after moment after moment. That is, gender has 'no ontological status apart from the very acts which constitute its reality' (1990:136). There is no female, male or other gender identity that preexists the 'expressions' of gender; rather, the female and the male are constituted through the acts that performatively achieve gendered bodies. It is impossible to achieve fully the norms that state what a woman or man '*is*', but to be an 'I' requires that we strive to achieve them, because the 'I' is 'the historically revisable possibility of a name that precedes and exceeds me, but without which I cannot speak' (ibid.).

Thus, as Butler summarises it (1993:2):

a) The appearance of substance is just that: an appearance;
b) Performativity 'must be understood not as a singular or deliberate "act", but, rather, as the reiterative and citational practice by which discourse produces the effects that it names';
c) Sexual difference is materialised through this multitude of repeated little acts that occur within regulatory norms of sex which materialize the body's sex;
d) Although the body is material (it is *matter* that *matters*), that materiality is an effect of power, so how the body is understood (why genitalia are seen as the determinant of sex) is an effect of power;
e) So 'sex' is 'not simply what one has, or a static description of what one is: it will be one of the norms by which the "one" becomes viable at all, that which qualifies a body for life within the domain of cultural intelligibility'.

Her famous analogy with the drag artist does not imply that we are all in drag: what it shows is that we are all imitating something, but what we are imitating had no original that we can copy. Drag performs 'the sign of gender', a sign that is, crucially 'not the same as the body that it figures, but that cannot be read without it' (1993:237), because

The critical potential of 'drag' centrally concerns a critique of a prevailing truth-regime of 'sex', one that I take to be pervasively heterosexist: the distinction between the 'inside' truth of femininity, considered as psychic disposition or ego-core, and the 'outside' truth, considered as appearance or presentation, produces a contradictory formation of gender in which no fixed 'truth' can be established. Gender is neither a purely psychic truth, conceived as 'internal' and 'hidden', nor is it reducible to a surface appearance; on the contrary, its undecidability is to be traced as the play between psyche and appearance (where the latter domain includes what appears *in words*). (1993:233–234)

So bodies, in Butler's formulation, are performatively constituted within regulatory norms, with subjects not preexisting the acts but brought into being through the reiterative power of discourse. 'Sex' is not a bodily given on which gender is constructed, as social constructionism argues, but a cultural norm which governs how bodies materialize. Bodies 'assume' a sex that allows emergence of a speaking 'I', but within constraints that not only limit the possibilities for what counts as 'sex' but also render abject those who cannot conform with the norms. They do this through constant reiteration of micromovements that constitute the body as male or female.

Gender, it can be seen, is a construction that conceals its genesis. We collude tacitly within a 'collective agreement to perform, produce, and sustain discrete and polar genders as cultural fictions . . . [whose] construction "compels" our belief in its necessity and naturalness. The historical possibilities materialized through various corporeal styles are nothing other than those punitively regulated cultural fictions alternately embodied and deflected under duress' (1990:140).

DECONSTRUCTING GENDER: A PSYCHOANALYTICAL APPROACH

In these early books, Butler is constructively critical of Lacan's perpetuation of the patriarchal, heterosexual matrix, and in more recent work she gains insights from the feminist psychoanalytical theorist Jessica Benjamin. I find Lacan's Seminar XX conducive to understanding Butler's account, so my reading differs from hers on this point. Benjamin offers similar conclusions, albeit via a different trajectory, to Lacan, and Copjec reads Lacan in depth to define masculinity and femininity in the modern Western psyche. I will briefly summarise these accounts as they not only influence the discussion later in the chapter but also illuminate Butler's observation, in the preface to the second edition of *Gender Trouble* (1999:xxv), that 'part of what is so oppressive about social forms of gender is the psychic difficulties they produce'.

Freud argued that the child is originally polymorphously perverse—capable of becoming any or no gender or sexual identity. The child has to pass through the Oedipal stage in order to emerge as coherently male or female and thus, in Lacan's terms in Seminar XX, line up before one of the doors marked 'male' or 'female' (Lacan, 1982). Lacan's thesis is that insertion into a sexual identity is problematic and, even when achieved, is symbolic or enjoined on the subject (Rose, 1982:41). It is essential to Lacan's argument, Rose writes (1982:41), that sexual difference be understood as a legislative divide which *creates and reproduces its categories*. Each speaking being must line up on one or other side of the divide. Sexual difference is then assigned according to whether individual subjects do or do not possess the phallus, which refers not to the penis but to the master signifier. Anatomical difference *is* sexual difference, for the one is strictly deducible from the other, but only because anatomical difference comes to *figure* sexual difference. Sexual difference for Lacan, Rose writes (1982:42), 'covers over the complexity of the child's early sexual life with a crude opposition in which that very complexity is refused or repressed. The phallus thus indicates the reduction of difference to an instance of visible perception, a *seeming* value'. Thus, Lacan talks about male and female speaking subjects rather than men or women—a male speaking subject may be biologically female, and vice versa (for a fuller analysis of Lacan's Seminar XX, and in particular its mixed reception by feminist theorists, see Fotaki and Harding, 2012).

The feminist psychoanalytical theorist Jessica Benjamin, (1988; 1995; 1998), although working in a different psychoanalytical tradition from Lacan, argues somewhat similarly. In analysing the subjectivity of the other (1998), she insists that 'masculine' and 'feminine' are descriptors which are too easily and simply mapped onto bodies. They are positions that can be occupied by subjects, and subjects can move between them, so ascriptions of 'masculinity', for example, as competitive, instrumentalist and careerist are discursive fallacies (Meriläinen et al., 2004). The mother may represent the security of home and the father the excitement of the outside world, but both 'mother' and 'father' are subject positions, representations, re-presentations. It follows that individual subjects desire both the mother and the father and their respective positions. Benjamin uses, as Butler often does, the Foucauldian reversal of causation: it is not the female subject who, say, provides care; it is the provision of care that constitutes the female subject.

But what are these positions, the masculine and feminine? To what are we referring when we use the terms 'male' and 'female'? Copjec's answer is that gender is painful, imprisoning and almost unbearable. In *Imagine There's No Woman* (2004), she uses Lacan's body of theory to develop a thesis of the form that masculinity and femininity take in their inscription in the psyche. Each is located in relation to the gaze. Female speaking subjects, Copjec argues, have to invent themselves as women, that is, *as objects different from themselves*. It is impossible, she argues, to live as a woman; rather, the person who is in the position of a female speaking subject is engaged in a masquerade by which she pretends to be a woman. The female body, that which says to the woman that she is woman, is a semblance—the body is female because the law requires that it be female. The woman can approach and enjoy what appears to be her own body only through an imaginary position from which she understands how it would be enjoyed by another: the woman's body is thus not hers. This body that tells her who she is (not) is therefore not her body, and in her encounters with it she constantly encounters her difference from herself. Further, the woman is everywhere looked at, object of a gaze she must pretend she does not know is directed at her. Think of the ubiquitous photos of the female body in magazines: she lies there, two-dimensional, existing only to be looked at and having no existence until she is looked at. The three-dimensional woman gazes upon and absorbs thousands of such images of women on screen and paper, and she is herself that image made flesh, walking about and working on itself and always subject of a gaze. Copjec argues that the only retreat from this excess of visibility is into hysteria.

The feminine therefore is a subject position where one constructs one's self as an object to be looked at and where one can grasp the self only as an object that exists for the other's gaze. To paraphrase a famous statement of Lacan's, where the female speaking subject is (an embodied presence), there she is not—there is no such thing as *the* woman, only a fantasy that she constructs for the gaze of others.

With regard to masculinity, Copjec (2004) argues that the superego is a judgemental gaze that insists on constant self-monitoring. The masculine ego is 'too full of sacred places, too full of ancestral dead, to make living there easy. Life is continuously sacrificed to the past and to the ancestral others by whose dreams the living judge themselves, measure and validate themselves' (176). The impossibility of living up to this judgemental gaze, a gaze that is nomadic and looks at masculine subjects from all sides, making them visible in the world, means that the masculine self is also the subject of a gaze, but one that infuses him with shame. The response of the female speaking subject is to pretend she does not know she is being looked at even though she desires that look; the masculine response is an escape into perversion, into a desire for domination and the ability to dictate what the law shall be. The masculine ego therefore attempts to conquer the world and to occupy the position of the big Other, from which position the actions of all others will be dictated (this is what you must do) and assessed (this is how you will do it, how you will be measured in your performance and punished for failure).

In summary, the interpretation of poststructural gender theory I offer here argues that there is no necessary relationship between biological bodies and male/female, masculinity/femininity; there is only a 'contingent, illicit, unsubstantiated' link (Hook, 2009:166) that is grafted on to bodies that are performatively constituted as gendered. Sex/gender emerges from neither biology nor culture but from a compulsory sexuation which precedes culture (and thus organizations) and allows entrance into the symbolic realm. There is nothing given about male and female, or masculine and feminine; rather, there are fantasies that are inscribed in the psyche. These fantasies govern what practices male and female speaking subjects must strive to maintain. The female speaking subject's agency arises from that work on her self through which she will make herself visible to the desiring gaze she desires; the male speaking subject's arises from imposing its will on others. Both positions are painful and debilitating.

THE PROBLEM

This period in the Euro-American part of the globe, as with that time around the industrial revolution in Britain, is a time of gender flux. Changes that take place in epochs such as this evolve slowly, over several generations, and are not immediately visible to participants, but poststructuralist gender theory is articulating something of what many of us perhaps sense is happening. In other words, I am suggesting that earlier studies of how organizations actively participate in the gendering of employees (Adler, Laney and Packer, 1993; Benn and Gaus, 1983; Benschop and Doorewaard, 1998; Cockburn, 1990; Duncan, 1996; Gherardi, 1995; Grant and Porter, 1996; Mills and Murgatroyd, 1991; Mills, 1992; Pateman, 1983; Trethewey, 1999) may need updating to take account of the woman as a speaking managerial or professional subject. Rather than using the constructionist approach of the studies just cited, which argues that behaviour follows biological sex, a poststructuralist thesis such as this argues that organizational gender discourses *constitute* the masculine and feminine. The exploration in this chapter explores current changes in organizational 'modes of existence' (Judovitz, 2001:1) occasioned by the influx of women into professional and managerial positions in organizations. The thesis that organizations were male public spaces, with women contained within the private space of the home (Pateman, 1983) has broken down. This does not mean, of course, that there is that elusive thing called equality between the sexes or that many occupations do not remain strictly identified as 'women's' or 'men's' (Lam, 2004). What it means is that women or, rather, those who occupy the speaking positions of women (Lacan, 1998) have become highly visible co-occupants of the public spaces in which professional and managerial work is undertaken. If gender is performatively constituted within a cultural, historical and psychic field where one seeks recognition, then one must ask whether changing gender structures of management and the professions offer different possibilities for constituting one's gendered organizational self. This leads to the questions, noted earlier, of what therefore 'is' gender in today's organizations. Does the distinction between labour and work hold good when discussing gender? Is the zombie-machine gendered, or the human, and where is gender in my aspirations for the me I desire to be(come) through/in work?

The empirical analysis ponders these questions. It has three sections. The first is a study of a science fiction drama, in which we see enacted very clearly and visibly the breaking down of the relationship between gendered attributes and biological bodies. The second is based on two interviews, in which I explore the gendering of the working self and show how one moves between gendered identities, even into non-gendered positions, but is always surprised back into one's culturally required gender. The third is a reinterpretation of data from a paper by Martin (2006) which I reread through the thesis developed here. This leads to the conclusion that organizations are places where, for some people at least, one constitutes the self as polymorphously perverse and where there is freedom from the pains of gender. However, this relief is temporary: one is always surprised back into gender and into its traumas. This has somewhat contradictory implications for the thesis of this book.

ANALYSIS ONE: HOW THE MALE BECAME THE FEMALE WHO WAS MASCULINE: REPRESENTATION OF GENDER FLUX IN POPULAR CULTURE

I start with an analysis, influenced by Rhodes and Brown's (2005) exploration of how fiction and social scientific narratives overlap and flow into each other, of the television series *Battlestar Galactica* to illustrate how representations of masculinity and femininity and thus possibilities for being male and female have changed in the past 30 years.

Popular culture provides not only interpretative frameworks for negotiating understanding of the social world but also both a lens for seeing the social and performative texts that inform how we constitute our 'reality' (Brewis, Hampton and Linsted, 1997; Hassard and Holliday, 1998; Bowring, 2004; Fuery and Fuery, 2003). *Battlestar Galactica* captures some of the ways in which gendering of organizational subjects has changed/is changing in jobs where women now share what was previously male organizational space. *Battlestar Galactica* is a science fiction television series that first aired in the late 1970s but ceased production after two series, to be resurrected extremely successfully 25 years later. In its new format, it ran for four series. In the 1970s, one of the leading characters, Starbuck, was played by a man; today, Starbuck is female, although she is a hard-drinking, tough and rebellious character, much more 'masculine' in many ways than the original Starbuck. It would have been difficult to cast a woman as a swashbuckling hero in the 1970s, so this change signifies shifts in sexed/gendered identities in the current period. The Starbuck character is, I will demonstrate, polymorphously perverse, that is, neither masculine nor feminine but having the potential at any moment to be either or both or many or none. As such, she symbolises changes in the gender regime currently taking place. The series' huge popularity, I suggest, arises in part from the ways in which it allows viewers to identify with aspects of the (gendered) self they sense but of which they are not consciously aware. However, when they see it imagined on the screen, it speaks to that unthought knowledge, articulating for them what they sense but cannot put into words (Silverman, 1988).

Starbuck

The time may be in the past, the future or indeed the present. Humankind lives on 12 linked planets and has invented robot-like creatures, cylons. Forty years previously, war between cylons and humans led to the vanquishing and exile of the cylons. The cylons have evolved and now can adopt an appearance so like that of humans that they cannot be detected, allowing the introduction into the story of a problematic often explored in science fiction, the question of what it means to be human. Indeed, some cylons have been placed as 'sleepers' in human society but do not know they are not human. The story opens with the cylons attacking the 12 colonies, intent on destroying the human race. The remaining humans flee into space aboard any space ship available. The only military spaceship not destroyed is the Battlestar Galactica. It is through the eyes of the people on board Battlestar Galactica that much of the story is told. The battlestar has a crew of fighter, or viper, pilots, one of the more senior of whom is a woman called Kara Thrace, whose call sign is 'Starbuck'. All pilots dress identically in boiler-suits.

Starbuck is a hard-drinking, cigar-smoking gambler. She is 'an accomplished viper pilot', who is 'self-reliant—and a bit of a loner'. Described on the official programme website as tough and rebellious, she has a 'take-charge' attitude and is 'always hungry for a good fight'. She is at the core of the combat team because of 'her guts, her brain, and a little luck'. (All quotations are from http://www.gateworld.net/galactica/characters/thrace. shtml, [2] accessed May 2007.) A gifted pilot, she is also a talented military strategist. In various episodes, she is seen to use her body in ways that could be regarded as masculine (Young, 1990). For example, in hand-to-hand fighting or in the boxing ring, she punches overarm, like a man. Now it may seem at this point that Starbuck represents here a woman who has to 'pass' as a man in order to be accepted in a masculine profession (Marshall, 1984; Wajcman, 1998). This is not the case, however, for Starbuck is shown often in a 'feminine' light, as weak, vulnerable and emotional.

Much of this description, except for the last sentence, is equally true of the male character called Starbuck who featured in the original series of *Battlestar Galactica*, which premiered in 1978 and ran for two series, ending in 1980 (see http://www.scifistream.com/battlestar-galactica/ for more information). Further funding was not available until 2003, after which the 'reimagined' story proved so successful that four series were commissioned. The show won numerous prizes, positive critical comment (except for the last episode) and larger audiences than any other series on the Sci-Fi channel, according to Wikipedia.

The numerous websites which discuss Starbuck do so in adulatory tones. Only a few references describe as controversial the decision to put a woman into what had previously been a male role. One such is an intriguing question asked by a journalist of actor Katee Sackhoff: 'I am somewhat concerned about Starbuck as a woman, since the "original" character was not just a man, but a Ladies [*sic*] Man with a big old phallic cigar and all that. What about now? Does Starbuck have something to replace the cigar?' Sackhoff replies: 'She still has the cigar. God, I must have smoked about 30 of the things' (http://scifi.about.com/cs/a/aa11203.htm, accessed 22 May 2007). Sometimes a cigar is just a cigar, but the phallic imagery here resonates with Butler's proposal (1993) of a lesbian phallus; that is, *contra* Lacan, she argues that the phallus (the master-signifier) need not be represented by something alarmingly similar to a male organ. The phallus is central to much of Lacan's thinking. It is the master signifier, holding a privileged position over all other signifiers, for it establishes the conditions for what can be signified. The phallus therefore determines what can be knowable. Butler (1993), having used Freud to show that bodily parts are imaginary, demonstrates that the phallus can be attached to any body part, leading to the question of why it should be attached to any body part. What would happen if the phallus became a lesbian body part? Any body part or, indeed, none could thus be the 'master' signifier. Following Butler's argument, it is possible to see Starbuck's cigar as a female phallus that establishes the conditions for what can be signified. As such, does it not suggest the possibility for signifying gender as a disembodied ascription that can, to a certain extent, be refused? That is, although my body is female, I may refuse some or many of the attributes of its femininity, refusing to acquiesce in the requirement that morphology becomes my destiny.

Battlestar Galactica was transmitted during a time of flux in which the very possibilities for gender are changing. The 21st-century version of the series, unlike its earlier incarnation, featured numerous strong female characters, including the president, Laura Roslin; the cylon who destroyed the 12 colonies, Number Six; and numerous fighter pilots. Starbuck's character is different: these other female actors are playing strong, powerful characters, so they articulate changes in women's lives that have occurred since legislation promoting equal opportunity was enacted in much of the Western world in the 1970s. Starbuck represents something more, because of the polymorphous perversity of 'her' character (language insists we must categorise the character as 'he' or 'she' and thus limits the possibilities for speaking about polymorphous perversity). Writers and actor have made a conscious attempt to replicate many of the mannerisms and characteristics of the original male character, whilst at the same time Starbuck is shown to be romantic, vulnerable and in other ways 'feminine'. That such moves are possible testifies to the major changes in the possible gender identities that have become available in the quarter-century between the making of the original and the 'reimagined' series. The success of the series suggests a public quite comfortable with characters whose visual appearance suggests their femininity whilst their behaviours suggest masculinity. Where 'women's films' of earlier decades taught women how to desire men, thus upholding the heterosexual matrix (Doane, 1988), such a popular television series today seems to encourage its audience to desire and enact not a masculine or a feminine but a polymorphously perverse subject position that refuses gender categorisation.

This, importantly, is a subject position that may be desired alongside the desire for an identity within a feminine or masculine subject position. By this I mean that the two are not in opposition, not an either/or; rather, a person can move fluidly between and, indeed, can refuse either or both of them. This is illuminated specifically in one episode in the first of the 'reimagined' series, when Starbuck is portrayed off-duty and away from the spaceship. She 'dresses up' as an alluring, sexually attractive woman, wearing a revealing red dress and makeup. Danger threatens, and she is a leading participant in the ensuing fight scene. This is the most overt demonstration, in this early episode, of how she can move easily between seemingly 'masculine' and 'feminine' subject positions. Meanwhile, the character who represents female sexual allure and the appearance of femininity, the character known as Number Six, is a cylon who is intent, it seems, on annihilating the human race. This character is Butlerian theory in action: the archetypal attractive, blonde, alluring woman is shown in the very first episode to be a creature that becomes a woman (rather than, say, a machine) only through the performativity of the feminine.

Now, the objection may be raised that what I am observing in *Battlestar Galactica* is, rather than a refusal of categorisation, an elision of difference between men and women and thus a return to an older feminism which encouraged or required women to become as masculine as men (Hekman, 1999). One of the major differences between this and earlier arguments is that I am neither advocating that this is what women should do nor suggesting some essentialised 'woman' beneath the portrayal of masculinity. Rather, I am saying *this is what is happening*, that new possibilities for gender have emerged and are informing the constitution of gendered identities in organizations. A second objection therefore is that I am observing a form of masculinity being practised by those with female anatomy and thus to some extent following Halberstam's (1998) analysis of female masculinity. If so, then women are conforming to organizational requirements that they practise their gender differently. This, I submit, is one part of the case, but I want to keep in tension the practising of both masculinity and femininity and polymorphously perverse organizational subjects. It is not a case of either one or the other but of both/and and, indeed, neither/nor. I develop this argument by turning to the two people who agreed to be interviewed for this book, Kara and Saul.

ANALYSIS TWO: EXPERIENCING GENDER

I interviewed Kara and Saul, two academics, and also observed them giving lectures, trying to discern the ways in which the performatively achieved body is constituted in its moment-to-moment repetitions of stylized gestures. My aim was to better understand how the gendered body interacts with the psyche to confirm one in what seems like a stable gender identity. I also reflected back on myself as I watched them and tried to observe myself auto-ethnographically in the process of giving a lecture: how is the embodied academic self constituted through the doing of academic activities? The observations initially confused me: there appeared to be few, if any, differences between how Kara and Saul used their bodies, save for the obvious differences of physical appearance. I observed other colleagues and speakers at conferences, keeping notes of how female and male lecturers moved, trying to discern those movements that are supposed to be specific to each gender (Young, 1990). I found I could not—both men and women keep their arms close to their bodies or use their hands a lot; some men move around and take up a lot of space, but so do some women. Some women take up little space, moving their bodies only in small ways, but some men do likewise. With a few exceptions (such as Judith 'Jack' Halberstam), the appearance of each speaker conformed to his or her biological sex: no man wore a skirt or lipstick, and none of the women wore a tie. After a while, it struck me that, beyond these superficial declarations of gendered identity, the people I was watching while they were working were not performatively constituting materially embodied gendered identities; there was a surface to the body that symbolised masculinity or femininity, dress, hair and other familiar codes, but, apart from the obvious distinguishing marks, there were few discernible differences. Rather, I realised, *I was imposing gendered identities on them*. That is, my subjective body was imposing gender on what are, to me, the objects that are their bodies (Leder, 1990).

The scene of recognition here was thus reversed: rather than their requiring that I recognize them as appropriately gendered so that I could confirm them in their gender identity, I was imposing on them the requirement that they appear to me as appropriately gendered. Butler alludes to this in her work: recognition can be granted only on the condition that one approximates the norms that allow the self to be recognised; therefore there is another party (including one's own self looking in the mirror or reflecting on [thinking about] its self) that judges whether one has reached the standards necessary for recognition. This implies that there is one who grants recognition, an Other whose subjectivity we know little of. My experience suggests something further: if I impose gender identity on an other, it means I can place myself in relation to that person and know myself as appropriately gendered and capable of recognition and therefore of being. In other words, I require others to be appropriately gendered so that they hold up a mirror in which I can know myself: in looking in that mirror I can see myself as 'like' them (we share the same sex) or the opposite of them (we do not share the same sex), and therefore I can know who I am. This must also apply when the other is the reflection of my own body in the mirror, a body that is outside of and separate to whatever it is I call 'me', but when I see a body reflected back at me on which I can put the label 'woman' I can know my gender. If I cannot place the other in an appropriate category, then my own position is confused. This perhaps explains what happened to Kara at the end of the semester, after her last tutorial, an incident (discussed below) which suggests repair work is necessary for organizational participants when a person does not conform to that imposed gender identity and is, in many ways, polymorphously perverse: we/they insist on regendering that person, surprising them back into gender.

Kara was 31 and Saul 32 at the time of the study. They both work in business schools in British universities. Saul was born and grew up in Britain, while Kara, although educated in Europe, grew up elsewhere. In order to maintain their confidentiality I will give no more than these few sketchy details. Kara is short and slim and has her own, unique, clothes style. When I watched her give a lecture, she moved about the stage little and used what I would call 'professional' body language, in that her movements related largely to the PowerPoint presentation and other visual aids, but her presence commanded attention as she spoke slowly and clearly in a voice that could be described as in the range of an alto singer. Saul is tall and slim, dresses conservatively in trousers and open-necked shirt and gives the appearance when lecturing of rigidly controlling his bodily movements.

Our discussion followed the timetable of a lecture: preparation, walking to the lecture theatre, setting up, beginning to speak, delivering the lecture and finishing. I will start with Kara's account of walking to the lecture theatre.

Walking to the Lecture Theatre

Kara's reply to a question about what she experiences as she walks to the lecture theatre was really surprising. She had started the discussion by saying that appearance is something that is a struggle, so she does not bother much with it:

> N: *Um, what's your philosophy with regard to looking after yourself?*
> K: *Um, minimalist, seriously. Er, like the least pain possible. Um so most of the time um I'm really lazy, I'm not very much bothered, I make an effort to kind of dress up and brush my hair for lectures and more or less appear in public, otherwise if I know that I'm going to go to work and sit in my office, even if I'm meeting students actually, I just wear jeans and um I don't know, . . . tennis shoes [laughs] for footwear, and sweaters and um and so I do have aspirations for dressing nicely and looking nice but most of the time it sort of falls through.*

When I asked, 'Walking to the lecture theatre and actually going into the lecture theatre. What is going through your mind?' her answer contradicted her earlier account, and there was therefore a breakdown in the logic of her arguments:

> K: *My primary thought is please please god do not let me fall off my heels [joint laughter, occasioned on my part because I share this dread]. Because I er, I'm very, I like wearing heels, but I don't do it too often because it's quite painful for me, I don't know why, I'm just not very good on them . . . er stumbling is a very common affair for me, exactly, and I've got these fantastic pair of platform shoes which I absolutely love . . . and especially when I go down those stairs at XXX Building, it's like okay, just take it slowly, focus on how you're walking [laughs] and er ah, and if I go through a crowd of students in in coming up to the lecture I know that I'm quite short and most of them are taller than me, so just please notice me and let me through, [laughs] so there is kind of like that feeling, yeah and once I get to they more or less see me and once I get to to to the desk [emphasis on desk] I can have something to hold onto and, you know, while they all sit, and there's no possibility of me getting lost in the crowd I start to feel better [laughs] yeah, but this transition is a dangerous thing. I have visions of myself like stumbling and crashing on the stairs and oh no [laughs].*
>
> N: *When you start to talk, how do you actually start to talk? What does it involve?*
>
> K: *Um, I just, I start by giving out the attendance sheets, so it's quite officious, and then say 'right, welcome to the lecture' so I start talking in quite a loud voice just to kind of give a signal to everyone okay that's the time to put mobiles away and stop talking and you know the lecture has officially started.*

The extended discussion of high-heeled shoes was startling, but its inclusion, as well as the length of the reference, suggests that Kara herself is here working with an as-yet unformulated theory of herself as lecturer. She shows that these shoes not only inhibit freedom of movement but are dangerous—if she falls her credibility as a lecturer is at stake because she would be put in the position of the frail woman needing to be rescued. Furthermore, as she discusses these shoes she talks about herself as invisible—it is only when she gets to the lectern that she feels safe from falling and able to silence the students with a few words spoken in a loud voice. What Kara is articulating here is, I suggest, a transition between what I will call for the moment the feminine and masculine speaking subject positions. The shoes make her vulnerable and perhaps in need of rescue, but they also symbolize, in their instability, the frailty of the gender she must sustain if she is to be recognized as a woman. However, when she gets to the desk or lectern, the signifier of the lecturer, she shifts rapidly from a vulnerable 'feminine' subject position to a dominant, 'masculine' one.

Copjec (2003), as outlined earlier, argues that woman constitutes herself as an object for the desiring gaze of others; Kara, when talking about herself as an academic, seems to be saying that she fails at this. Using a female signifier (high heels) makes her invisible (the students are all taller than she is, even though she is wearing high heels). To me, what Kara is articulating here is, first, the precarity of gender as symbolised by the feminine shoes: it is something that may fail us and so undo us, unravelling all the work necessitated in sustaining a sense of self. Second, she is espousing a theory about the impossibility of being a female speaking subject in academia: we lose our female gender identity (fall off the shoes) when we occupy the masculine speaking position of 'the academic': that is, we must move out of the position of female speaking subject and in some ways regender ourselves. To be academics we must abandon the normative construction of the female self: we fall off our heels and become logical, rational, non-emotional, powerful and in command; we do not exist to be looked at. We are 'safe' when we reach the lectern, which acts similarly to Lacan's famous toilet door in allowing us to claim the appropriate gendered position: we line up behind it and can assume the position of male speaking subjects. I have previously argued that the manager's suit is a form of control over male managers (Harding, 2002) and have often been asked how that account applies to women managers who dress very differently. Kara gives an answer to that question: women working in what have traditionally been masculine professions are in drag, masculine minds in feminine attire perhaps, if we briefly use a Cartesian binary. As such, female professionals are controlled in ways very different from their male counterparts. Dominant representations of women in European cultures are of embodied creatures: semi-naked female bodies stare out at us from magazines, adverts and billboards. The woman remains tied to its body (de Beauvoir, 1949/1997); she is always-already naked, a nudity covered over by clothes. For men, the professional suit eliminates the body. If the woman who works in a professional career is in drag, then she is controllable through the threat to tear off the dress to reveal her as a woman, to make her conform to the archetypal female position.

Saul wears smart trousers and sharply ironed shirts to work. He does not use the phallolinear mark that is the tie, but his clothes otherwise, in their severity and lack of adornment, bespeak the rationality and non-emotionality signified by the manager's suit (Harding, 2002). For him, the walk to the lecture theatre passes without hindrance:

> N: *Walking to the lecture theatre and going into the room—what goes through your mind, what do you do in those moments?*
> S: *Umm. It depends actually, not a lot actually, if I'm going in on my own, I tend not to have anything in my mind. Partly because you're in that social environment and you might be seeing people you*

> *know and typically before I've gone to the class I know what I'm*
> *going to talk about so it isn't in the front of my mind.*

Masculinity has often been described as the unmarked gender—men do
not think about what it is to be gendered. The absence of thought here suggests that Saul is a 'typical' male speaking subject traversing the corridors
from office to lecture theatre, so confident in the identity accorded by masculinity that he does not have to think about it (Seidler, 1994). However,
arrival at the lecture theatre is traumatic:

> S: *I do like to have ownership of the room, though. If I can be there*
> *before the students, I like to be um or before the majority of the*
> *students. . . . I don't like it if for whatever reason they're early or*
> *I'm running a few minutes late, I don't like to get in there when*
> *everybody is there. [He needs to organize the technology and his*
> *lecture notes.]*
> N: *How does it feel standing there in that sort of minute?*
> S: *I tend to use my notes then, just to flick through, I always come in*
> *with a highlighter, because as I'm talking I might want to scribble*
> *something down as I'm talking to them. . . . As much as anything as*
> *if that act of highlighting commits it to memory rather than when*
> *I'm actually in front of the lectern that I'm going to read it. Because*
> *it's a bit of a blur, anyway, when I'm live. Um . . . it means I don't*
> *have to stare looking at the students and them thinking 'oh what's*
> *he looking at?' and looking back, you know what I mean.*

He had talked earlier of feeling so anxious about lecturing that his body
temperature rises. Here we see first a need to take control, to be in charge,
to prevent chaos ensuing if anything goes wrong. This is a masculine subject
position. But note also two statements: things become a bit of a blur when
he is 'live' and his references to being gazed at.

With regard to 'when I'm live', the metaphor of 'live' refers both to an
electrical charge flowing through a cable and to television or radio appear-
ances where, rather than being prerecorded, speakers are heard by listeners
as they talk and there is no opportunity to make corrections. Saul is speaking here of a major transition, from a quiet, introspective and *invisible* person who is about to become a lecturer to an active performer (lecturer) who
is able to carry out tasks without conscious thought ('it's a bit of a blur').
When Saul goes 'live', when the electrical charge courses through him and
brings him to life (Frankenstein's monster?), he stops refusing the students'
gaze ('I don't have to stare looking at the students') and actively invites it:

> N: *When you start to talk what does that involve?*
> S: *First of all, I'll draw people's attention to me, cos I'm in charge.*
> N: *How do you do that?*

S: *Um I might just sort of say 'okay' or 'okay good evening', and then
I'll wait for them to die down and say 'okay, yeah, good', and then
'what we're going to look at this topic'.*

Now all eyes have to be on him, in this swift change of subject position.
In other words, he, like Kara, moves from being invisible to being visible, to
inviting the gaze of the other, a gaze that desires the other's desire, which, as
Copjec argues, is the place of the feminine. However, we will see next that
how Kara and Saul respond to that desired gaze differs and positions them
in unpredictable ways: Saul, the male speaking subject, responds to the gaze
in what we may regard as a 'female' way, whereas Kara responds in what
is commonly regarded as a 'masculine' way. For now though, the conclusion at this point is that the transition from office to lecture hall is one in
which Kara, a female speaking subject, experiences that speaking subject's
self from a female position, while Saul, a male speaking subject, experiences
that speaking subject's self from the unmarked male position. This changes
when they begin lecturing.

Giving a Lecture

To be the subject of a gaze has powerful resonance for academics who, by
definition, must be looked at, as can be seen in Saul's return to a question
he could not answer until the issue of being looked at was raised. Early in
the discussion, in response to something Saul had said, I had asked him,
'So who are you then?' His reply had been very bland, if not evasive. When
asked what it is like to have 'all those faces' looking at him as he lectured, he
suddenly returned to that earlier question, signalling the turn in the discussion with an emphatic 'So':

*So. Going back to this idea of who am I, I suppose, there's a degree
to which you project an image and it can be quite playful at times and
you can sort of do a little parody of yourself and everyone laughs, you
know, that the lecturer, you know, I don't know, plays computer games
or whatever and doesn't go down the pub every night, and they all go
ha ha ha isn't that funny? And it's fine, but it's one that you're willing
to give, you know, it's like I'll check out my vulnerability, and it's not
manipulative, it's just a way of moving the class along. But clearly that
degree of openness is measured and it's appropriate, and it's not 'oh did
I tell you what happened last year, because it was a really tough time for
me' cos you're just thinking, well, you know, or whatever, you know,
there's a degree to which you don't bring that to work particularly with
the students because, yeah.*

At this point, Saul articulates how he moves into a passive feminine
speaking position, one that desires to be desired by the other (making all the

students laugh and identify with him as a person rather than a lecturer as he performs a 'little parody'). He is constructing an image of himself that is to be looked at, in which he acknowledges that he is being open and 'checking out' his 'vulnerability'. Compare this to Copjec's thesis of the masculine: the gaze there is hugely judgemental, constituting in the male speaking subject a psychic pain at its inadequacies having been found out. With 'all those faces looking at him', Saul puts himself in the position of a female speaking subject, constructing a self that is not him but that requires the gaze of the other so as to approximate an identity.

Kara, on the other hand, when asked about how she felt as she starts giving a lecture, describes herself as a seducer.

> *At that moment. I feel quite sexy actually [laughs]. There's there's definitely, cos there's always there's always this part in lecturing—is it performance, although I don't. I mean. Prior to this interview I was kind of thinking about that. Is it, you know, talking about the body of a lecturer, is lecturing a performance or whatever? I mean, I, it definitely is, right now, it's definitely a performance . . . and I know I'm gonna give give a give a good one, cos I know I'm good at it.*

When Kara gives a lecture on a subject she likes, she talks about feeling sexy, about giving a good performance—she will 'give a good one'. Sometimes, it seems, the seduction fails, but this is on the occasions when she does not feel sexy. This is the only time in the discussion that she mentions a philosopher's name, a male philosopher who, it seems, takes over the position of the seducer but who gets it wrong and insists on dry sex, sex as duty, not sex as pleasure. Obviously, the man is not up to the job of seduction: it needs a powerful woman in a masculine speaking position—she laughs in the place where the word 'orgasm' might have appeared, but then changes her tone to show that she 'does' very few that are so unproductive of excitement:

> *It's definitely an oppressive feeling. . . . You know, it doesn't feel as pretty, as elegant, you know, it feels messy somehow, em, and that's and that's what bothers me a bit. I don't see the beauty in it so much, er, the beauty of the performance and the beauty of the communication, and and the vibe that is created, you know, I just, when I'm talking about what is it, er, you know Adam Smith for example, there are some good things to say about that, but overall when I explain the theory of comparative advantage it's very difficult to get the (she laughs), it's not a very sexy theory, it's just [laughs] um so that that particular aspect, that particular excitement is not quite there, and I do I do very few you know [pause and a stumble] education and sex are very intimately connected.*

Sex is everywhere in organizations (Burrell, 1984; Hearn and Parkin, 1987). Sinclair (2009), for example, has explored how the sexual energy of male students puts her in a vulnerable, female position. Such arguments are located in a heterosexual matrix that presumes essentialist identities of male and female (Butler, 1990; 1993). Halberstam (1998) has shown that forms of desire are not attached to biological bodies; a biological female may experience desire as if she were a penetrator rather than penetratee, a speaking position that Kara seems to be taking up here, a position of 'female masculinity': she is the masculine seducer who generates libidinal energy for the transfer of knowledge. On the stage of the lecture theatre, she has kicked off her high heels and looks at the students from a dominant, assertive male position; in so doing, she demands that they look at her from their passive female position.

However, perhaps these continuing references to male and female, masculine and feminine, go too far—why is the male regarded as active and the female passive, save for its metaphorical relationship to a particular position adopted by two parties during the act of having sex? Indeed, through continuing to refer to them, am I not performatively constituting a relationship where there should be none? Sjöholm (2010) has looked to *The Antigone* and to Sappho for an alternative to Foucault's history of Eros. Her argument is that we should distinguish between active and passive rather than between male and female and speak of an erotics that goes beyond sex. Is that what we are seeing here, that is, rather than moving between male and female speaking subject positions, Kara and Saul are moving in and out of passive and active positions? We are now getting 'caught up in ontological thickets and epistemological quandaries' (Butler, 2004:16), but we must fight our way through them.

So, one interpretation of the foregoing is that we have what we can call, for simplicity's sake, *a biological male* who makes a transition from male to female speaking subject position in the course of carrying out his work and *a biological female* who transits in the opposite direction, from female to male speaking subject. This suggests something of that polymorphous perversity identified by Freud and posited by Lacan's statement in Seminar XX about subjects being able to occupy speaking positions that do not conform to their biological sex. We see here the condition of the infant being re-experienced in adulthood, in places where female and male speaking subjects now share public space and so the terms and conditions of what we understand as 'gender' may have changed. Another interpretation might be that we have two speaking subjects who move between active and passive speaking positions. In this case, sex is not ascribed to bodies. Either interpretation suggests that something revolutionary is taking place in the ascriptions of sex and gender within the spaces and places of organizations.

It would seem that such changes are not occurring in non-work situations. Neither Kara nor Saul could talk about being embodied at the workplace, but this did not apply to their talk about their off-duty selves. The body is difficult to speak as a labouring body but is not so absent when one is discussing non-work activities. I started each interview by asking about the participant's height, weight and philosophy of care of the body.

Each has a conscious relationship with their body in non-work situations. Saul's relates to control of a machine that will allow him to function well—he seeks a healthy body that will allow him to carry out his job. This is a masculine body familiar to those who study the sociology of health: the man takes his ill body to the doctor much as he would his car to the garage: fix it please (Courtenay, 2000). Kara, on the other hand, enjoys having a body and looking at her reflection as an embodied being: she admires in a mirror the way she can make it move and how it looks when dressed up.

Table 5.1   Table Title

Saul	Kara
I am 5'11, I am [pause] 13 stone 9 normally, give or take a couple of pounds, target weight is 13 7 [laughs] and, in terms of my philosophy about looking after myself, I suppose physically I go to the gym at least three times a week, not just for weight training which is something I do a lot less of now that I am getting a bit older and don't see much point in having lots of muscles to sit at a desk and do a sedentary job. I might do some cross-training or running or some resistance training, circuit training, and that's what I do physically, I suppose, I play football once a week.	I am 31 and, er, I am about a 160, er, no, yes, 160 centimetres high and weight about 60 kilos. N. Why do you go belly dancing? Er, just because it's fantastic, the fun, um, we have a nice troupe of people, there's my teacher and two other girls, we do dancing in my teacher's living room and all four of us go absolutely crazy. We do things like impersonating trolls [laughter]. And it's just an enormously relaxing activity. We do the dancing, we just socialise, we eat cake all the time, so every session starts with cake and tea [laughs], and we watch films, and we do performances for charity and so it's just, I don't know, I just like it. I like it for the dancing, it puts you in touch with your body really. I can feel it, I enjoy my body, it's really, it's a beautiful feeling when you can make your body do interesting sort of things and make it look good and there's a giant mirror, you know, in the room where we can admire ourselves, so it's. Dress up in sequins and skirts and scarves, so it's like whee it's brilliant, yes.

Outside work, she is immanent to her body (de Beauvoir, 1949/1997), and she enjoys that sensation of being embodied. This is in sharp contrast to her relationship with it when at work, where it is something that has to be covered up rather than enhanced.

Surprised into Gender?

Wondering why it might be so difficult to talk about one's labouring body, I observed myself while lecturing to try to come to grips with this issue in the manner that Ronai (1999) does so well. She explored, during an auto-ethnographic study in which she became a mud-wrestler, how the movements of her body in interaction with the gaze of others evoked buried traumas: mind, body and psyche were invoked together. However, even though trying to consciously think about the body and its movements while lecturing, I found myself forgetting to be aware of being embodied and reminded of it only if a physical impediment (such as needing to avoid tripping over a step) appeared in my way. The lecturing academic body becomes very much an absent body, to use Drew Leder's terms. That is, 'one's own body is rarely the thematic object of experience'; rather, it is experienced as a 'corporeal absence', a 'ground of experience [that] tends to recede from direct experience' (Leder, 1990:1). If the body is absent and gender is written on the body, then is gender or our awareness of being gendered also often absent?

Now, following Butler, gender is constituted in part by means of a body that performatively constitutes its sexed identity through moment-to-moment reiterations of movements inscribed on the psyche. As I type this account, I am using fingers whose nails are painted (today in a fashionable coffee colour), and each movement of each finger as it hits the keyboard follows a culturally mandated rule of how a woman's fingers, rather than a man's fingers, should move. To balance my laptop on my lap, I have crossed my legs in a way that is becoming of a woman (my mother told me when I was ten years old that women do not sit with their legs apart), and, as I stretch my neck to relieve the tension of staring at the monitor, I run my hands through my (longish) hair as I do so, in a movement that, allied with all the others, performatively achieves my female gendered identity. But, most of the time, I perform these acts without being aware that I am doing so: I am unaware of the female body that is moving, so deeply engrossed am I for much of the time in this thing we call 'the mind'. Any observer who sees these acts of moment-to-moment constructions of the embodied self can, however, locate themselves as a result of my act in an appropriate place on the gender map: hair, nail varnish, physical stance, all these say, to an onlooker, 'woman', even though I am absent to my embodied self (Leder, 1990). *The subject that I am is often unaware of its body, which is then present as an object only to others.* So, returning now to my observation that I was imposing gender on colleagues as they gave their lectures, I suggest that for much of the time we are unaware of gender or of being gendered, even while the body performs the acts that constitute that gender. Its constitution, all of Butler's work tells us, requires confirmation from another, recognition that the construction is 'successful' in some ways, that we are coherently gendered. That is, gender is for much of the time subjectively an absent-presence. It is only as object of another's gaze (including my own reflection in a mirror) that I know that I am gendered, that my body is identifiable (in my case) as that of a woman.

In other words, when carrying out the labour of lecturing and many other such acts besides, the body that is constituted is one on which other subjectivities will inscribe a gendered identity. As subject, however, I often am not aware of the body or of gender. I become subjectively ungendered or degendered or indefinably gendered or perhaps polymorphously perverse.

However, I have suggested that Kara and Saul moved between masculine and feminine, active and passive, positions. To the audience that looked down at them, such movement was invisible: Kara, to them, must be female and Saul, male. Yet, that there is at some level some awareness in onlookers of a subject's refusal to conform to the onlookers' desire that s/he constitute the requisite gender identity was suggested by a later incident. Something traumatic happened to Kara at the end of the last lecture of the semester which suggests, firstly, that the person whose body is biologically female but who takes up occupation of what appears to onlookers to be an active, male speaking subject position, even while s/he may be subjectively somehow outside of gender, tears the heteronormative organizational matrix. Secondly, other actors who, I have suggested, require that s/he occupy the appropriate gendered subject position if they are to be confirmed in their own gender identity feel enjoined, whether they know it or not, to repair those tears. She sent me an e-mail:

> Hi Nancy,
>   I thought I'd add one more little vignette on bodily interactions with the student body. It happened just now:
>   After the XXX tutorial that I conducted, I was left in a room with three of my mail [*sic*] students. One of them (Student 1) was asking me a coursework question, another (Student 2) was just hanging around and the third (Student 3) one wanted to take a photo with me. After Student 3 asked me for a photo and I said ok, Student 1 said he wanted one too. I said all right. When the photo was taken he stood quite close to me—not too close, but probably closer than I would have liked. When the photo with Student 3 was taken, Student 3 (who is quite a bit taller than I am) put his arm around my shoulder, but very lightly, barely touching me. After this happened, Student 1 said he would really love another photo, and in this 2nd photo put his arm around me too (somewhat more firmly than Student 3).
>   I sense that something is going on here with all these arms. I think Student 1, seeing that Student 3 got away with putting his arm around

me, also decided to give it a go. I did not awfully mind, but I was not very comfortable and still (I am writing about 20 minutes after the incident) do not feel very comfortable. I felt very small and fragile with these big arms around me, and this is not how I see myself as a lecturer. As a lecturer, I am big, strong and authoritative. If there are arms being put around things, they are my arms, as opposed to other arms being put around me. It also makes me quite uneasy knowing that while all these students are very polite (I even got a bow from Student 1), some of them are wanting to put their arms around me.

So here we go. Now I am thinking about how to avoid arms in the future. (or should I? . . . is this an expression of my insecurity?)

Picture the scene. Kara has just finished giving a lecture in which she has occupied an active, 'male' speaking position, one of authority, dominance and control. The students who approached her and put their arms around her returned her immediately to a passive, 'female' speaking position, one in which she is inferior and where she exists to buttress the frail masculine ego (Brennan, 1993). Kara is switched from being the superior to the subordinate, from the powerful to the powerless, from the active to the passive, and in that moment she becomes subject to the inferiority that is the heritage of women in the West. From being unaware of her body, from having an absent body, she is made aware again that her body is small, weak and leaky (Shildrick, 1997). Kara is therefore surprised back into gender.

I want to suggest that this is not an unusual event but one that happens repeatedly. Sitting here typing this account, my body recedes from my conscious knowledge, as does my awareness of my gendered identity. A glance at the nail varnish on my fingers reminds me swiftly and sometimes brutally that I am a woman. Every time we catch sight of our reflection in a mirror or are positioned as male or female in the eyes of another person, we see the visible signifier of our gendered position so, having lapsed out of it, we are always surprised back into it. There is a violence for women in being surprised back into what we know consciously as an inferior, subordinate identity and for men and women alike in what we know unconsciously is a baleful, depressing position requiring much work in the maintenance of something we really do not want to maintain. We thus continually taste the freedom from gender and have it snatched away, taste it again and have it snatched away again. To be forced back into gender is traumatic, at both the conscious and the unconscious levels. Consciously, norms of how we should behave as men or as women can be oppressive and overdemanding, and we are always subject to failure. We may be judged on our gender rather than on our achievements, categorised and forced into uncomfortable boxes. Copjec's analysis shows how gender in the psyche is a torment. This becomes clearer through re-reading an incident reported in Martin's (2006) research.

ANALYSIS 3: SURPRISED INTO GENDER

Paula was the only woman manager present at a meeting where an incident occurred that was so upsetting that it led her to leave the company
six months later. She recounted to Martin (2006) what had happened. At a
meeting, a new member of the managerial staff, Bob, had just been introduced. He 'pulled a pair of bikini undies [from his coat pocket] and tossed
them on the table and said, "I'm always ready". Only one of the men present did not burst into laughter, and this man, Jeff, walked out of the room
with Paula. Paula made numerous formal and informal complaints, but
Bob's only punishment was the withdrawing of some promised perks. Paula
left and established her own 'flourishing financial services firm'.

Martin (2006) uses this and other examples to argue that men in organizations are insufficiently reflexive about how they practise their masculinity
and the effect this has on women's continued subordination. I fully support
her in her conclusion but suggest the incident says something more about
organizational gendering.

Paula has been cursed by psychoanalytical theory's buttressing of Western culture, so she has no option but to construct herself as female and thus
subordinate. She evades those demands by constituting herself within an
active, managerial speaking position. Martin indeed argues that gender is
a tacit, liminal practice that may be largely subconscious. Paula thus may
'forget' she is a woman and join with the men in the meeting as an equal.
She, like them, may be 'agendered', or non-gendered, or have all sorts of
possible gendered identities potentially available as, in the company of the
men with whom she works, she forgets about culture's requirement that
she be female. However, the throwing of the women's underwear onto the
table surprises her back into gender, for if Bob had tossed onto the table,
say, a handkerchief, the incident would have been meaningless. Underwear,
in an office, is 'matter out of place' and thus has disruptive, performative power (Douglas, 1966). A garment that clothes the genital area, it has
sexual associations. Its sudden appearance, I suggest, reminds Paula that
she is a woman, with all the connotations of inferiority, subordination and
powerlessness that are the heritage of women in the West. She is surprised
back into gender.

Further, women's underwear symbolises that supposed fear of castration
which Freud argues results in the male child aligning himself with the masculine. So the 'uproarious' laughter of the men in the room may have been
less about humour and more the result of shock at their being surprised
back into gender as well. They are reliving that earlier trauma, that earlier
imagined threat of castration, through what Freud termed *nachträglichkeist*,
most commonly interpreted as "deferred action" or "retroaction". By this
term is meant memory traces that are given new meaning as a result of being
'relived' in specific situations in the present. In other words, an episode that
occurred in infancy will return again and again, to be reconstructed and

reexperienced in the present (Barzilai, 1999). Lacan (1977) proposed that human subjects live *nachträglich* perpetually, not extraordinarily, and, in so living, they encompass three temporal stations: past, present and an anticipatory dimension.

The sudden appearance of a symbol of symbolic castration therefore would plunge all parties present back into the trauma of becoming gendered. The men's laughter is thus less laughter than a rictus response which may have had little to do with humour and much to do with the return of the repressed.

In this reading, Paula the manager, polymorphously perverse and confident in her non- or agendered identity, is reminded that she cannot evade the powerless position of the woman. She is sentenced to entombment in a symbolic cave, that of gender, the trouble and confusion of which is apparent in Brewis's (2005) painful exploration of the subjectified identity of the female academic.

CONCLUSION: WHAT IS WORKPLACE GENDER IN THE EARLY 21ST CENTURY?

In this chapter I have explored the fluidity of gender identities in jobs that women now share with men. Gender is in flux in these jobs: it is perhaps more appropriate to talk about organizational speaking subjects, untied from the descriptors 'male' and 'female', than about men and women. These positions have no more than tentative connections with biological sexes, and 'male' and 'female' are active and passive positions through which individuals move. The person whose genitalia are female may practise itself as rational, logical, avoiding of intimacy, active, all those things regarded as 'masculine'. The person whose genitalia are male may practise itself as caring, emotional, passive, all those things regarded as 'feminine'. These descriptive categories are arbitrary but normative. We are trapped by language when trying to capture some of what is going on today, because we are inevitably returned to 'she' and 'he' when we are surprised into gender. It may be more appropriate to talk about, say, active and passive subject positions, but even here we return to the grammar of 'he' and 'she', and we cannot escape the centuries-long view of activity as masculine, and passivity as its female other.

Furthermore, I have suggested that for much of the time we are, to ourselves, ungendered or outside gender, but others impose gender upon us, require that we be gendered so that they are confirmed in their own gender identity. Repair work may be taken by those others if we do not conform to their requirements of how we should be gendered, and indeed we may shock ourselves when we see our reflections in mirrors—we return to embodied movements that confirm us in our culturally mandated gendered identities. We are therefore regularly surprised into gender, returned to the traumatic identity whose norms are unattainable and whose practices may render us abject or put into painful and untenable positions. Then we lapse back out of gender, only to be returned to it; then we lapse back into that comfortable position in which the requirements of our gender are forgotten as more immediate tasks and activities take precedence. But only for a while.

In attempting to move beyond the no-longer-tenable distinctions between organizational masculinities and femininities, there is the possibility of subjectivities that are about *being*. Rather than there being a 'he' and a 'she', there will just be an 'is'. Ending that sentence with a copula, not linking the verb 'to be' to anything, signifies the meaning of that sentence. It is about not being male, not being female, not being gendered, but just being a subject. Indeed, Foucault's *The Order of Things* (1970) should have led us to ask why traits have been organized into two lists of 'male' and 'female'. Are they not, as Foucault suggests, fundamental codes of a culture which allow the ordering of things and disallow other possibilities? Does it not behoove us therefore to challenge them rather than to continue listing them?

In terms of the argument of this book, organizations here have a potentially emancipatory stance: they offer the possibility, perhaps to only some of the people and only some of the time, of freeing the self from the dire controls of gender. There is a cultural requirement to be identifiable according to gender in order to be capable of recognition (Butler, 1990; 1993), but organizations may be illuminating ways in which it is possible to escape from such a requirement. To be able to absorb one's self in one's task or to work with others in a position of mutual respect about the self as a person, with no judgements being made on the basis of whether one is fulfilling the norms of masculinity or femininity—that is the possible future of organizational (un)gender. Organizations currently show us a promised land, even though we are currently allowed to enter for only sufficient time to know what it must be like to become a citizen. The self that is outside gender is a self we might hardly know we desire to be, because gender appears as natural and as inescapable as the air that is breathed. However, having experienced the freedom of being non-gendered, I may feel a visceral knowledge that the me I wish to be would be freed from the constraints of gender.

I will therefore posit the notion that, when working on the self as an organizational subject, we work on a self that will be outside gender, freed from its constraints. But, when we labour, then, we labour as men or women, with no freedom from gender's constraints. The human is or should be treated very differently. The terms of the question I posed earlier about whether the distinction between labour and work holds when we are discussing gender are turned on their head. The question should have been: what can gender tell us about the distinction between labour and work? The arguments in this chapter suggest that gender should be equated in some ways with imprisonment and in other ways with freedom. There can be pleasure in performatively constituting a gendered self, but also the terms of gendering may be imposed in such a way that we become incarcerated in a traumatic prisonhouse of a body/identity. If this is the case, then labouring as a gendered person, with the terms of that gender imposed by the organization, means that labour equates to fixed gender categories. On the other hand, through work, we may (sometimes) escape from that prison and become outside gender for a while. So work equates to constituting a self freed from gender's constraints.

The next question was: is the zombie-machine and/or the human gendered? The answer would appear to be that the zombie-machine is clearly marked as sexed and judged accordingly. It may be channelled into jobs that are the domain of its requisite gender (such as nursing or caring jobs for women, hard manual labour for men). The zombie-machine becomes judged on how it upholds its ostensible (fixed) gender identity. The human, on the other hand, may move in and out of gendered identities, *choosing* how to constitute itself as female or male and refusing to be judged according to the norms of either category.

These are tentative conclusions, but they point to a somewhat unexpected observation in a critical text. This is that organizations may, in some ways, offer some people some of the time a revolutionary potential for becoming free of the constraints of gender.

6 A Hyperbolic Theory, a Theory in Drag: Organizations and the Murder of the Me's-I-Might-Have-Been

This book, located within a sociocultural philosophical framework that incorporates Judith Butler's work and that of several lay philosophers, develops a theory of the damage caused to individuals because of the power of organizations to impose their desires upon staff, thus ignoring, suppressing, stunting, frustrating or killing the desires of people who, as Julie showed in Chapter One, go to work to do more than labour. Organizations seek to employ less than human zombie-machines, and individuals seek employment in which the selves they aspire to be can be worked on. The tension here is between the less-than-human and the human. Though staff twist and turn to escape from the organization's desires to reduce them to the less-than-human, the organization imposes limits on the possible selves they can be. Previous chapters have argued that the manager cannot even imagine any existence other than as zombie-machine and so in many ways is the most controlled. Through Shakeel, Alex, Kara and Saul, we have seen how employees' intelligence may be refused expression and their enthusiasm and skills ignored or turned against them and used to control them; the straitjacket of the organization's desires prevents their flourishing. We do the best we can do in such circumstances to constitute a sense of self, seeking recognition through friendships, escaping temporarily from the constraints of organizational norms, etc., but so many compromises must be made that the dreams of who we could be(come) through our work are killed off. Even those of us in relatively privileged jobs, such as that of the academic, are restricted in what we can do and what we can be for much of our working days.

This book's conclusion is therefore that organizations murder the-me's-that-might-have-been. This is in some ways what Butler (1997:149) calls 'a hyperbolic theory, a theory in drag, as it were, which overstates the case but overstates it for a reason'. The language used, of murder and death, is hyperbolic but allows articulation of the damage that organizations do to working people in an era where work on the self is fundamental to a sense of being human.

The modus operandi of this chapter differs from that of the previous chapters, in that it turns to popular culture for its 'lay philosophy' and does not use Butler's work for its theoretical framing. Again, the source of its arguments arises from personal experience. I voraciously read or watch detective stories, or 'whodunits', and so gobble up accounts of violent and gruesome deaths. This contrasts markedly with my weak and stumbling attempts at vegetarianism, Buddhism and pacifism and my horror of horror stories (they give me nightmares), but somehow I am drawn again and again to the whodunit. I am not alone: Euro-American culture is saturated with images of fictional violent death that cater for a seemingly insatiable appetite for the whodunit. I therefore wondered if the whodunit could be articulating something that is otherwise unsayable, as Parker (2011) argues of the outlaw. An immersion in the literature about the whodunit, allied with some previous reading of film theory, suggests this could be the case (pun intended), while an excursion into philosophical and other explorations of death allows elaboration of the theory.

This chapter therefore argues that the detective genre articulates on our behalf an unspeakable knowledge, which is that the limitations imposed on self-making in organizations is a form of death, the *deaths of the me's-who-might-have-been*, the me's I dream of becoming; organizations are guilty of the murder of these possible selves. This, of course, is not biological death, death of the body, but neither is it social death (Glaser and Strauss, 1968), that is, becoming a nonperson while biologically still alive, because social death remains tied to the material ending of the body. 'Organizational death', the death of the me-who-might-have-been had the organization not killed my potential self/selves, is the murder not of the body but of selves-in-the-making, so that what remains is a zombie stunted by the vile and poisonous toad, work, that squats on our lives (Larkin, 2003).

My thesis concerning organizational death starts with imagining the feelings Frank, Alex, Shakeel, Saul and Kara might have but for which there is no easily available vocabulary. There is something that is experienced as a sense of loss and dissatisfaction, of boredom with work and the wish to escape, of frustration with the boss and dreams of starting anew. It is described as a midlife crisis, a period when one realises that many of the things one had planned to do have failed to materialise. Like physical pain, it is an experience of which we are aware but for which words fail us (Scarry, 1988). However, this knowledge that cannot be expressed makes itself known elliptically, through eruptions in other fields to which we are drawn. One field of such eruption is the entertainments consumed in our leisure times, many of which seem to focus almost obsessively on violent death. To relax, we immerse ourselves in fictional death, and this, I suggest, is a symptom of that which is felt but cannot be articulated while at work. Whodunits are home to an understanding of death that 'remain[s] unknown not because [it is] occluded or unspoken, but because [it] circulate[s] constantly and visibly as commonplaces' (Dollimore, 2001:xii). The detective story or whodunit deals in both death and organizations and so articulates for us our unsayable knowledge that the me's-who-might-have-been are murdered by the organization.

The chapter begins with an overview of academic theories of death. It then explores the whodunit and what it is articulating for us, its readers/viewers, that we otherwise could not say. The discussion then returns to Dollimore's thesis on death, first discussed in the chapter's review of literature on death, to weave Dollimore's thesis on disessentializing with Marx's theory of alienation. This leads to a discussion of how work could allow not only self-making but also opportunities for escape from dread anxieties surrounding death.

WHAT IS DEATH? THEORIES WITHIN MANAGEMENT AND ORGANIZATION STUDIES

There is as yet very little analysis of death by organization theorists. The bulk of that which does exist takes a psychoanalytical stance (Smith 2006). For example, Wolfram Cox (1997) points out the similarity between the mourning that follows organizational change and the mourning that follows someone's death. Ways in which the psyche, notably the unconscious death drive, Thanatos, influences behaviours in organizations have been explored (Fotaki, 2005; Menzies, 1960), allowing development of a thesis of the merger of organization and self (Schwartz, 1987; Clark, 1993) such that the individual's ethics and code of conduct become overridden by those of the organization, and staff carry out acts that they would otherwise find unacceptable. Sievers (1994), for example, argues that organizations require that staff remain immature and thus oblivious to their own inevitable deaths, so organizations inculcate a generalised feeling of immortality, while Feldman (2004) sees this denial of death as freeing the professional person to act without any morals other than those given within a professional herd mentality. Feldman argues that denial of one's own death estranges one from life. Carr and Lapp (2005) similarly draw on Freud but argue almost the contrary, that it is death which gives meaning to working life. They argue that Eros and Thanatos, respectively the life and death drives, are dialectically related, with life and death, pleasure and displeasure, always imbricated each in the other.

One body of sociological theory, represented most passionately by Bauman (1989), regards organizations as machineries of death. The argument here is that those rational rules which generally enable organizations also facilitate genocide; they allow participants to distance themselves from their actions (see also Burrell, 1997; Browder, 2003). In an intriguing argument, Willmott (2000) looks to sociological theories of death to argue that organizations sharpen death's sting because they provide the products, services and sense of self that make life worth living. Fear of death is therefore a form of grieving in advance for what we will ultimately lose. Willmott thus turns on its head sociologists' argument that institutions have developed to help us cope with fear of our own deaths. His argument, in other words, is that social institutions developed to stave off knowledge of our death actually constitute fear of death. Smith (2006), meanwhile, critiques a dominant thesis within sociology, of the sequestration of death. This argues that modern Western societies shut the dying away, so that death has become private and hidden. Smith starts with the proposition that although ways of dealing with the material effects of death have been removed from day-to-day life, death itself remains shatteringly omnipresent, so that the bereaved are, literally, devastated and have to rebuild themselves and their memories of those they mourn. This rebuilding requires *organization*.

An important recent paper (Reedy and Learmonth, 2011) introduces to organization studies philosophical thinking about death. Reedy and Learmonth develop a Heideggerian organizational ethics in which they argue the need to acknowledge mortality, an acknowledgement that should lead to different ways of being and of being employed while at work. Through turning the knowledge of one's inevitable demise back on itself, the self, they argue, can learn to live ethically, alive to every moment of its existence; such a self demands an ethical organization aware of the need to value every single one of those moments. Organizational responsibilities in regard to its treatment of staff are therefore highlighted.

These disparate works cannot be woven together into a coherent argument or meaningful categories. Organizational death theory (organizational thanatology?) is thus in its infancy, in contrast with its exploration in other disciplines.

WHAT IS DEATH? ANSWERS FROM THE ARTS, HUMANITIES AND SOCIAL SCIENCES

The death of God in the increasingly secularised world of 19th-century Europe was a 'sociological fact' (Young, 2003:3) by the time of Nietzsche's announcement of this death in *The Gay Science* (1882/2001). It is difficult, enmeshed in a culture that has long been secularised (albeit not atheistic [Chadwick, 1990]), to comprehend the hole left in people's lives as religion lost its place and the certainty of life after death faded. If God is dead, then the meaning of life has disappeared, and if nothing takes its place then all that remains is nihilism. In light of this gargantuan bereavement, how are we to cope with life and death? Twentieth-century philosophers answered that we cope with it by ignoring death even while we know of its omnipresence; they warned against such neglect.

Simmel (1910/2007), for example, argued that death should not be seen as a single act but rather must be recognised as being there, in every single moment of our lives, for the human subject is an organism that knows it must die. Death gives form to and colours life, but it does this through an aversion to death. Therefore, 'earning a living and enjoyment, work and rest, and all other activities considered to be natural, are instinctively or consciously flights from death' (ibid.:75). Similarly, but more influentially, Heidegger (1926/1962) argued that the temporary and transitory reality of being a biological creature is so horrendous that knowledge of our forthcoming death is suppressed beneath compulsive activities which keep that knowledge from us. To imagine not being, not existing, is so fearsome and anxiety-provoking that we indulge in all sorts of pursuits that distract us from our dreaded mortality. For Heidegger, the recognition that we are all someday going to die should bring with it a strong ethical stance: we must be authentic, acknowledge our finitude and thus choose the best way in which to live. As noted earlier, Reedy and Learmonth (2011) argue that Heidegger's insights make it even more imperative that working lives not be blighted by organizations.

Sociological theories of death echo philosophers' arguments regarding its absent presence, but with the focus turned towards understanding how the precariousness of human existence conditions social action. The horror of death cannot be avoided: 'Death remains the great extrinsic factor of human existence . . . [it is] the point zero: it is nothing more or less than the moment at which human control over human existence finds an outer limit' (Giddens, 1991:162). This 'consuming dreadfulness' of death and dying, Small (2001, in Smith, 2006:226) suggests, 'take[s] us as individuals, to a place that exists at the brink of the crisis of modernity. We are not in control, we do not understand. Our sense of self, our relations with others, even the way we experience time is challenged'. This explains why we cut death out of conscious awareness, sequestering it, moving its 'consuming dreadfulness' into institutions such as hospitals, care homes and hospices that care for the dying and dispose of bodies (Giddens, 1991). Death is therefore an 'absent presence in social conduct' (Willmott, 2000:654) which haunts our understanding of our selves and our lives (Bauman, 1992), challenging the possibility of ontological security (Giddens, 1991). Although we are not overtly aware of its constant presence, it sends us to the gym and diet books as we attempt to defer dying (Shilling, 1993).

There is thus a major body of theory which argues that death is ignored or hidden away in Western cultures because it is too fearful to comprehend. There are some suggestions that this perspective is now changing. For example, the social historian Audrey Linkman (2011) argues that it applied to the earlier part of the 20th century but that the taboo was challenged in that century's last two decades, when a 19th-century tradition of taking photographs of the dead was resurrected.

A body of theory that is difficult to comprehend intuitively (until perhaps in midlife, as one's own meeting with the Grim Reaper starts to etch itself into one's diary) is that which, influenced by Freud, argues that the human animal's fear of death is matched by an equally powerful attraction towards it. Freud (1914/2009; see also de Lauretis, 2008) argued that the subject has two fundamental drives, those of Eros and Thanatos. Eros is the drive towards life, the creative life force, and Thanatos the drive that seeks a return to the inorganic state from which life emerges. It is only in death that we can escape from the burdens and fears of life. This uncomfortable thesis permeates Western culture: Shakespeare's *Hamlet*, a play that influenced Freud's thinking, articulates it for us:

> To die, to sleep,
> No more; and by a sleep to say we end
> The heartache and the thousand natural shocks
> That flesh is heir to,—'tis a consummation
> Devoutly to be wish'd. To die, to sleep—
> To sleep, perchance to dream:—aye, there's the rub;
> For in that sleep of death what dreams may come,
> When we have shuffled off this mortal coil
> Must give us pause.

For, Hamlet continues, it is only the dread of something that awaits us after death, 'the undiscover'd country from whose bourn no traveller returns', which prevents our killing ourselves.

Where Freud explored an unconscious desire for death, Baudrillard (1976/1993) dismisses psychoanalytical theory as a myth of our time, but he argues similarly that death is omnipresent. Baudrillard traces modern Western concepts of death to the 16th century and, by contrasting them with those of other cultures, suggests reasons for Westerners' deep anxieties about death. 'Every other culture', he writes (158–159), 'says that death begins before death, that life goes on after life, and that it is impossible to distinguish life from death'. The dead do not disappear in other cultures as they do in the West, but remain active participants in daily life. We must therefore, he argues, grasp 'the radical indeterminacy of life and death, and the impossibility of their autonomy in the symbolic order' (ibid.), because we in the West are not so different in many ways from those in other cultures. Even during life, 'whole parts of "ourselves" (of our bodies, our language) fall from life to death' (ibid.). Identity is also continually falling apart, so that 'only in the infinitesimal space of the individual conscious subject does death take on an irreversible meaning' (160). Death is thus not an event but a myth which is experienced as anticipation and which serves to form identity by adding to the myth of origin another myth, that of ending. When we mourn the death of others, we also mourn our own anticipated death. Importantly for the arguments in this chapter, for Baudrillard, *contra* Heidegger and Simmel, death is everywhere in life and its localisation on the body as a single, traumatic event nothing but a Cartesian desire to blame the body for 'taking its revenge [for its subordinate status] by dying' (160). Mortal body and immortal soul are therefore both equally unreal.

Theories of death from other disciplines can thus be divided roughly into two contradictory categories: death is hidden away and ignored; death is omnipresent. A far more penetrating and intense study of Western European ideas about death, which encompasses the theorists noted here and many,

many more, is given in Dollimore's (2001) monumental study *Death, Desire and Loss in Western Culture*. Dollimore analyses discussions about death in the scraps that remain of the writings of the earliest Greek philosophers and their successors in Greece and Rome. He explores its importance to understanding Christianity and Buddhism, its appearance in drama, novels and poetry from the Renaissance to the late 20th century (Shakespeare, of course, and the metaphysical poetry of John Donne, with Lawrence, Conrad and Mann representing the 20th century), and theories of death embedded in the works of philosophers and psychoanalytical theorists (Bataille, Freud, Hegel, Heidegger, Kojève, Lacan, Marcuse, Marx, Nietzsche, Sartre and Schopenhauer). His list of sources and the depth of his reading make my 'literature review' here pale into insignificance. In what follows, I summarise the theory he develops but draw on it directly only towards the end of the chapter, after I have set out the thesis that organizational death is the killing of my hopes and dreams of the me's-I-might-have-been.

DOLLIMORE ON DEATH

This is the thesis I disinter from Dollimore's (2001) book. Death and desire have been mutually informative throughout the entire history of Western European cultures. Fear of death, of dissolution of the self, is so great that the only release from it is death itself. Temporary, fleeting release can be found in disessentializing the self through activities in which one loses one's subjectivity and the I, or the ego, dissolves. In such evanescent moments, there is no 'I' that can fear its own demise. (Where Dollimore finds possibilities for such momentary transcendence of the self in the anonymous sexual encounter, I will later use Marx's theory of alienation to posit another scene in which the self may disappear.)

Dollimore traces (sexual) desire's embedment in Western Europe's conceptualisation of death to the scraps remaining of the writings of the first Greek philosophers and tracks the continuing marriage of death and desire through millennia of Western European thought. Western Europeans are individuated, that is, 'separate, differentiated, alone' (xx); self-consciousness of individuality is formed through a knowledge of the end of one's life and informed by a feeling that the only release is death (xxi), that is 'oblivion, . . . the cessation of desire, the still point of the turning world' (10). There is thus embedded in the European psyche a desire for death, one that is intensified, thwarted, deflected and exploited by theology. Freud's theory of the death drive brilliantly reworks and challenges theology's grip on death (xx).

Death and desire are connected, Dollimore argues, because of 'mutability—the sense that all being is governed by a ceaseless process of change inseparable from *an inconsolable sense of loss somehow always in excess of the loss of anything in particular*' (xiii, emphasis in original). Over millennia, mutability becomes internalised as the inner dynamic of desire. 'Fragmented, unstable and death-ridden' (83), the human subject is driven forward reluctantly by that very 'deeply regressive desire for oblivion' (83): the desire for death is what propels us towards a life in which the knowledge of our own death foments 'a restless, agonized energy' towards the sustenance of life. The Western European subject is therefore always 'a subject in crisis', obsessed with control and expansion so as to deal with that crisis but instigating forms of control that always exceed and break down the very order that is restlessly quested (92–93).

Hegel, whose work informs the ideas of so many thinkers in the 20th and 21st centuries, understood this. Dollimore writes that Hegel, in analysing how 'we live stretched across a fierce dialectic in which identity is dependent upon otherness or difference—dependent, that is, upon what it is not' (154), on an other that can never be kept other because part of what I *am* is that I am *not that*, so that what I am not is not only alongside and independent of what I am, but is also interior to what I am. However, for Hegel, *being* presupposes *not being*, and vice versa. In order to be, everything must undergo a dialectic sublation or negation by, in or as its opposite, so the negation of death is not exterior but intrinsic to the subject. Thus, Kojève, interpreting Hegel, could write that 'the human being itself is no other thing than . . . (a) death that lives a human life'; 'Man [*sic*] is not only *mortal*, he is *death* incarnate; he *is* his own death'; Man not only knows that he will die, 'he is the consciousness of his death' (164).

Freud, Dollimore writes, evolved a new language, almost a new mythology, to articulate the absolute interiority of death to life. Freud's 'ancient, shocking vision' was that death is not the termination of life (that 'mystifying banality by which we live' [192]) but life's animating and driving force. Thanatos, or the death drive, arises from a desire for the complete calm of the grave, free from the troubles of life. Life is merely 'an enforced substitute for death, a movement in the only direction available, which is forward and one always undertaken against the more fundamental desire to regress, to die (186–187).

In the 20th century, Dollimore argues, death was not so much repressed as 'resignified in new, complex and productive ways which then legitimate a never-ending analysis of it' (126). One of these is the marking upon homosexuality of death. Homosexuality becomes a 'symbolic focus for cultural preoccupations which far exceed it'. Homosexuality, defined by desire, comes to figure death. (Another of these figures of death, I will argue later, is the whodunit—by reading novels or watching films or television programmes about murders and the search for the murderer, we immerse ourselves in analysis of and fantasies about death. Thus we will return to organizations.)

Now we come to what is most shockingly productive in Dollimore's thesis. The only freedom from knowledge of death that we have in that time between cradle and grave is when we become 'disessentialized' (325), that is, when we so forget the ego or the I that we are lost to ourselves. Postmodernism's anti-essentialism, he writes, 'as a merely theoretical statement about identity is misleading to the point of being useless' and 'what needs to be recovered is the experiential dimension of anti-essentialism' (325). Dollimore finds this in homoerotic writing and in the anonymous homosexual encounter, in which the self is 'disidentified' as 'the divide between reality and fantasy momentarily shifts and even dissolves, as do other divisions too, including those between public and private, self and other' (327). In the momentary suspension of individuality, of the individuated self, there is a temporary release from Thanatos, from the compulsion towards death.

This would seem to take us a long way from much that goes on in organizations, but there is a link to be made via Marx's theory of alienation. I will return to this argument in the conclusion to this chapter. For now, however, I turn to the detective novel to explore how death informs working lives.

Just as the homosexual, in Dollimore's thesis, is a symbolic focus for Western Europeans' fear of death, I suggest that the detective story offers a cultural focus through which we put ourselves face to face with death. It has been pointed out that there are strong similarities between the work of fictional detectives and that of academics—each is concerned with discovery, with finding out and with resolving dilemmas (Nicolson, 1946, Porter, 1981, both in Hühn, 1987); further, fictional detectives are a useful proxy for scientists and academics more generally (Czarniawska, 1999). Czarniawska (1999) explores in depth the complementarity between detective fiction and academic writing, while Salzer-Morling (1998) mimics the hard-boiled detective novel to explore the relationship between academic papers and organizational life, but there are no papers which analyse the detective story's performative relationship between reader, text and organizations. That is, there is no exploration of how the detective story constitutes the author/reader/viewer, who, we have seen, is long argued to be a creature not only endowed with the fearful knowledge of its own finitude but in many ways driven towards its own ending. I will use film and literary theorists to show that our delight in observing, over and over, the fictional portrayal of death arises from our attraction to a genre that says, on our behalf, albeit elliptically and through symbols, metaphors and images, something which we cannot put into words. This is, we know we are going to die, so we know how precious is the time available to us. In that time, we wish to constitute selves that will have made our lives worth living. Organizations, as the previous chapters and much research in labour process theory and critical management studies have shown, severely restrict the possibilities for constituting selves because they require that we spend much of our time in work needlessly made boring and aimless. That organizations thus limit our potential and stifle the selves we could be is a form of murder—the murder of our dreams of who we could and might have been.

THE DETECTIVE THRILLER AS ARTICULATION OF AN EPOCH'S UNSPEAKABLE TRAUMA

The detective:

> *Wallander rushed down into the mud. He stumbled into the ditch and scrambled up the other side. When he saw Hoglund [a fellow detective] on her back in the mud he thought she was dead. . . . And it was all his fault. For a split second he saw no way out but to shoot himself. Right where he stood, a few metres from her. Then he saw her moving feebly. He fell to his knees by her side. She was deathly pale and stared at him with fear in her eyes. 'It'll be all right,' he said, 'It will be all right'. . . . Wallander could feel the tears running down his face. He called for an ambulance. Later he would remember that while he waited, he had steadily murmured a confused prayer to a god he didn't really believe in. In a haze he was aware that [two colleagues] Svedberg and Hamren had arrived. Ann-Britt was carried away on a stretcher. Wallander was sitting in the mud. They couldn't get him to stand up.* (Mankell, 2009:557)

In this section I outline the history of the detective story and its relevance for understanding organizations. The detective story, with its focus predominantly upon violent death, is hugely popular. To take one week at random, beginning 25 April 2010, British television's five terrestrial channels offered each evening a minimum of two programmes (including films) that featured violent crimes and their resolution. Satellite television channels offered numerous offerings on the same theme. The terrestrial channels' programmes included reconstructions of actual crimes; a drama in which a police officer has been transported back to the police force of the 1980s; 'reality' programmes in which police officers are accompanied by camera crews; a film about a fictional 18th-century detective; a futuristic series in which the whole of the human race is at risk; and numerous episodes of North American crime dramas. The top ten paperback titles in terms of sales that week included seven crime novels, two historical novels and one book combining both genres through its exploration of an unexplained crime from the 15th century (the murder of the princes in the Tower of London). There was little difference in the proportion of television programmes, films and books devoted to crime and its detection in August 2010 and in March 2011. In the US, six of the ten highest-selling books in 2008 (the latest year for which statistics were available at the time of writing) dealt with violent death and its detection. [1]Many of these books are translated into numerous languages, so their stories are known internationally. For example, two Swedish authors whose books are read worldwide are Stieg Larsson, whose *Millenium Trilogy* has sold more than 40 million copies, and Henning Mankell, whose *Wallander* series, featuring the eponymous detective, has sold 25 million copies.

The BBC television films of the *Wallander* novels were watched by more than 20 percent of the viewing audience on their first airing in the UK, that is, by between 5.2 and 6.3 million people, 10 percent of the entire population[2]. Many more will have watched the programmes via other formats. Television programmes based on Ian Rankin's *Rebus* detective novels have achieved viewing figures of up to 8.4 million people.[3] Crime dramas, notably those concerning murder and attempts to discover the murderers, are therefore the entertainment of choice of many millions of people. When six million people sit down to watch *Wallander*, they sit down to watch a portrayal of murder.

Detective fiction appeared in the mid-19th century alongside an emergent scientific interest in deductive logic and, indeed, manufactories. A newly literate reading public which was experiencing the cultural upheavals of industrialisation, the move from rural to city living, mass literacy and secularisation, found in detective fiction some sort of ontological security (van Dover, 2005). Edgar Allan Poe's two short stories *The Murders in the Rue Morgue* (1841) and *The Purloined Letter* (1844) established the 'twin fountainheads' (Rzepka, 2005:74) of detective fiction: 'whodunit?' and 'how is the criminal to be discovered and captured?' As the scientific method developed, so also did the focus in the crime novel on deduction through a careful accumulation of facts: the amazingly insightful detective could emerge. It was Sir Arthur Conan Doyle's *Sherlock Holmes* books that institutionalised the format, which was to continue for a century and more: the somewhat troubled but brilliant and astute loner, dependent on a good friend, who has powers of observation far beyond those of the average person (Rzepka, 2005; van Dover, 2005). The detectives featured in the classic detective novels (and, later, the films and television programmes) offer, in the scientific age, the assurance that someone knows infallibly what has happened to us and knows the mysteries that surround the beginning and the ending of our lives (van Dover, 2005). There is nothing in this first incarnation of the detective genre to relate it to organizations: the detective operated independently, demonstrating a sparkling intelligence far in advance of that of the police officers, whose role was that of the inferior other to this superior form of being.

Classic detective fiction revolves around two stories: the story of the crime and the story of its solving, often recounted by a companion to the hero-detective. Its successor, American hard-boiled detective fiction, emerged in the first half of the 20th century: now the companion disappears and the detective becomes the narrator. Dashiell Hammett's Sam Spade, who appeared in *The Maltese Falcon* in 1930, and Raymond Chandler's Philip Marlowe, who featured in a series of novels beginning with *The Big Sleep* (1939), typify the hard-boiled detective. Whereas previously there were two overlapping stories—the committing of a crime and its solving—now the two stories merge, and through the very process of searching for the criminal the detective causes the criminal to commit more crimes. Often the hard-boiled detective has to battle against not only the devious criminal but also the corrupt organizations that employ them. The heroic detective of the classical novel is replaced in the hard-boiled novels by a detective who is damaged, disillusioned, and 'in a paralyzed state of profound weariness and melancholy' (Hühn, 1987:461) but who can, like the heroic detective, 'reintegrat[e] the aberrant event, [and so] the narrative reconstruction restores the disrupted social order and reaffirms the validity of the system of norms' (425). It can be seen that, as with the classic detective story, the hard-boiled detective story does something far more than entertain, because it addresses the traumas of an age. However, there is again little about organizations in this period: the detective is a solo operator, and any organizations encountered are shadowy, criminal and dangerous, symbolic perhaps of the world wars of the 20th century and the West's fear of Soviet communism but not of workplaces.

Classic and hard-boiled detectives have been challenged by the post-modern detective story. Whereas literary theorists have argued that this generation of whodunits is one, typically, in which each person's story of the crime is just another version of what happened, with little possibility of discovering 'the truth', I suggest that the distinction between the post-modern detective story and its predecessors is the importance of organizations to the analysis, because today's detective works for an organization, usually a police force, and often deals with murderers who work for other organizations. Like that of the hard-boiled detective, this detective's reading of the story changes the story itself, and the detective, battered and bruised, is left to suffer the consequences of a damaged ego. However, this detective is not so much disillusioned as traumatised at being unable to control everything going on around him/her (Czarniawska, 1999), and much of what goes on around the detective is organizational life. Although one story—the teleological journey towards discovery of perpetrators of the crime—continues, alongside this runs another story in which teleology is defeated and all around is chaos and uncertainty. This is signified in material (organizational) objects such as the furniture in the detectives' offices. Where the aesthete Holmes has a comfortable study and his body remains barely touched by his encounters with criminals, Philip Marlowe is the possessor of a modest office consisting of two rooms (one for his secretary, one for himself) that is sometimes ransacked. Marlowe himself is often beaten up, captured, threatened or bruised, and his body aches as he pursues the perpetrators. The postmodern detective shares a cramped office with other officers, in an organization upon which s/he depends for his/her livelihood and is often engaged in finding murderers who work in other organizations or who commit crimes on behalf of those organizations. As the level of privacy and comfort in the detectives' offices diminish and the detectives' engagement with organizations increases, the detective becomes more vulnerable.

Today's detectives are flawed, fallible people, just like their readers. Where Marlowe suffered no more than a hangover from drinking his favourite bourbon, his successors now suffer the problems of alcohol abuse; their bodies ache from lack of exercise and poor diets. Mankell's Wallander worries about his weight and has to take a day off work when he has flu, he is too cold if he has not worn the right jumper, is often aware that he needs a shower, has trouble finding the time to do his washing, shopping or cleaning, and is eventually diagnosed with diabetes and, later, Alzheimer's disease. Rankin's insomniac Inspector Rebus is increasingly unfit and cannot keep up when chasing criminals, while Billingham's Detective Inspector Thorne stares in his mirror at his bloodshot eyes and, like Rebus, is racked with guilt and haunted by past cases, and, unlike Rebus but like Wallander, has a nervous breakdown. Larsson's Blomqvist, the journalist who acts as detective in the *Girl with the Dragon Tattoo* trilogy, is put into the position of the female (he almost dies at the hands of a mass murderer of women) and, emasculated, is rescued by a woman. Jo Nesbo's Finnish detective Harry Hole is an emaciated alcoholic. These detectives often are seeking love but unable to find it. Again it is organizations that are responsible for this failure in the detectives' lives—they are unlovable because of the jobs they do. Those detectives with friends and families find their relationships damaged, and often organizations, work and family intrude into one another's sphere in ways that endanger not only family life but the life and health of family members. Rebus's daughter is disabled as a direct result of his job; Wallander's daughter is, in several of the novels, held at knifepoint by deranged murderers, and D.I. Thorne's only friend, a pathologist (it is notable that pathologists often have a major role in these stories), is targeted by a murderer because of their friendship. Everything around these detectives that relates to organizations appears unreliable or dysfunctional. They drive cars that seem always on the point of breaking down. Wallander's office contains a rickety chair which is perpetually in danger of collapse, a chair that seems symbolic of both the organization in which he works and of Wallander himself. Rebus and D.I. Thorne loathe the buildings in which they work, and Thorne constantly hurts himself on the corner of his desk. All are worn down by their jobs and the organizations against which they struggle.

Not only do organizations feature prominently in the postmodern whodunit, but also their integrity is often challenged. Blomqvist is editor of a magazine that is put under severe threat, a scenario which instigates his exploration of another organization which perpetrates utterly vile acts. Harry Hole works with totally corrupt police officers; while Donna Leon's Venetian Commissario Brunetti is, unusually, happily married but oppressed by corrupt governmental and private organizations. Brunetti's private happiness contrasts with public despair: the crime is solved, but the criminal often goes unpunished because of influence from 'higher-ups'. Postmodern detectives have no respect for those more senior than they in the organizational hierarchy, and indeed it is almost a hallmark of these detectives that they despise their managers.

Where the brain of the classical detective solved crimes and brain combines with brawn in the hard-boiled detective novels, the postmodern detective relies on the stolid work of the team, on the brilliance and intuition of the bruised and battered detective and also on luck. These detectives are inescapably embroiled in organizations: those they work for (and rail against) and those they battle, pursue and attempt to bring to justice.

This history is important because detective fiction reflects dominant societal discourses in any epoch and *also explores the unsayable at any particular time* (Rzepka, 2005). The classic detective novel, written during the certainties of imperialism and the uncertainties of industrialisation, could articulate the fears of a collapse of social order and could promise its restoration. Readers of the hard-boiled detective story lived through two world wars and were threatened with nuclear armageddon: the hard-boiled detective signalled, through his isolation and his vulnerability, the loss of certainty and the fear that social order would always be tentative (Rzepka, 2005). The postmodern detective is a flawed, suffering and fallible human being who works for one organization while often battling the crimes committed by other organizations or criminal employees. What does this detective articulate about the current epoch that is otherwise unsayable?

I suggest that in an era when the self is a project to be worked on, an achievement that is always ongoing, always in process and offered to the self for its own consumption (Foucault, 1979; 1986; 1992), the whodunit articulates issues around the project of the self. Technologies of the self 'permit individuals to effect by their own means, or with the help of others, a certain number of operations on their own bodies and souls, thoughts, conduct, and way of being, so as to transform themselves' (Foucault, 1997b:225). The liberatory potential articulated here by Foucault is quashed by organizations: work, for many, remains a place where the self cannot be transformed. The body of literature on identity in MOS is too big to summarise here (see Alvesson, Ashcraft and Thomas, 2008, for a statement on the state of the field), but the detective story, given the size of the reading and viewing audience, must constitute one of the discourses or technologies of the self that makes available ways of being and identity within postmodern Western organizations. It articulates attitudes and feelings that have a performative potential, informing work on the self through the circulation of interpretations that are invested in the becoming of the self. I next explore how the taken-for-granted presence of organizations in today's detective stories alerts us to the unsayable that these stories articulate for us, albeit through a glass darkly, and which become part of the ongoing working self. The unspeakable secret is that organizations are imbricated with death.

IMMERSION WITHIN (POPULAR) CULTURES OF DEATH

The victim:

> *With a tremendous effort, he had managed to wrench his bound hands up to his mouth so he could gnaw on the rope. At first he ripped and tore at it like a beast of prey gorging on a kill. Almost at once he broke a tooth on the lower left side of his mouth. The pain was intense at first, but quickly subsided. When he began chewing on the rope again—he thought of himself as an animal in a trap who had to gnaw off its own leg to escape—he did it slowly. . . . Twice each day or night he was given water and food. Twice he was also dragged along the floor by his feet until he came to a hole in the floor. . . . [There was nothing except] a pair of hands with gloves on. Hands that dragged him to the hole in the floor. . . . The hands had no body no ears, no mouth. . . . He foresaw his own end. The only thing that kept him going was his chewing.* (Mankell, 2009:50–51)

I turn now to outlining how and why all this watching of fictional death, portrayals of something that is so awful it is supposedly sequestered, denied or repressed, is not a passive occupation but one in which the watcher/reader is actively engaged in *becoming* through this immersion in the whodunit. This attraction towards portrayals of death, notably portrayals that are imbricated within and through representations of organizations, does something far more than entertain us: it articulates a relationship between the self, death and organizations.

The thesis that fear of death is suppressed or repressed seems to me to ignore technological developments which, over the course of the second half of the 20th century, turned Western cultures into image-saturated cultures (Jameson, 1991), where the self is constituted through and within omnipresent visual images, both static and moving. In the arts, media and culture, 'high' and 'low', death is prodded at, poked, interrogated, analysed, pondered, laughed at, analysed and inserted into plot lines, newsreels, poetry, plays, films, novels, short stories, photographs, paintings and sculpture, so that images and representations of death, real or imaginary, are inserted willy-nilly into our lives whenever we turn on the television, read a newspaper or glance at a billboard. We are immersed in a mediatised and visualised culture that is saturated with images of death.

Literary and film theory shows that all this watching and reading is far from being passive and is, rather, performative of the self (Bal, 2000). In Western 'looking cultures' (Denzin, 1991), subjects possess a visual literacy which, Denzin argues, has displaced literacy based on orality and print. It is through looking that we construct our 'postmodern selves', which have become signs of themselves, where media representations and everyday life interact in 'a double dramaturgical reflection': our understanding of films and other visual images thus bleeds into our 'everyday lives'. Literary theory, brushing aside Denzin's observation regarding the displacement of the written text, explores how interactions between reader and text involve a reader who writes the text as she reads and how she too is 'written' through engagement with the story (Lodge, 2000; Iser, 2000). Denzin's thesis suggests that readers interpret written texts in a manner informed by their engagement with the visual media, and so readers and lookers constitute a sense of self through engagement with both types of texts. Similarly, Mieke Bal (2000) suggests that narrative modes which combine visual images with the thought processes of the viewer instigate a subjective recall of things suppressed and one's own life narrative, so that there is within 'the mind' no distinction between imagery and the spoken—they so intertwine and interweave that an appreciation of a work of art may be felt viscerally and articulated to the self-as-viewer through the media of both words and images.

Film theory draws from Lacan (1977) the perspective that we want the gaze of the text to see us so that we know of our own presence. Thus, the relationship with the text involves a two-way flow, and our subjectivity becomes 'a text for the text', where readers and texts are caught up in each other and where, through *suture*, readers enter into or project themselves into the text whilst simultaneously operating from the place of the gaze (Silverman, 1988; 1996).[4] It goes further: it examines how we do not sit passively in the cinema seat or on the living-room settee but project ourselves into the screen, locating ourselves on the camera's lens and entering ourselves into the characters portrayed on the screen. When we watch or read a whodunit, we can therefore *identify* with detective, murderer and corpse. Our engagement with film and novel is performative: through interaction with images and words, we construct a sense of self and learn how to be in the world (Doane, 1988).

Living in image-saturated cultures (Jameson, 1991) in which we actively invite dramatisations of mortality into our leisure hours, read avidly about them and view images that bring them to life, we are therefore ourselves produced as subjects who are cognisant of and interact with death. For example, in the opening shots of the filmed version of Mankell's *Faceless Killers*, we see two elderly people, husband and wife, eating their supper, laughing and talking. We firstly observe them through a window, from the vantage point of their murderers; the camera then locates our vision within the noose the murderer is carrying, and we see Mrs. Lovgren's terrified face as she sees the intruder. From our vantage point, we too are intruders. We know what is to happen, and our bodies react viscerally (Marks, 2000). The scene changes—we are taken into a restaurant where the detective, Wallander, is having dinner with his daughter, and we relax with him but struggle as he tries not to damage his family relationships. The next time we see Mrs. Lovgren is as she dies in Wallander's arms. We are both Wallander holding her and Mrs. Lovgren as she dies. We breathe a breath that mimics her last breath and feel the despair of the detective.

However, the deaths we consume while sitting on our settees or cinema seats or in bed before going to sleep are fictionalised deaths. In filmed versions of the novels, we see bodies lying on the floor, soon to be outlined in chalk marks by crime officers (we have become schooled in such police procedures), but these are the bodies, we know, of actors who picked themselves up, wiped off the fake blood and got on with the rest of their lives after the camera stopped rolling. They are people, just like us, doing a job of work. We can watch dramatisations of the murder of hundreds, if not thousands, of fictional people and know that each body we see laid out will get up and resume daily life. In reading the novels, we enter into the selves of the victims, but we turn the page and are resuscitated back to life after the imaginary death we have momentarily experienced. What the detective genre therefore does is educate us into an experience of death followed by life followed by death followed by life, over and over, until we finally stop reading or viewing.

So, in absorbing the stories of violent deaths, we *experience* being the victim, the murderer and the detective, and we experience being the observer—the eye of the camera observing everything except the vital clues that have been deliberately withheld from us. This experiencing is not intellectual but is comprehended and felt 'with our entire bodily being, informed by the full history and carnal knowledge of our acculturated sensorium' (Sobchack, 2004:63). We move among the positions of the terrified victim, the calculating murderer and the confused but ultimately successful, albeit damaged, detective. So, as viewer or reader of detective stories, we experience the possibility of our own deaths. The untimeliness of a violent death portrayed in detective stories, Sobchak (2004:240) writes, can thus be appreciated as potentially mine. But, in knowing that we have survived the murderer's attack—indeed, in knowing that the actor who played the victim got up, took off the 'blood' and had dinner—we know that death is put off until another day. Some of our understanding of death is therefore Lazarus-like: we can be killed and we can rise up again, immediately, to be killed again the next time we open the novel or turn on the television.

In such ways, through processes of projection and introjection of the stories in which we immerse ourselves, we experience death and put it behind us until, that is, the next programme or the next chapter of the novel. At the same time that we have experienced the situation of the corpse, we have projected ourselves into the position of the detective searching for the murderer and often, especially in novels, into the place (mind) of the murderer. In the quotation that opened this section, we find ourselves inside the terrified mind of someone who is about to be murdered, and in the quotation that follows below we are taken into the mind of the murderer. Very shortly after this account, Mankell takes us into the mind of the detective, and with that we are plummeted back into the world of organization and work. Through the power of the image or the written word, we imagine that we know something of what it is to take life and to be dead and the frustrations of the work that results from those twinned acts. Always, in the postmodern detective story, we are located within organizations—they are an omnipresent although hardly noticed aspect of the stories. Their taken-for-grantedness is perhaps what makes the import of the whodunit so powerful: the images work on our conscious minds while we remain hardly aware that they are doing so. When we watch the detective film or read the book, we are not escaping from the daily grind of the workplace but are taken back into it, albeit while hardly noticing because we are more concerned with whodunit. In that workplace, then, we experience our own murder, then rise back up from it, to experience it again. It is through culture and its articulation in the imagination that organization and death become imbricated. I turn now to film and literary theory to develop the thesis that this experience articulates that which is otherwise unspeakable: that organizations murder the me-who-might-have-been.

ANALYSING THE TEXT: THE DETECTIVE WALLANDER

The murderer:

> *In an hour her guests would arrive. Before then she would have to give the man in the oven his food. He had been there for five days. Soon he would be so weak that he wouldn't be able to put up any resistance. . . . She had not yet decided how she was going to kill him. There were several possibilities, but she still had plenty of time. She would think about what he had done and then resolve how he was supposed to die.* (Mankell, 2009:54–55)

Although the relevance of novels for understanding organizations has been demonstrated by Knights and Willmott (1999), there is perhaps more interest in films as a vehicle for interrogating organizations and working lives. Edited texts (Hassard and Holliday, 1998) and monographs (Bell, 2008; Rhodes, 2007), alongside special editions of journals (*Organization*, 2008, 15:4), suggest a potential for developing intellectually subtle theories that complement those found in the work of the better film theorists. Within management and organization studies, the stories contained in films, novels and television programmes have been analysed as historico-cultural texts that provide insights into organizations and working lives. For example, an analysis of *Star Trek* provides an account of the changing status of women in the late 20th century (Bowring, 2004), and one of *Priscilla, Queen of the Desert* (Brewis, Hampton and Linstead, 1997) facilitates an understanding of the fluidity of gender identity, while a close reading of the film *Jarhead* (Godfrey, Lilley and Brewis, 2012) allows analysis of the masculine military body. British television comedy series of the 1970s contain a cultural history of organizations that might otherwise be unavailable (Hancock, 2008).

A constructivist account of culture and organizations, meanwhile, explores how 'reel life' and 'real life' are closely connected (Parker, 2008); that is, the performative dialectic through which depictions of organizations on screen inform the 'reality' of organizations (leading to changes in the depictions of organizations on screen, and so on) is interrogated.

Film philosophy, however, encourages an analysis of the cultural text not only for an understanding of the ostensible subject matter of the text but also for an understanding of issues circulating within wider culture that, although remaining on the periphery of consciousness, gnaw away at viewers/readers (Conard, 2007; Wartenberg, 2007). In relation to organizations, for example, Parker (2009) has shown how representations of pirates allow dreams of utopias that contrast with 'our lives of constrained labour' and, furthermore, how they articulate the porosity of the boundary between 'legitimate' (dominating, constraining, rule-bound) and 'illegitimate' (anarchistic, carnivalesque, egalitarian) organizations. Parker (2008) has explored the lessons for organization theorists to be learned from representations of the Mafia in books, films and television series, especially depictions of eating that feature in all explorations of the Mafia. Here again, boundaries between domains become the focus of attention, but this time the lesson is the importance of maintaining boundaries, of not letting organizations confuse the firm with the family. The following analysis builds on the thesis of boundaries between domains: here the question becomes one of exploring what is and what is not regarded as a crime, which emerges from the chapter's thesis that death should not be limited, in our understanding, to biological death but should incorporate an understanding of what we could call the death of our dreams, that is, the death of the desired, imagined, anticipated selves that we could become.

Although the faces of people who have died in 'real life' are rarely shown in close-up in news programmes, those who have suffered a fictional death in the whodunit are pored over by the camera. We are invited to gaze on the twisted body at the place where the murderer left it and then as it lies on the pathologist's slab. Indeed, a stock scene in the detective story is that of the new recruit who vomits at the first sight of the body that is being cut open by the pathologist.

When we look at these dramatised images of fictional deaths, what do we see? In her magisterial, existential phenomenology of film-watching, Sobchack (2004) argues that death is signified by two states of bodies: the lived body and the corpse, 'a thing of flesh unintended, inanimate, static' (236). The corpse horrifies because it is an object denied subjectivity. It 'engages our sympathy as an indexical object existentially connected to a subject who was once an intentional and responsive "being", and it generates our horror as a symbolic object bereft of subjectivity and responsiveness that stands for a condition we cannot existentially know and yet to which we must succumb' (236). It is this distinction between subject and object that is relevant to the present discussion. If Sobchack is correct and corpses are able to occasion 'visual and metaphysical reflection on being and not-being' (237), on the difference between being a subject and an object, then the corpse will also allow reflection on subjectivity: what it means to be quick rather than dead. The horror of the zombie, of a fictional body that lives but has no subjectivity, suggests that it is not only death of the body that horrifies but death of whatever it is that animates and was animated by that body, what we may call 'the self' (Bollas, 1993; 1995). The corpse therefore symbolises the loss of all that would have been had the person continued living: of the me-who-might-have-been.

So, when we engage in the pornography of death that is detective fiction, when we look at the bodies laid out on the fictional pathologist's slab, we are plummeted unawares into a meditation on the me who animates and is animated by the body. We may be reminded of the horror of the eventual but inevitable mortification of our own flesh as we look at that of the fictional corpse, but the capacity of the subject for imagination and the ability to project one's self into the future involves knowledge not only of the flesh but of one's subjectivity. In other words, the possibility of no longer being a me appals us just as much as the possibility of becoming putrefying flesh. Film theory suggests that when we glance at the supposedly dead bodies in whodunits, we know what it is like to be a corpse, for the corpse has invited us to share its end. We thus know something of what it is like to cease being a being, all hopes, plans, adventures and joys ended. It is not just the future of the body that ceases but the future selves that could have animated that body if death had not been visited upon the self. In Mankell's *The Man Who Smiled*, for example, the murdered solicitor will never enjoy his retirement; the ex-policeman seeking to rejoin the police force will never again be a police officer; the aid worker blown up in an explosion will never become all those future selves she might have been. These victims are identified by their job titles and by the organizations they work for. In *The Man Who Smiled*, as in so many postmodern detective stories, organizations are implicated in all these murders. As we project ourselves into the corpses in this story and back out from those dread positions, our future selves are there in this ekstatic dance: the me's-who-might-have-been had they not been bludgeoned, strangled, or bombed by the organization. All that potential, all wiped out.

But where are the detectives when we need them? The detective is charged with finding the murderer before s/he can commit any further crimes but time and time again fails to do so before more people die terrifying deaths. In *The Man Who Smiled*, Wallander fails to save the lives of at least three people: we see graphically that it is the very organization which has charged the detective with this task that impedes him in his duties of saving them. In the BBC's filmed version, the organization does not want Wallander to return to work after his nervous breakdown, even though that breakdown has been caused by the organization's very desires for what that person must do. In the novel, colleagues welcome Wallander back warmly, and it is he himself who feels alienated, an outsider, a stranger who does not know his way around. He is in the organization but not, at this point, of the organization. His identity, that of police officer, is tentative, uncertain, capable of being changed in a moment from that of detective to that of ex-detective. It is the detective who should save me, the viewer, from the murders that may be visited upon me, but the detective is frail, vulnerable and in need of rescuing himself. It is the job and the organization that have ground him down. And thus it has ground me down.

I want to suggest next that it is the organization, through all this, which is the murderer. This is signalled in various ways: organizations employ today's detectives and demand that they commit acts and live lives that destroy them. Wallander, Hole, Stone and numerous others often contemplate leaving the police force but are trapped: they are unemployable elsewhere. There is no way out: their potential to be something else has been slain. Indeed, the BBC dramas *Life on Mars* and *Ashes to Ashes* are set in a limbo world where police officers, on the point of death, refuse to die but battle on perpetually against organization and criminals: for them, there is no way out whatsoever; their choice is either the organization or the grave. Even though we may not know the denouements of these series, they articulate for us at some level the despair occasioned by working lives that allow no exit and impose major impediments to joy, pleasure and work on the self.

The detective speaks for us about being in an organization and trapped by that organization. Murderers work for organizations that have charged them with the task of murder. In our reading/viewing, organization and criminal merge, each inseparable in its identity from the other. The organization with which we are presented as we turn the pages of the book or watch the television is therefore one that both imprisons and murders. We are trapped within that organization, which symbolises for us the company for which we work.

This, then, is my argument. I live in an epoch and a culture when, in order to be a me, I must work on the self as if it were a work of art. Working on the self as a work of art requires work that is congenial to the identity I would be, but the organization limits what I am allowed to be. It compresses me within narrow boundaries, labouring at tasks that prevent me from working on the other possible selves I would be if only there were the opportunities. I go home at night, tired and disenchanted, and turn on the television or sit reading a novel. If I have chosen a whodunit, as many people will have done, then I enter into a scene where I experience being a murderer, a victim and a detective charged with finding the murderer. Again, I plummet into an organizational world—there is no escape. As I engage with the text and experience these imaginary subject positions, I know the despair of having no future (the corpse), with all the me's-that-I-might-have-been having been murdered. I also experience the position of the murderer and so feel culpable. I am the person who has murdered all the me's-that-I-might-have-been. But the detective saves me from that knowledge, because, as I experience the mind of the detective, I am told, over and over, that it is the organization that hired the killer and wished the victim dead. I, like many others, may feel frustrated and dissatisfied by my work but can articulate those feelings only in terms of things that may appear relatively trivial. But there is a deeper sense of frustration, one that is there at the edge of my consciousness and for which I have no language. I am thus drawn irresistibly to cultural artefacts that articulate it for me. Through watching the detective I am reaching towards an understanding: it is not so much that my work is tedious, boring, controlling, frustrating, albeit shot through with moments of pleasure or achievement; my work may indeed be all those things. More fundamentally, the current organization of work, in hierarchical organizations that try to control my movements, thoughts and feelings, murders the me-I-might-have-been, all those dreamed of, aspired to 'I's' that could have existed were work organized differently.

CONCLUSION: TOWARDS A THEORY AND ETHICS OF ORGANIZATIONAL DEATH

This chapter has used the whodunit to explore our fascination with fictional portrayals of death. I have argued that the location in organizations of the postmodern detective illuminates the whodunit's articulation of thoughts and ideas that can be expressed only tangentially, through artefacts or products that symbolise what it is we cannot put into words. The thesis of this chapter has been that the organization in demanding that we labour as zombie-machines so limits opportunities for working on the project of the self that it murders the selves who might have been. A regretful looking back at one's teens, with all their promises, hopes, aspirations and dreams, perhaps comes closest to saying this unsayable thing, because we speak about death only in terms of the biological ending of the body. However, there is so much individuals could do, so many people they could be, if they were not required, every working day, to constrain themselves within the straitjacket of the particular function, task or identity required by the organization, so there must be another form of death, one which is not biological but is *organizational*. Organizational death is that murdering of the me's-who-might-have-been, selves perhaps with greater capacity for joy, wonder and achievement, and of the production of things of beauty and of the maintenance of family and community than can be expressed in bureaucratised, clock-watching, rule-bound, profit-oriented production processes.

Now it might be objected that the form of the self I am outlining here limits the possibilities of the self to those available within post- or late modern capitalism. Work on the self is therefore limited to that which fulfils capitalism's needs (Bauman, 2007). There is that possibility, of course, although Foucault's perspective is very different. He advocates a politics of pleasure, one in which work on the self (as a work of art) is an end in itself. I will return to his arguments, along with Butler's more recent theorising about recognition, in the concluding chapter. For now, I will preface that discussion by returning to Dollimore's (2001) analysis of how death and desire have been interwoven into the Western European psyche and to his arguments concerning the disessentializing of the self as the only means by which the dread fear of death can be put aside, if only for a short while. I will suggest here that his advocacy of means of dissolving the ego can illuminate further the distinction between zombie-machine and human.

DISESSENTIALIZING THE WORKING SELF

There is in Dollimore's thesis a moral imperative towards finding ways of experiencing freedom from individuation and thus its spectral DNA, the dread anxiety of death. This goes beyond the possibility of the fantasised I who I would be if work facilitated the constitution of such an I. This is an I that we can grasp only with difficulty, because it is an I that ceases to be an I, that lets go of its ego and becomes disessentialized, to use Dollimore's term. I am now going to use this possibility as a thought experiment, so to speak, to explore its potential for a new politics of organization studies, one that fights on behalf of the me's-I-might-become. Barthes has suggested that disessentializing occurs when one is immersed in literature. I suggest the contrary: the self does not disappear while we read a novel or a film; we might be taken outside ourselves, but we become another I, another ego, and that is not what disessentializing means. I will start this discussion on disessentializing with a short vignette from my own experience, in which the ego dissolved while the body was immersed in its work. I will relate that to Marx's theory of alienation and then turn Marx's theory on its head to suggest ways in which disessentializing of the self would be an aspect of work as it should be experienced. In this regard, work (not labour) concerns not only working on the identity of the self but also constituting selves that are (fleetingly, temporarily) freed from the traumatic knowledge of our own mortality.

A Vignette: An Oppressive Disessentializing of the Working Self

Many years ago, in what now seems like another life, I was trying to find a job in the Welsh Valleys during one of the regular depressions of the 20th century's economic cycles. There was little employment available for a 17-year-old with a handful of 'O' levels save for work on the production lines in a factory that made components for electrical products. I worked on a machine making capacitors that became parts of transistor radios (which shows how long ago this was). The work was piecework; that is, we were paid only for the number of pieces we made each week. We started at 8 a.m., finished at 5 p.m., had two 15-minute tea breaks and a 30-minute dinner break. The high windows of the capacitor room were covered in newspaper to keep out the sunlight, on the odd days that the sun shone, making unbearably hot the huge, high-ceilinged space. Music blared from a record player, and later Radio One's pop music station, as a way of keeping the boredom of the work at bay. Each of the women and girls working in this section of the factory sat at a machine that had a footboard; rollers on which two large skeins of ribbon, one metal and one plastic, were located; two cups, one to left and one to right, that held strips of wire; and a peg across which stretched a short strip of metal that glowed red-hot and was used for sealing the components. The process, so far as I can remember it, was as follows:

- With the left hand, place the ends of the plastic and metal ribbons around the end of a spinner, and then press a button on the footboard with the left foot to spin the ribbons around the spinner until they catch;
- With the right hand, lift a piece of wire, place it on the metal ribbon (which is much narrower than the plastic ribbon which will eventually encase it), lower an arm of the machine, and double-click with right foot so that an electrical current seals the wire to the plastic ribbon;
- Repeat with a piece of wire to the left;
- Click left-foot button to roll further ribbon around the spool, holding it with the left hand to ensure that it takes shape properly;
- Almost immediately, lift the red-hot sealer with the right hand, taking care to move the left hand just in time to avoid burning your thumb instead of sealing the wires;
- With the right arm, move another arm of the machine across to free the new capacitor so that it slides down into an awaiting tray, and at the same time click a counter with the left hand;
- Repeat 2,400 times a day for five days so as to earn £12 for the week's wages.

With practice, you could establish a rhythm: move right arm, move right foot, move left arm, move right foot, and so on and so on. One of the fascinating things was that, despite the noise and the always-present danger of burning one's thumb (the smell was very similar to roasting pork), we could somehow, sometimes become absent from our bodies, and time would pass without our having any awareness of it. The evidence for this was the counter: we watched them anxiously to check we were keeping up sufficient speed to earn a living wage, and sometimes a few hundred suddenly seemed to have been added to the count. The clock would show that 20, 30 or more minutes had passed without our having any conscious awareness of having been there, as an embodied person making those components.

This is one aspect of what I think Dollimore is referring to when he uses the term 'disessentializing'. One is alive but is absent to one's self; the ego disappears, and in its place there is the calm of the grave, all fear of death forgotten because the ego that experienced that fear has ceased, for a short time, to exist. However, that this absence from the self was instigated through becoming the ultimate zombie-machine, where the dexterity of the human animal melded with the machine so that maximum efficiency was obtained, suggests that Dollimore's thesis will help flesh out the distinction between zombie-machine and human. Marx's thesis on alienation, read through the lens Dollimore offers, will assist in this exploration.

I was introduced to Marx's theory of alienation as an undergraduate a few years after working in this factory, and it seemed to me to capture that experience of making capacitors, where forgetting the self for a short while was a bonus because it meant not having been consciously aware of the passing of the 20, 30 or 40 minutes of tedium in the noise and dirt of the factory. This is a thesis outlined by the young Karl Marx (1988) who, in his 26th year, wrote the scraps that remain of the *1844 Manuscripts*. He outlined a theory of a subject alienated by, from and within work, one whose mirror image is the self that could and should emerge through work. Work should be productive of a radiant self constituted through crafting of objects within an aesthetically pleasing physical location and a strong social network. In 1911 the then-55-year-old Frederic Winslow Taylor published *The Principles of Scientific Management*, which put what seems to have been the final nail in the coffin of the implicit dream in the *1844 Manuscripts*. Marx's thesis on alienation haunts the text you are reading now. It is time to acknowledge it openly.

Marx wrote that the human is alienated from the product s/he makes, from him/herself, from his/her 'species being' and from his/her fellow (wo)men.

I will start with Marx's exploration of alienation from 'species being', which is in many ways the most difficult part of his discussion but which is easier to understand if one thinks of a cow chewing the cud or grazing in the field all day. The cow exists only to exist; it labours only to continue being alive. It has no consciousness (so far as we are aware) over and above the need to continue chewing and grazing. It has no 'conscious life-activity' (Marx, 1988:76). The human, in contrast, is a species being that is conscious of its own existence: a human can ponder itself as if it were an object and so is a 'Conscious Being' (76). (Wo)Man does not exist in isolation from other people but is an active participant in the species that is the human animal (77) and so contributes to the sustenance of humankind as a whole (77). S/he goes beyond his/her own immediate physical needs so as to contribute to the greater good, producing 'the whole of nature' (77). S/he 'forms things in accordance with the laws of beauty' (77). However, under capitalism, (wo)man's life activity is reduced to a means to staying alive and no more—s/he becomes like the cow, working only to sustain physical existence. S/he moves but does not think or create. S/he exists only to exist and so, rather than contributing to mankind or community, focuses only on the means for his/her own immediate sustenance. S/he is thus estranged from his/her species being.

Further, under capitalist conditions, workers are alienated both from the products they produce and from themselves as producers of that product. The products they make are whipped away from them to be sold elsewhere. The worker also 'must sell himself and his human identity' (1988:25) in order to survive. Workers thus 'sink . . . to the level of a commodity' (69), a commodity that they themselves produce through their labour and which is itself sold. This commoditised self, like any other commodity produced through labour, is 'the objectification of labor' (71); that is, the object in which work is 'congealed' or in which immaterial practices become material—real, physical objects. In the factory, blindly producing capacitors, we were not allowed to talk to each other and had to have permission to go to the toilet. We were thus infantilised but, more than this as Marx explains, we existed only as extensions of machines that made meaningless products. We moved our hands, arms and feet, but our minds were disengaged, and the capacitors that rolled down into the collecting trays were taken away—alien objects that belonged to the employer. Our 'inner worlds' were impoverished, as the work required no thought, skill or imagination, and yet we were so busily occupied in such very mundane activity that we could not produce anything that seemed meaningful or that would contribute to the good of the community. Yet we could not stop producing the capacitors, one after the other, 2,400 each day, 12,000 each week. The machine governed all our movements, with those damned capacitors dictating how we sat, thought and behaved. They 'exist[ed] *outside [me]*, independently, as something alien to [me]' and became 'a power on its own confronting [me]' (72). Each of us had 'become . . . a slave of his object' (72). This could occur because the only means of earning a living, of maintaining ourselves as physical subjects, was through paid employment of this kind, but it was only through being physical subjects that we could be workers: to be a subject, I must labour; to be a labourer I must be a subject who can labour (73).

Further, in the act of doing the work itself, workers estrange themselves from themselves. First, because the worker is him/herself one of the products that s/he makes and all products s/he makes are owned by someone else, s/he is estranged from herself. Second, because labour is *external* to the worker, a form of activity that is imposed upon him/her and which makes him/her feel 'outside himself', the I becomes an object just doing the mundane activities it has been told to do. 'The worker therefore only feels himself outside his work, and in his work feels outside himself' (74). The body sitting at the machine making capacitors had no separate existence from the machine: it was a labouring body sans mind, sans motivation, sans a sense of being human. There was no me but a body to which I 'returned' at the end of the day. However, what or who was this me to which I returned? In Marx's words (1988:74), 'man (the worker) no longer feels himself to be freely active in any but his animal functions—eating, drinking, procreating, or at most in his dwelling and in dressing-up, etc; and in his human functions he no longer feels himself to be anything but an animal. What is animal becomes human and what is human becomes animal' (74). That is, eating, drinking and procreating become the acts of animals because they are undertaken only to sustain the self as a labourer. This is self-estrangement, because capitalism takes over the life-world of the worker.

Finally, it follows that (wo)man is estranged from (wo)man. The people with whom one works become no more than fellow cogs in the machine.

As people are reduced to working only so as to sustain the physical body, Marx argued that work becomes something to be shunned 'like the plague' (74) when we do not have to do it. Sitting at the machine, churning out capacitors, we counted out the hours and minutes before we were free to leave for the day. Those odd moments when we were absent to ourselves, when ego had ceased to exist and the body performed the required duties as an extension of the machine, were times of blessed relief. In the terms of the arguments in this book, we were pure zombie-machines, with no investment in the products we were making, no opportunity to work on the self as anything other than an extension of the machine; no interaction with others save for supervisors who treated us like schoolchildren; and no sense of making a contribution to the good of humankind. We worked solely to earn money to pay the rent, buy food and clothing, pay for heating, raise our children and, if there was anything left over, go out one or two evenings a week in search of entertainment. There were no dreams of the me's we might become: the future stretched out in front of us, as attachments to machines who laboured to contribute to the household budget.

However, the zombie-machine is not disessentialized, in Dollimore's terms, because, although it escapes temporarily from its mundane existence as it forgets its own existence, it is a self whose humanity has been stripped away.

There is an alternative possibility for disessentializing the self through one's work, but this requires that work be undertaken differently (that is, as work rather than labour). Marx regarded work as 'satisfaction of a need' (74), a need which goes far beyond the mere sustenance of the physical body. This need is that of expressing one's self through one's work, of contributing to the community and living as a social being. This is alienated work turned on its head; it is a model of what our jobs *should* be like. It involves work in which we can invest ourselves with pride: the objects that we make attest to who we are, and we invest ourselves in them. When I look at this book, for example, whatever others may say about it, I will be proud to have written a book—I will have invested myself in it, and I am happy to see that self looking back at me. We therefore can constitute ourselves as human in the making of products and services that allow us to use our talents and skills in the best possible way, in a social environment in which the human can flourish. Engagement with our colleagues, friends, customers, clients and managers, recognition from them of our skills in making bread, growing crops, devising art works, caring for children, cleaning toilets, not under the watchful eye of managers but in a shared endeavour in which each gives what s/he can—that is the sort of utopian work space Marx seemed to envisage. Through such labour, we would contribute to culture, society and the welfare of all. Conscious of ourselves as humans, we would also be aware of and recognize all the frailties that accompany membership in such a species.

Another form of disessentializing of the self would be possible here. It is one that people sometimes talk of when they discuss their hobbies or leisure pursuits, that is, the things they want to do and in which they develop skills different from those they must use in their paid jobs. They talk of, say, painting and 'not noticing the time go by' or 'forgetting about everything because I got so absorbed'. This form of forgetting is another way in which one becomes disessentialized, if only for a fleeting time. If it were to occur in the (utopian) workplace because of the pleasure in making the object or delivering the service, then the disappearance of the ego would not be of the sort that reduces one to a zombie-machine, allowing one to forget not only the immanence of one's mortality but also the dire circumstances of life itself. It would be one in which the dread knowledge of one's own mortality ceased for a while as the ego dissolved, and the product or service in which one was absorbed could be all the better for that forgetting, because one's talents would be set free. As Pirsig argued, in *Zen and the Art of Motorcycle Maintenance* (1999), rather than a rider driving a motor bike on which he had painstakingly worked, rider and machine become one—motor bike in motion.

It does not seem likely that many people would say that they dream of jobs in which they become so absorbed in their work that they forget themselves; we articulate our desires in other ways, perhaps because this sort of language is not easily available to us. So, we can say that we dream of being an astronaut or a chef or a cake baker, and with those aspirations we dream of the people we would be while working in those jobs. We cannot say, 'I want a job where I can forget myself for hours at a time'. However, I suggest that this form of forgetting the self is an aspect of being human, of being freed to work on the self through a job that allows one's expression of one's skills and talents. When the zombie-machine forgets itself while, say, making capacitors, it escapes not only from the awful knowledge of its own inevitable demise but also from a working life that presses down on the self. On the other hand, when the human forgets itself through its work, it escapes only from the awfulness of the ego; its return to its 'self', to being essentialized, is to a place where pleasure accompanies the self who works.

To conclude: this chapter has focused on death and has used the whodunit to argue that our fascination with death articulates a knowledge that we cannot otherwise put into words: that organizations murder our dreams, all the me's-I-might-have-been. Jonathon Dollimore's thesis on death allowed me to bring in the young Marx's theory of alienation, which haunts this book. I have argued that the zombie-machine can sometimes become disessentialized and escape from the terrible knowledge of its own mortality but that dissolution of the ego reduces it to a machine that must return to a consciousness of itself as a zombie-machine. The human, however, would be working in a job that not only allowed work on the self, on the constitution of a desired identity, but also would allow the self to become unaware of itself and so forget its inevitable demise because of the sheer pleasure taken in its tasks. That is, work should be enjoyable and should give a sense of achievement. The 'work of art' that Foucault spoke of, that which we are ideally forever constituting, could thus be one that is achieved through one's work.

There are some (to my mind) crass arguments in contemporary leadership studies which recommend that leaders become 'servant leaders', devoted to ensuring that staff can contribute their best efforts to the organization. There are perhaps elements of what I am arguing for in this chapter in that body of work. However, the difference is the context. Servant leaders work in organizations whose aims are those of maximising return for shareholders or, in public-sector organizations, the government or community. Servant leadership, in such a context, remains exploitative, another attempt at securing more wholehearted commitment (and thus hard work) from staff. What I am imagining is a very different organizational context, in which other objectives are subordinate to the major priority of the flourishing of staff.

POSTSCRIPT: HYPERBOLIC THEORY IN DRAG

Can death be used as a metaphor for what is not biological death? Patrick Reedy and Mark Learmonth's (2011) Heideggerian reading of death and organizations suggest it should not be: I may take away its full horror and let organizations off the hook of their ethical responsibilities, while at the same time so exaggerating my arguments that they lose their force. To answer this question, I return to Butler's (1997) reference to the need sometimes for 'hyperbolic theory', one that overstates its case for a reason. Organizations have certainly been complicit in atrocities which caused death and suffering for millions of human beings (Bauman, 1989), and the sort of suffering I am exploring in this book is nowhere akin to the depths of barbarity of which organizations are capable. However, the identity politics of the past 40 years has shown that forms of suffering exist that were not recognised until a language emerged that allowed labels to be put to them and thus an activist politics to develop. I am attempting in this book to identify another form of suffering for which we currently lack labels. Feminism, queer theory, postcolonial and crip theories are all testament to the power of language to inform politics, change the symbolic order and thus have real, positive impacts on people's lives. An earlier politics based on class and grounded in Marxist theory focused on working lives but eventually came to little in the West, perhaps because, as Lacan (2007) observed, it would have done no more than replace one master with another. Feminism challenged *patriarchy*, queer theory *heteronormativity*, and postcolonial theory *empire*, and it seems to me that we need a new language, beyond that of control and resistance, that allows us to challenge what organizations do to the people who work in/for them, including those of the relatively privileged people of 'the West'. I have used the terms 'murder' and 'death' because of their power to arrest attention. I have used the detective because s/he combines in the same symbol both organization (the employer) and death (detectives' job is to deal with death and find murderers), and so the whodunit provides a bridge that links death and organizations. Furthermore, this bridge is a person who is ground down by *unnecessary* organizational limitations that add to the burdens of the messiness of everyday life. I am not arguing for the possibilities of a Utopia where all suffering disappears, only for a means of reducing the strains upon lives that will always be in many ways less than perfect.

Conclusion: From Poverty of Aspiration to a Politicised, Ethical Me-I-Might-Become?

The thesis of this book is that in late capitalist or postmodern cultures where the self has become a project to be worked on, we look to our jobs as a means of constituting the selves we aspire to be. Organizations, however, so limit the possibilities for being that the most many of us can achieve is a shade of the selves that might have been, a ghost of a life that has never been lived. Organizations therefore murder the selves that might have been. This is a hyperbolic theory, a thesis in drag, as Butler would have it, which uses the language of violent death as a political manoeuvre.

I have used a sociocultural philosophical approach that analyses the working-life stories of individuals through the lens of Judith Butler's theoretical perspective, treating the life stories as if they were lay philosophies of work (Introduction). The argument can be summarised as follows. Organizations desire staff who are zombie-machines, that is, intelligent machines totally focused on achieving organizational aims and objectives and thus lacking any agency beyond that required in contributing to organizational goals (Introduction). Such staff would be somewhat less than human and, it follows, would be and are devoid of certain rights that attach to being human. Julie showed us in Chapter One that individuals, unsurprisingly, approach work with aims and desires different from those of their employers. Among the outcomes we desire from our work is the constitution of a desired self or selves, selves we could become through our jobs. Inherent in aspirations for opportunities to work on the self is a theory of the self as human. Julie's ideas, illustrated further by Alex's working life story (Chapter Four), suggest that labour and work should be distinguished from each other. Labour involves doing the tasks required by management but, as it excludes anything that serves in the constitution of the self, labour is what is undertaken by zombie-machines. Work involves those activities, often over and above the tasks required of the zombie-machine, that facilitate constitution of selves that are fully human. Alex illuminated how the friends and colleagues with whom we work, rather than management or the organization, contribute that recognition which is vital in the constitution of selves.

Frank, the boss, demonstrated (in Chapter Two) the difficulty for managers of granting recognition to employees as anything other than zombie-machines, because his thesis is of a selfhood that is so intertwined with the organization that the self is no more than a constantly labouring, managerial zombie-machine. Just as the lord, in Hegel's dialectic, does not seek recognition from the bondsman, so Frank does not look to staff for recognition, although he requires that staff labour as zombie-machines in order that he can demonstrate to himself and others that he is a manager. At the same time, if his staff are perfect zombie-machines then Frank's psyche is challenged. The manager is on the horns of an impossible psychic dilemma. Shakeel (Chapter Three) blurs the boundary between managers and staff, because he shows how staff speak in the idiom of management, have firm ideas of how work should be carried out and are frustrated by managers who are seen as inefficient intruders into working space. Staff therefore cannot grant recognition to managers because they do not recognise managers as anything but imposters who disrupt the efficient flow of work. Although staff of necessity give the impression that they are working like zombie-machines (and thus, in their own perception, inefficiently), the impression is superficial, unstable and abandoned whenever possible. Managerial and staff 'realities' are so different that they cannot be said to occupy the same space. An implication of Shakeel's account is that he, like Alex, turns to colleagues and friends for recognition of the self as human. Such a recognition is impossible outside the terms of gender; gender is compulsory but also debilitating. Kara and Saul (Chapter Five) showed how fluid are gendered identities and how the self that is lost in the doing of its work escapes from the prisonhouse of gendered identity. Reparative organizational work is then undertaken, in this case not by management but by students ('customers'), to line up gendered subjects with biological bodies. This causes shock and trauma to organizational subjects freed, for a time, from the constraints of gender, but time and again they are surprised back into them. I suggested that the labouring zombie-machine has to conform to traditional gender categories, whereas work on the self incorporates opportunities for freedom from the trauma of gender. These explorations of the limitations imposed on constituting aspired-to working selves were brought together in Chapter Six, where theories of death, the detective novel, and Marx's theory of alienation were used to argue that organizations murder the me's-that-might-have-been.

In summary, in late or postmodern capitalism, we look to our work for a means of constituting an ideal(ised), aspired-to self, but organizations negate that aspiration. Staff find ways of escaping from organizations' most dire demand that they be reduced to less than human zombie-machines and thus discover ways of constituting a sense of a workplace self that is human, albeit one whose potential for being is so constrained that it is only a shadow of the dreamed-of, aspired-to self. Organizations therefore murder the me's-that-might-have-been.

What I have not yet explored is who that desired, dreamed-of self might be. Julie (Chapter One) suggested that her aspiration is to be freed through work: work would give her a face to show to the world, and she would then be able to go out and explore that world. Frank waits for a retirement from work that will give him the time to do those things he has put aside so as to devote himself totally to his managerial labours. Shakeel has aspirations to be a writer and become politically active, but labour gobbles up so much of his time that those aspirations are left to wither on the vine of his dreams. Alex comes closest to constituting the desired self of the glamorous, exciting professional archaeologist, but the conditions of employment (short-term, temporary assignments without many employment rights) means she has to live much of her life exasperated by administrative jobs that she loathes. As to Kara and Saul, as academics they work in a profession whose members love their work but are constantly frustrated by creeping managerialism, increasing administration and the impossibility of working on the aspired-to academic self (Harding, Ford and Gough, 2010; Clarke, Knights and Jarvis, 2012).

But there is something narcissistic in our dreamed-of selves, and indeed late or postmodern culture would appear to provide the terms in which our dreams are focused on the 'me'. Bauman (2007), as we saw in the Preface, is perturbed that work on the self is devoted to constituting nothing but a commodity to be sold to the highest bidder (see also Sennett, 2006). The self that is constituted is also a product for one's own consumption (in front of the mirror, I ask myself do I look gorgeous/good enough?) and that of others (have I constituted a self that my peers will value and which they can use in positioning themselves—am I academic enough for students, managerial enough for workers?) (Falk, 1994). This commodity that is the self is a work-in-progress which staves off death—if I work hard enough to make my body immune to illness and dying, I may live for a thousand years (Shilling, 1993). Although self-absorbed, this is a self that is positioned within normative requirements of how one should be, and so failure to constitute a desired self can reduce one to a position of abjection. There is little of that ecstatic, ek-static self that Marx dreamed of, whose self is caught up in giving to its society and taking from it only what it needs.

This is perhaps therefore another form of the murder-of-the-me's that might have been: that is, in late or postmodern capitalism, we have impoverished, deracinated aspirations of who we can be or what we might become.

Can we aspire to be something more? Foucault's late work and Butler's recent work points to alternative possible selves.

WHAT IS THE WORKPLACE 'ME' I COULD BECOME?

Can we constitute workplace selves that are ethically alive and alert to a politics of microrevolutionary change that, while it would not challenge capitalism per se, could change the norms that govern workplace identities and thus contribute to the flourishing of working selves? Marx (1988) hinted at this self, as discussed in Chapter Six. For Marx, the communist workplace should be a welcoming place that would facilitate workers' contribution to the greater good while they made aesthetically pleasing products. Those objects would reflect an investment of a self that flourished through its labours. Foucault's question concerning why we should not turn ourselves into works of art is redolent in some ways of Marx's conception of a non-alienated worker, although it is a question framed for the conditions of late or postmodern capitalism rather than of Marx's industrial capitalism. Both theorists help us understand that one of the objects produced through work is the self.

Where Marx conceived of persons with what we would now define as homogeneous identities, Foucault distinguished between the subject and the self, observing different forms of the subject emerging in different places: 'The subject is not a substance but a form', one that is

> not primarily or always identical to itself. You do not have the same type of relationship to yourself when you constitute yourself as a political subject who goes to vote or speaks at a meeting and when you are seeking to fulfil your desires in a sexual relationship. . . . In each case one plays, one establishes a different type of relationship to oneself. And it is precisely the historical constitution of these various forms of the subject in relation to the games of truth which interests me. (Foucault, 1997a:290–291)

Marx could not conceive of a self that was not, within capitalism, itself a commodity, but we have seen in this book how workplace subjects can have a number of different relationships to themselves, in Foucault's terms, in that they can be at one time a less-than-human zombie-machine and at another time lay claim to their humanity. Workplace selves (with the exception, it would seem, of the manager) can thus move between (more or less) alienated and (more or less) non-alienated subject positions, or what I have called the zombie-machine and the human. The question thus becomes one of exploring how to expand the space of the latter. There has been limited but promising work in management and organization studies drawing on Foucault's later work on aesthetics of existence, which offers 'a movement of hope, giving fresh meaning to political ideals that occupy a vital position in contemporary political discourse and a way out from the confinements of the new knowledge based enterprise' (Barratt, 2008:525). Butler's recent work on ethics adds insights to Foucault's thesis on constituting one's self as an ethical subject. Both thinkers work within the constraints of a capitalism that is unlikely to be overturned by direct, revolutionary challenges. Their work on ethics, when combined, can suggest how each one of us could become a microrevolutionary (Gibson-Graham, 1996), doing what we can within the conditions of possibility of capitalist workplaces to change those conditions of possibility.

FOUCAULT AND AN AESTHETICS OF THE SELF

Foucault (1997a:262), informed by intense studies of the Greco-Roman world, arrived at 'the idea that the self is not given to us, [and so] I think that there is only one practical consequence: we have to create ourselves as a work of art'. This involves far more than working on one's appearance: beauty and virtue are conflated; the person who works on the self so that it becomes a virtuous self is thence a thing of beauty (O'Leary, 2002). The practice incorporates a politics and an ethics arising from the ascetic practice of 'an exercise of the self on the self by which one attempts to develop and transform oneself, and to attain to a certain mode of being' (Foucault, 1994:282). There are four major aspects of the relation to one-self (Foucault, 1997b:238) (i) the aspect of myself or my behaviour which is concerned with moral conduct; (ii) the mode of subjection, or the way in which people are invited or incited to recognise their moral obligations; (iii) the means by which we change ourselves to become ethical subjects; (iv) the kind of being to which we aspire when we behave in a moral way. These are all aspects of the relationship to oneself, and the distinction be-tween morals and ethics is important because moral codes are no more than rules or precepts, whereas ethics is the relation of the self to the self. What Foucault is articulating here is a need to identify how discourses of morality, although performative of the subject, prevent one from act-ing ethically. We could say that Frank, in striving to maintain a profitable business, is acting morally (he keeps staff employed, provides a service val-ued by customers, and contributes to returns to shareholders). This book's thesis suggests that he is, however, acting unethically in that he operates within managerialist discourses within and through which he requires that staff become zombie-machines. For Foucault, through working on one's relationship with oneself, one can reach out to others more ethically and develop new relationships with them: the ethical act does not precede the ethical actor.

What is sought is a practice of freedom, where 'Freedom is the onto-logical condition of ethics. But ethics is the considered form that freedom takes when it is informed by reflection' (Foucault, 1997a:284). The free-dom that is sought is freedom from a disciplinary practice that 'categorizes the individual, marks him by his own individuality, attaches him to his own identity, imposes a law of truth on him which he must recognize and which others have to recognise in him. It is a form of power which makes individuals subjects' (Foucault, 1982:212). There is evil at play here, but evil is to be understood not as the law-breaking actions of immoral agents but 'as arbitrary cruelty installed in regular institutional arrangements taken to embody the Law, the Good or the Normal' whereby 'systemic cruelty flows regularly from the thoughtlessness of aggressive convention-ality, the transcendentalization of contingent identities, and the treatment of good/evil as a duality wired into the intrinsic order of things' (Connolly

1998:109). In this light, the suffering produced by organizations in requiring that staff become zombie-machines should be understood as an evil. One's duty becomes development of a form of subjectivity that could be the source of effective resistance to such organizational power (Bernauer and Mahon, 1994:147). This 'remove[s] ethics from the quest for universal standards of behaviour that legislate conformity and normalization' (ibid.); it encourages escape from 'those prisons of thought and action that shape our politics, our ethics, our relations to ourselves' (ibid:152) and thus facilitates engagement in a struggle for freedom within the confines of one's historical situation, against forces that work to subordinate human existence.

The work on the self advocated by Foucault, in this reading, becomes a micropolitics of localised struggles in which each individual works on its self to produce an aesthetic self that reaches out ethically to others. The point of this, as summarized by Connolly (1998:115), is 'to ward off the violence of transcendental narcissism: to modify sensibilities of the self through delicate techniques. . . . The goal is to modify an already contingent self—working within the narrow terms of craftsmanship available to an adult—so that you are better able to ward off the demand to confirm transcendentally what you are contingently', that is, to resist the discourses that position one as zombie-machine or anything less than human and within which one positions others similarly.

That is, one must struggle to identify the discourses that position one as a subject and then work to free oneself from those discourses, questioning all the time how they position one in response to others. How can we do this? There are few guidelines in Foucault's work, and indeed there cannot be because it must be left to the individual to find his/her own way to constituting the self as a work of art. However, in the Preface to Deleuze and Guattari's *Anti-Oedipus*, Foucault called for the need to struggle against 'the fascism in us all, in our heads and our everyday behaviour, the fascism that causes us to love power, to desire the very thing that dominates and exploits us' (Bernauer and Mahon, 1994:154–155). This emphasises that we should start to observe how we conform within norms that are injurious to others and how the discourses that speak through us are harmful to those others. It would seem that one must own up to and change one's racism, homophobia and tendency to judge others by arbitrary rules of beauty; we must give up our wish to dominate, our habits of being judgemental about others' behaviour and so forth. One must, in short, continually question the taken-for-granted modes of being of/within 21st-century organizations.

Butler's recent development of a left-wing politics in *Frames of War* (2009), which I examined in some depth in Chapter One, helps expand upon this. Foucault and Butler alike unsettle us in that they urge us to recognise our 'dark side'; for Foucault, it is our affinity with fascism, and for Butler it is our urge to destroy the other.

BUTLER, ETHICS AND POLITICS

To reiterate, in *Frames of War*, Butler critiques the violence perpetrated by the US and its allies in retribution for the 9/11 attack on US territory and its citizens. She asks why the loss of American lives is something to be grieved and avenged, while those anonymous people killed in the subsequent wars in Iran and Afghanistan are not subjects of Western mourning. She argues that *framing*, that is, how dominant interpretations organize our thinking, comes to position us so that we regard some people as human and worthy of grief and others as less than human. My arguments in this book have explored how a form of violence very different from that analysed by Butler is perpetrated every day in the organizations in which we work. This is a violence that is in no way akin to the sheer dreadfulness of war, but to be required to become a zombie-machine and to have one's possibilities for selfhood greatly impoverished should not be regarded as normal, even normative, but *should be framed as a form of violence*. Butler works with photographs of prisoners at Guantanamo Bay and Abu Ghraib to develop her arguments. She writes (2009:64):

> Whether and how we respond to the suffering of others, how we formulate moral criticisms, how we articulate political analyses, depends upon a certain field of perceptible reality having already been established. This field of perceptible reality is one in which the notion of the recognizable human is formed and maintained over and against what cannot be named or regarded as the human—a figure of the non-human that negatively determines and potentially unsettles the recognizably human.

Those in power *frame* our understanding such that war becomes regarded as justifiable on the grounds of national protection and the citizens of those countries against which war is waged become understood as nonhuman. Capitalism has so long *framed* our expectations of how organizations function that the capillary form of violence I have analysed in this book, the murder of the me's-that-might-have-been, is regarded as an everyday necessity rather than the violence that it is.

Where Butler can work, in *Frames of War*, with visual images that project very directly and without qualification the inhumanity of which she is speaking, organization theorists have to work with words spoken from within a discourse that has no language for the form of oppression I am exploring in this book. If 'framing presupposes decisions or practices that leave substantial losses outside the frame' (Butler, 2009:75), then we must explore what is or cannot be said. The ways in which labour and work are currently conceived do not allow everyday articulation of the possibilities for a being at work that is positioned 'outside the frame'. In other words, I am extrapolating from Butler's thesis to argue in favour of contesting the 'ontological given' of what being at work *means* and thus, like many authors working in what we loosely call 'critical management studies', challenging the normative framework in which governance of 21st-century organizations is located. It follows that the argument also involves a desire for a language that allows articulation of the currently inarticulable. Hence the hyperbolic choice of the terms 'death' and 'murder'.

Unsurprisingly, given the influence of Foucault on Butler's work, we see here similarities in his arguments and hers: we need firstly to identify how our thinking and talking are constrained to what is available within dominant discourses, so as, secondly, to break free of the chains in which they have bound our thoughts and speech.

Where Butler differs markedly from Foucault is in the final chapter of *Frames of War*, when she explores the challenge of nonviolence. Butler's argument throughout that book follows a neo-Buddhist path: we are all ek-statically constituted in relation with others and so are inextricably bound up with others; we cannot exist and cannot have an identity without others, so that the harm I do to another is harm done to myself. We inhabit 'animated fields of differences' wherein the social ontology of the subject is one that affects and is affected by another, such that ' "the subject" ' is less a discrete substance than an active and transitive set of interrelations' (147). Our ontological interrelation with others is prior to any calculation of how that interrelation should work.

From this flows an ethical stance towards the other.

However, Butler cautions against any easy presumption of a moral self that can be turned towards the other. We are, each of us, 'mired in violence', that is, in the violence that formed us and a violence that inhabits us. First, we are all at least partially formed through violence, because against our will we must conform to norms that confer intelligibility or recognisability (167). Although we are born within a matrix of power, the repetition inherent within performativity means that we do not have to repeat the violence of our formation, even though we continue to be assaulted by relations we never chose and that 'are impingements that are injurious, acting forcibly on the body in ways that provoke rage' (171). Indeed, we must 'assume responsibility for living a life that contests the determining power of that production' (170) *because* we are 'mired in violence'. Just as Foucault argues that we must recognise our fascist desires, Butler, drawing on Levinas and Melanie Klein, advises the need to recognise that to be a subject is to acknowledge that one is 'injured, rageful, disposed to violent retribution and nevertheless struggles against that action' (171). We must acknowledge that we are, even those of us who are ostensibly peaceable, pervaded by aggression. We must recognise the injuries that we ourselves cause others and engage in an active struggle against our own aggression, because

> To say that we have 'needs' is thus to say that who we 'are' involves an invariable and reiterated struggle of dependency and separation, and

does not merely designate a stage of childhood to be surmounted. It is not just 'one's own' struggle or the apparent struggle of 'another' but precisely the dehiscence at the basis of the 'we', the condition under which we are passionately bound together: ragefully, desirously, murderously, lovingly. (183)

Moral responsibility thus includes protection of the other from one's own aggression. This involves the fallible practice of trying to attend to the precariousness of life (177) and being wary of moral sadism, which is a form of persecution that passes itself off as virtue (177).

Although Butler is here referring to a political stance that preaches the necessity of war in order to secure peace, I suggest that 'moral sadism' can be applied to understanding organizations. Where Butler is concerned with living and dying, I am concerned with how we define 'life' in organizations and how that life is denied when subjects are reduced to zombie-machines. The attempt to understand 'the boss' in Chapter Two shows how managers are so caught up in dominant organizational discourses of the need to devote oneself singularly and wholeheartedly to the organization that they cannot separate themselves from 'the organization'. I have argued previously (Harding, 2003) that management textbooks and thus management degrees are complicit in constituting such a managerial subject position. In the language that Butler now provides us with, one must charge business schools, management textbooks and the discourses of managerialism that circulate more broadly as a form of *moral sadism*. That is, they preach *the virtue* of profits and duty to shareholders and subordinate all other claims beneath those overarching impositions, arguing that we will all benefit if we serve the needs of profit making.

If so, then we work within conditions of moral sadism. How does one care for one's self and others in such a context? The art of caring for the self, in Foucault's terms, would involve, in Butler's terms, 'an understanding of the possibility of one's own violent actions in relation to those lives to which one is bound, including those whom one never chose and never knew' (179). As with Foucault, this involves being alive to understanding the ways in which we have been educated to see the world, that is, how our understanding of it has been framed. This requires the hugely difficult task of challenging the very terms through which we have learned to think and to act. We must educate ourselves so that we can challenge the frames through which representations are given to us.

CONCILIATION

Foucault and Butler combined lead us to ethical practices in which we (i) identify how we are subjected and subjectified by dominant moral discourses and how our responses are framed so that the breadth of our thinking and understanding is constrained within narrow limits; (ii) find ways of moving beyond those discourses into more ethical positions; (iii) work on the self to identify and acknowledge the meanness and nastiness within the self and to find ways of limiting its effect on others but abjuring any claim to have rid the self of its dark side; (iv) work on the self to change the terms within which one works and acts and so to reach out to others ethically.

These are ethical practices of the individual who is always given over to others. To practice such techniques of the self would be to constitute selves that perhaps surpass those of which we had previously dreamed. It is a political action because such a self refuses the terms within which organizations seek to subjectify us and insists on the right to constitute selves that are nourished and can flourish through our work.

This is where I struggle. In this chapter, I have singled out Frank, the boss, to illuminate the absence of ethics in management. If the overall aim is to develop an ethics of organizations in which each person can flourish, constituting selves that perhaps surpass those of which they/we had dreamed, then the most obvious target for change would be managers, and perhaps we could reach them through our teaching and our writing. But how would a Shakeel, a Julie, an Alex, a Kara and a Saul respond to these ideas, and how could or would they work on themselves? Would they be able, given the presumptions of hierarchy and the pressures on them to be zombie-machines, to educate their managers? I must include myself in this list: how do I challenge those discourses of the moral codes to which I cling and move towards more ethical practices of the self? How could I sustain them when I feel tired and grumpy and want to escape from the world and back into my books?

For now, perhaps our focus should be on the first two of the steps outlined here, that is, identifying and changing or moving beyond the organizational discourses that inhibit our flourishing. That is what this book has aimed to do: to develop a hyperbolic theory that uses the language of murder and death to introduce different ways of articulating the harm that organizations do when they inhibit the flourishing of their staff.

Appendix

SOPHOCLES'S TRAGEDY, *THE ANTIGONE*: A PRÉCIS

Many versions of the stories of Oedipus and his family would have circulated in Athens, passed on by word of mouth and woven into presentations for the theatre. The version with which we are most familiar is that given by Sophocles,[1] who presents the story in three plays written many years apart. Oedipus is the son of Laius and Jocasta, king and queen of Thebes. Following a prophecy that the boy will kill his father, the parents charge a shepherd with the killing of their infant son. The shepherd cannot go through with the deed and passes the child to another shepherd, who takes him to Corinth, where the childless king and queen adopt him. Told by the Oracle at Delphi that he, Oedipus, now a grown man, will kill his father and marry his mother, Oedipus decides he will avoid the curse that is on him by never returning to Corinth. At a narrow pass on a mountain range, there is a violent dispute over who has right of passage, and Oedipus kills the man who has obstructed him. He later encounters the Sphinx. This monster is oppressing the citizens of Thebes and will stop its tyranny only when someone answers its riddle correctly. She asks Oedipus, as she has asked many others: what is it that goes on four feet, three feet and two feet and is most feeble when it walks on four? Oedipus's answer is 'man': on all fours as a baby, on two feet when grown, and on three (with the aid of a walking stick) in old age.[2] The Sphinx throws herself to her death, and Oedipus's reward is marriage to Jocasta, the widowed queen. She and Oedipus rule happily for many years, producing a family of two daughters, Antigone and Ismene, and two sons, Eteocles and Polyneices. Eventually the fate that has been awaiting him all along intercedes, and Oedipus discovers that the man he slew at the mountain pass was his father and that he is married to his own mother. Jocasta hangs herself, and Oedipus takes the long pins from her robe, puts out his eyes and goes into exile with his daughters. Jocasta's brother, Creon, assumes the throne until his two nephews come of age, at which time there is an agreement that the brothers, now under a curse from Oedipus, will share the throne. Eteocles, taking his turn first, refuses to give up the throne to his brother at the due time, and Polyneices summons an army from another city-state and sets out to attack Thebes. Oedipus's curse is fulfilled because in the ensuing battle the brothers kill each other.

It is at this point that *The Antigone* begins. Creon, returning to the throne, dictates that Polyneices's body shall not be buried. Antigone refuses to obey this edict and twice sets out to scatter earth over the carcass. Discovered, arrested and taken to Creon, she refuses to obey his law, and he condemns her to the slow death of entombment in a cave. Creon's son, Haemon, betrothed to Antigone and heartbroken, begs for her freedom, and eventually Creon cedes to his son's wishes. He has delayed too long, for when they get to the cave they find the body of Antigone swinging from the cloth she has used to hang herself. Haemon, the wretched lover, kills himself, and, hearing the news, so does his mother, Creon's wife. Creon is himself soon to die.

Notes

CHAPTER 1: WHAT IS 'WORK'?

1. I distinguish between management (the function) and managers (the people who do management tasks).
2. Whenever possible, our mother used to dress all five of us sisters alike.
3. At that time, median gross weekly earnings for full-time employees in the UK were £489, that is, £531 for men and £426 for women: *Statistical Bulletin: 2009 Annual Survey of Hours and Earning* (London: Office for National Statistics).
4. George A. Romero, director of this film, has developed a cult following for his films since this one, made in 1968.
5. A scene of recognition of the academic self: I read Butler's chapter at a pavement café in Avignon, so my response is partly caught up in my construction of my self as a sophisticated traveller (I omit all reference to the wrinkles and the middle-aged spread—it countermands the image of the self I wish to present to myself. Indeed, they are 'the' rather than 'my' wrinkles and middle-aged spread) who can sit at a pavement café, ignoring the cigarette smoke that is now absent from British cafés (but, then, so is the sun), reading a philosopher discussing the work of another philosopher and thinking, 'Wow, I think I can understand this'. I interrupted my reading every so often to demand that my friend listen to a choice phrase or two. He did similarly with the book he was reading. As we read, sipped and chatted, did we not project ourselves forward to a time of telling others about sitting at a pavement café in Avignon's morning sunshine, eating croissants, drinking strong coffee, breathing in the smoke of Gitanes, images of generations of French philosophers having done likewise informing our images of ourselves, making our images of our selves visible to self and other? This is an observation that we, of course, discussed, in that scene of recognition, in which we *became*, moment to moment to moment, academics.
6. People from South Wales typically insert a 'by' before 'here' or 'there', and indeed the whole phrase ('by here' or 'down by there') is perhaps a heritage of the Welsh language that informs the English spoken there, 'Wenglish'. It took me a long time to learn not to do this when I took up my first lecturing post, and I still often forget. On the other hand, my grandsons tell me off for not talking proper Wenglish when we are together.
7. In the succeeding chapters, I will argue that there is a workplace realm, away from management, in which people can work as well as labour and, in so doing, construct themselves as human.

CHAPTER 5: BECOMING AND NOT BECOMING GENDERED

1. Women now work in large numbers in professional and managerial roles that once were the sole domain of men. Where, in the UK, women occupied 10 percent of professional jobs in the 1970s, in 2005 they occupied 42 percent of managerial positions (although only 17 percent of directorships and chief executive posts). In 2005, 37 percent of the medical profession and 58 percent of medical students are female, 32 percent of financial managers and 47 percent of the legal profession are women, and women occupy 30 percent of management consultants and related roles, 41 percent of academic positions in higher education and 43 percent of financial institution management roles (Equal Opportunities Commission, 2006).
2. That web address is no longer available. Details about *Battlestar Galactica* can now be found at http://www.scifistream.com/battlestar-galactica/.

CHAPTER 6: A HYPERBOLIC THEORY

1. See http://en.wikipedia.org/wiki/Publishers_Weekly_list_of_bestselling_ novels_in_the_United_States_in_the_2000s#2008.5B4.5D (accessed 10 August 2010).
2. See http://www.yellowbird.se/index.php?option=com_seyret&task=videodire ctlink&id=219&Itemid=4 (accessed 10 August 2010)
3. See http://www.dailyrecord.co.uk/news/uk-world-news/2007/06/03/rebus-rebuff-78057-19237980/. (accessed 10 August 2010).
4. 'Suture' refers to procedures whereby cultural texts confer subjectivity upon their viewers or readers (Silverman, 1988:195).

APPENDIX

1. I have used the version introduced by Knox and translated by Fagles (1982).
2. I cannot resist quoting from Muriel Rukeyser, 'Myth' (in Cavarero, 2005:49):

> Long after, Oedipus, old and blinded, walked the roads. He smelled a familiar smell. It was the Sphinx.
> Oedipus said, 'I want to ask one question. Why didn't I recognize my mother?'
> 'You gave the wrong answer,' said the Sphinx.
> 'But that was what made everything possible', said Oedipus.
> 'No', she said, 'When I asked, What walks on four legs in the morning, two at noon, and three in the evening, you answered, Man. You didn't say anything about woman'.
> 'When you say Man', said Oedipus, 'you include women too. Everyone knows that'.
> She said, 'That's what you think'.

References

Adler, S., Laney, J. and Packer, M. (1993) *Managing women*. Buckingham: Oxford University Press.

Alvesson, M. (2003) Beyond neopositivists, romantics, and localists: A reflexive approach to interviews in organizational research. *Academy of Management Review*, 28:1, 13–33.

Alvesson, M., Ashcraft, K. and Thomas, R. (2008) Identity matters. *Organization*, 15:1, 5–28.

Alvesson, M. and du Billing, Y. (1992) Gender and organization: Towards a differentiated understanding. *Organization Studies*, 13:1, 73–103.

Alvesson, M. and Skoldberg, K. (2009) *Reflexive methodology*. London: Sage.

Alvesson, M. and Willmott, H. (1996) *Making sense of management: A critical introduction*. London: Sage.

Alvesson, M. and Willmott, H. (2002) Identity regulation as organizational control: Producing the appropriate individual. *Journal of Management Studies*, 39:5, 619–644.

Anderson, B. (2010) Migration, immigration controls and the fashioning of precarious workers. *Work, Employment and Society*, 24:2, 300–317.

Anderson-Gough, F., Grey, C. and Robson, K. (2000) In the name of the client: The service ethic in two professional services firms. *Human Relations*, 53:9, 1151–1174.

Andrew, A. and Montague, J. (1998) Women's friendship at work. *Women's Studies International Forum*, 21:4, 355–361.

Anouilh, J. 1951/2000. *Antigone*. London: Methuen.

Bal, M. (2000) Visual narrativity. In G. Coulter-Smith (Ed.), *The visual-narrative matrix: Interdisciplinary collisions and collusions*, 7–16. Southampton: Southampton Institute.

Barratt, E. (2008) The later Foucault in organization and management studies. *Human Relations*, 61:4, 515–537.

Barry, J., Berg, E. and Chandler, J. (2006) Academic shape shifting: Gender, management and identities in Sweden and England. *Organization*, 13:2, 275–298.

Barzilai, S. (1999) *Lacan and the matter of origins*. Stanford, CA: Stanford University Press.

Bass, B.M. and Steidlmeier, P. (1999) Ethics, character and authentic transformational leadership behavior. *Leadership Quarterly*, 10:2, 181–217.

Baudrillard, J. (1976/1993) *Symbolic exchange and death*. London: Sage.

Bauman, Z. (1989) *Modernity and the Holocaust*. Cambridge: Polity Press.

Bauman, Z. (1992) *Mortality, immortality and other life strategies*. Cambridge: Polity Press.

Bauman, Z. (2007) *Consuming life*. Cambridge: Polity Press.

Bell, E. (2008) *Reading management and organization in film*. Basingstoke: Palgrave Macmillan.

Benjamin, J. (1988) *The bonds of love: Psychoanalysis, feminism and the problem of domination*. New York: Pantheon.

Benjamin, J. (1995) *Like subjects, love objects: Essays on recognition and sexual difference*. New Haven, CT: Yale University Press.

Benjamin, J. (1998) *Shadow of the other: Intersubjectivity and gender in psychoanalysis*. London: Routledge.

Benn, S.I. and Gaus, G.F. (1983) The public and the private: Concepts and action. In S.I. Benn and G.F. Gaus (Eds.), *Public and private in social life*, 3–30. London: Croom Helm.

Benschop, Y. and Doorewaard, H. (1998) Covered by equality: The gendered subtext of organizations. *Organization Studies*, 19:5, 787–805.

Bernauer, J. and Mahon, J. (1994) The ethics of Michel Foucault. In G. Gutting (Ed.), *The Cambridge companion to Foucault*, 141–158. Cambridge: Cambridge University Press.

Bernstein, J.M. (2010) 'The celestial Antigone, the most resplendent figure ever to have appeared on earth': Hegel's feminism. In F. Söderbäck (Ed.), *Feminist readings of Antigone*, 111–132. Albany: State University of New York Press.

Blundell, S. (1995) *Women in ancient Greece*. Cambridge, MA: Harvard University Press.

Bollas, C. (1989) *The shadow of the object: Psychoanalysis of the unthought known*. New York: Columbia University Press.

Bollas, C. (1993) *Being a character: Psychoanalysis and self experience*. London: Routledge.

Bollas, C. (1995) *Cracking up: The work of unconscious experience*. London: Routledge.

Borneman, J. (1996) Until death do us part: Marriage/death in anthropological discourse. *American Ethnologist*, 23:2, 215–235.

Bowring, M.A. (2004) Resistance is not futile: Liberating Captain Janeway from the masculine-feminine dualism of leadership. *Gender, Work and Organization*, 11, 381–405.

Braverman, H. (1974) *Labor and monopoly capital. The degradation of work in the twentieth century*. New York: Monthly Review Press.

Brecht, B. (1984) *Antigone. In a version by Bertolt Brecht*. Trans. J. Malina. New York: Applause Theatre and Cinema Books.

Brennan, T. (1993) *History after Lacan*. London: Routledge.

Brewis, J. (2005) Signing my life away? Researching sex and organization. *Organization*, 12:4, 493–510.

Brewis, J., Hampton, M.P. and Linstead, S. (1997) Unpacking Priscilla: Subjectivity and identity in the organization of gendered appearance. *Human Relations*, 50, 1275–1304.

Brocklehurst, M., Grey, C. and Sturdy, A. (2009) Management: The work that dares not speak its name. *Management Learning*, 41:1, 7–19.

Browder, G. (2003) Perpetrator character and motivation: An emerging consensus. *Holocaust and Genocide Studies*, 17:3, 480–497.

Budgeon, S. and Roseneil, S. (2004) Editors' Introduction: Beyond the conventional family. *Current Sociology*, 52:2, 127–134.

Burrell, G. (1984) Sex and organizational analysis. *Organization Studies*, 5, 97–118.

Burrell, G. (1988a) Modernism, postmodernism and organizational analysis 2: The contribution of Michel Foucault. *Organization Studies*, 9, 221–235.

Burrell, G. (1988b) Modernism, postmodernism and organizational analysis: The contribution of Michel Foucault. In A. McKinlay and K.E. Starkey (Eds.), *Foucault, Management and Organization Theory*, 14–28. London: Sage.

Burrell, G. (1997) *Pandemonium: Towards a retro-organization theory*. London: Sage.
Burrell, G. and Morgan, G. (1979) *Sociological paradigms and organizational analysis*. London: Heinemann.
Butler, J. (1990) *Gender trouble*. London: Routledge, Chapman and Hall.
Butler, J. (1993) *Bodies that matter*. New York: Routledge.
Butler, J. (1997) *The psychic life of power*. Stanford, CA: Stanford University Press.
Butler, J. (2000) *Antigone's claim*. New York: Columbia University Press.
Butler, J. (2002) Capacity. In S.M. Barber and D.L. Clark (Eds.), *Regarding Sedgwick*, 109–120. London: Routledge.
Butler, J. (2004) *Precarious lives*. New York: Verso.
Butler, J. (2004) *Undoing gender*. New York: Routledge.
Butler, J. (2005) *Giving an account of oneself*. New York: Fordham University Press.
Butler, J. (2009) *Frames of war*. New York: Verso.
Cabantous, L. and Gond, J-P. (2011) Rational decision making as performative praxis: Explaining rationality's *éternel retour*. *Organization Science*, 22:3, 573–586.
Cabantous, L., Gond, J.-P. and Johnson-Cramer, M. (2010) Decision theory as practice: Crafting rationality in organizations. *Organization Studies*, 31:11, 1531–1566.
Calas, M.B. and Smircich, L. (1991) Voicing seduction to silence leadership. *Organization Studies*, 12:4, 567–602.
Calas, M.B. and Smircich, L. (1992) Re-writing gender into organizational theorizing: Directions from feminist perspectives. In M. Reed and M. Hughes (Eds.), *Rethinking organization: New directions in organization theory and analysis*, 227–253. London:Sage.
Carr, A. and Lapp, C. (2005) Wanted for breaking and entering organizational systems in complexity: *Eros* and *Thanatos*. *Emergence: Complexity and Organization*, 7:3–4, 43–52.
Carr, A. and Lapp, C. (2006) *Leadership is a matter of life and death*. London: Palgrave Macmillan.
Cavarero, A. (2005) *For more than one voice*. Stanford, CA: Stanford University Press.
Chadwick, O. (1990) *The secularisation of the European mind in the nineteenth century*. Cambridge: Cambridge University Press.
Chambers, D. (2006) *New social ties*. Basingstoke: Palgrave.
Chandler, J., Barry, J. and Clark, H. (2002) Stressing academe: The wear and tear of the New Public Management. *Human Relations*, 55:9, 1051–1069.
Chanter, T. (2010) The performative politics and rebirth of Antigone in ancient Greece and modern South Africa. In F. Söderbäck (Ed.), *Feminist readings of Antigone*, 83–98. Albany: State University of New York Press.
Chia, R. (1994) Decision: A deconstructive analysis. *Journal of Management Studies*, 31, 781–806.
Chia, R. (1995) From modern to postmodern organizational analysis. *Organization Studies*, 16, 579–604.
Chia, R. (2000) Discourse analysis as organizational analysis. *Organization*, 7, 513–518.
Clark, D. (1993) *The sociology of death: Theory, culture, practice*. Oxford: Blackwell.
Clarke, C., Knights, D. and Jarvis, C. (2012) A labour of love? Academics in business schools. *Scandinavian Journal of Management*, 28:1, 5–15.
Clarke, C.A., Brown, A.D. and Hailey, V.H. (2009) Working identities? Antagonistic discursive resources and managerial identity. *Human Relations*, 62:3, 323–352.
Clegg, S., Kornberger, M. and Rhodes, C. (2007) Business ethics as practice. *British Journal of Management*, 18, 107–122.

Cockburn, C. (1990) Men's power in organizations: 'Equal opportunities' intervenes. In J. Hearn and D.H.J. Morgan (Eds.), *Men, masculinity and social theory*. London: Unwin Hyman.

Cole, A. (2004) What Hegel's master/slave dialectic really means. *Journal of Medieval and Early Modern Studies*, 34:3, 577–610.

Collinson, D. and Hearn, J. (1996) 'Men' at work': Multiple masculinities/multiple workplaces. In M. Mac an Ghaill (Ed.), *Understanding masculinities: Social relations and cultural arenas*, 61–76. Buckingham: Open University Press.

Conard, M.T. (Ed.) (2007) *The philosophy of film noir*. Lexington: University Press of Kentucky.

Connolly, W. (1998) Beyond good and evil: The ethical sensibility of Michel Foucault. In J. Moss (Ed.), *The later Foucault*, 108–128. London: Sage.

Cooper, R. and Burrell, G. (1988) Modernism, postmodernism and organizational analysis: An introduction. *Organization Studies*, 9:1, 91–112.

Cooper, R. and Burrell, G. (1989) Modernism, postmodernism and organizational analysis 3: The contribution of Jacques Derrida. *Organization Studies*, 10, 479–502.

Copjec, J. (2004) *Imagine there's no woman: Ethics and sublimation*. Cambridge, MA: MIT Press.

Costas, J. (2012, forthcoming) 'We are all friends here': Reinforcing paradoxes of normative control in a culture of friendship. *Journal of Management Inquiry*.

Courtenay, W.H. (2000) Constructions of masculinity and their influence on men's well-being: A theory of gender and health. *Social Science and Medicine*, 50, 1385–1401.

Critchley, S. (2012) *The faith of the faithless*. London: Verso.

Crotty, M.J. (1998) *The foundations of social research*. London: Sage.

Cummings, S. (1996) Back to the oracle: Postmodern organization theory as a resurfacing of premodern wisdom. *Organization*, 3:2, 249–266.

Czarniawska, B. (1999) Management she wrote: Organization studies and detective stories. *Culture and Organization*, 5:1, 13–41.

Da Cunha, J.V. and e Cunha, M.P. (2002) Reading between the lines: Unveiling masculinity in feminine management practices. *Women in Management Review*, 17:1, 5–11.

De Beauvoir, S. (1953/1997) *The second sex*. London: Vintage.

De Lauretis, T. (2008) *Freud's drive: Psychoanalysis, literature and film*. Basingstoke: Palgrave Macmillan.

Deleuze, G. and Guattari, F. (1977) *Anti-Oedipus: Capitalism and schizophrenia*. Trans. R. Hurley et al. New York: Viking.

Delmestri, G. and Walgenbach, P. (2012) Mastering techniques or brokering knowledge? Middle managers in Germany, Great Britain and Italy. *Organization Studies*, 26:2, 197–220.

Denzin, N.K. (1991) *Images of postmodern society: Social theory and contemporary cinema*. London: Sage.

Denzin, N.K. and Lincoln, Y.S. (Eds.) (2002) *The qualitative inquiry reader*. Thousands Oaks, CA: Sage.

Dick, P.K. (2007/1962) *Do androids dream of electric sheep?* London: Gollanz.

Dickie, C. (2009) Exploring workplace friendships in business: Cultural variations of employee behaviour. *Research and Practice in Human Resource Management*, 17:1, n.p.

Doane, M.A. (1988) *The desire to desire: The woman's film of the 1940's*. Basingstoke: Macmillan.

Dollimore, J. (1991) *Sexual dissidence: Augustine to Wilde, Freud to Foucault*. Oxford: Oxford University Press.

Dollimore, J. (2001) *Death, desire and loss in Western culture*. New York: Routledge.

Douglas, M. (1966) *Purity and danger*. London: Routledge.

Douglas, M. (1997) Deciphering a meal. In C. Counihan and P.V. Esterik (Eds.), *Food and culture: A reader*, 36–55. London: Routledge.

Duncan, N. (1996) Renegotiating gender and sexuality in public and private spaces. In N. Duncan (Ed.), *Body space*, 127–145. London: Routledge.

Elfring, T. and Hulsink, W. (2007) Networks in entrepreneurship: The case of high-technology firms. *Small Business Economics*, 21:4, 409–422.

Ellis, C. and Bochner, A. (2000) Autoethnography, personal narrative, reflexivity: Researcher as subject. In N. Denzin and Y. Lincoln (Eds.), *Handbook of qualitative research*, 733–768. Thousand Oaks, CA: Sage.

Elsesser, K. and Peplau, L.A. (2006) The glass partition: Obstacles to cross-sex friendships at work. *Human Relations*, 59:8, 1077–1100.

Ely, R.J. and Meyerson, D.E. (2000) Advancing gender equity in organizations: The challenge and importance of maintaining a gender narrative. *Organization*; 7:4, 589–608.

Equal Opportunities Commission (2006) *Facts about women and men in Great Britain*. http://www.unece.org/fileadmin/DAM/stats/gender/publications/UK/Facts_about_W&M_GB_2006.pdf, accessed 13 November 2012.

Essers, C. (2009) Reflections on the narrative approach: Dilemmas of power, emotions and social location while constructing life-stories. *Organization*, 16:2, 163–181.

Falk, P. (1994) *The consuming body*. London: Sage.

Fanon, F. (2008) *Black skin, white masks*. New York: Grove Press.

Feldman, S.P. (2004) The professional conscience: A psychoanalytic study of moral character in Tolstoy's 'The Death of Ivan Ilych'. *Journal of Business Ethics*, 49, 311–328.

Fleming, P. (2005) Workers' playtime? Boundaries and cynicism in a 'culture of fun' program. *Journal of Applied Behavioral Science*, 41:3, 285–303.

Fleming, P. and Spicer, A. (2003) Working at a cynical distance: Implications for power, subjectivity and resistance. *Organization*, 10:1, 157–179.

Fleming, P. and Spicer, A. (2008) Beyond power and resistance: New approaches to organizational politics. *Management Communication Quarterly*, 21:3, 301–309.

Fletcher, A.J. (1995) *Gender, sex and subordination: England 1500–1800*. London: Yale University Press.

Foley, H. (1995) Tragedy and democratic ideology: The case of Sophocles' Antigone. In B. Goff (Ed.), *History, tragedy, theory*, 131–150. Austin: University of Texas Press.

Ford, J. and Collinson, D. (2011) In search of the perfect manager? Work-life balance and managerial work. *Work, Employment and Society*, 25:2, 257–273.

Ford, J. and Harding, N. (2003) Invoking Satan or the ethics of the employment contract. *Journal of Management Studies*, 40:5, 1131–1150.

Ford, J. and Harding, N. (2004) We went looking for an organization but could find only the metaphysics of its presence. *Sociology*, 38:4, 815–830.

Fotaki, M. (2005) Choice is yours: A psychodynamic explanation of health policy-making and its consequences for the English National Health Service. *Human Relations*, 59:12, 1711–1744.

Fotaki, M. (2011) The sublime object of desire (for knowledge): Sexuality at work in business and management schools in England. *British Journal of Management*, 22:1, 42–53.

Fotaki, M. and Harding, N. (2012) Lacan and sexual difference in organization and management theory: Towards a hysterical academy? *Organization*, http://org.sagepub.com/content/early/2012/02/05/1350508411435280.abstract.

Foucault, M. (1966) *The order of things: Archaeology of the human sciences.* London: Routledge.

Foucault, M. (1977) *Discipline and punish: The birth of the prison.* Harmondsworth: Penguin.

Foucault, M. (1979) *The history of sexuality, Vol. 1.* London: Allen Lane.

Foucault, M. (1982) *Afterword: The subject and power.* In H.L. Dreyfus and P. Rabinow (Eds.), *Michel Foucault: Beyond structuralism and hermeneutics,* 229–252. Chicago: University of Chicago Press.

Foucault, M. (1985) *The use of pleasure.* Trans. R. Hurley. New York: Pantheon.

Foucault, M. (1986) *The history of sexuality, Vol. 2.* Harmondsworth: Viking.

Foucault, M. (1992) *The history of sexuality, Vol. 3.* London: Penguin.

Foucault, M. (1994) Theatrum Philosophicum. In J. Faubion (Ed.), *Michel Foucault: Aesthetics: The essential works 2,* 343–368. Trans. Robert Hurley et al. London: Penguin Books.

Foucault, M. (1997a) *Ethics: The essential works 1.* Ed. P. Rabinow. Trans. R. Hurley et al. London: Penguin.

Foucault, M. (1997b) Technologies of the self. In P. Rabinow (Ed.), *Michel Foucault: Ethics, subjectivity and truth.* New York: New Press.

Fournier, V. and Grey, C. (2000) At the critical moment: Conditions and prospects for critical management studies. *Human Relations,* 53:1, 7–32.

Freud, S. (1914/2009) *Beyond the pleasure principle.* Harmondsworth: Penguin.

Freud, S. (1915–17/1973) *Volume One: Introductory lectures on psychoanalysis.* London: Penguin.

Friedson, E. (1986) *Professional powers.* Chicago: University of Chicago Press.

Fuery, P. and Fuery, K. (2003) *Visual cultures and critical theory.* London: Bloomsbury Academic.

Gabriel, Y. (2003) Your home, my exile: Boundaries and 'otherness' in antiquity and now. *Organization Studies,* 24, 619–632.

Gatrell, C. and Swan, E. (2008) *Gender and diversity in management.* London: Sage.

George, J.M. and Jett, Q.R. (2003) Work interrupted: A closer look at the role of interruptions in organizational life. *Academy of Management Review,* 28:3, 494–507.

Gherardi, Sylvia (1995) *Gender, symbolism and organizational cultures.* London: Sage.

Gibson-Graham, J.K. (1996) *The end of capitalism (as we knew it): A feminist critique of political economy.* Oxford: Blackwell.

Giddens, A. (1991) *Modernity and self identity.* Cambridge: Polity Press.

Gilley, A. Gilley, J.W., McConnell, C.W. and Veliquette, A. (2010) The competencies used by effective managers to build teams: An empirical study. *Advances in Developing Human Resources,* 12:1, 29–45.

Glaser, B. and Strauss, A. (1968) *Time for dying.* Chicago: Aldine.

Godfrey, R., Lilley, S. and Brewis, J. (2012) Biceps, bitches and borgs: Reading *Jarhead*'s representation of the construction of the (masculine) military body. *Organization Studies,* 33:4, 541–562.

Grant, J. and Porter, P. (1996) Women managers: The construction of gender in the workplace. *Australian and New Zealand Journal of Sociology,* 30:2, 149–164.

Grey, C. (2009) *A very short, fairly interesting and reasonably cheap book about studying organizations.* London: Sage.

Grey, C. and French, R. (1966) Rethinking management education: An introduction. In R. French and C. Grey (Eds.), *Rethinking management education,* 1–16. London: Sage.

Grey, C. and Sturdy, A. (2007) Friendship and organizational analysis: Toward a research agenda. *Journal of Management Inquiry,* 16:2, 157–172.

Grey, C. and Willmott, H. (2005) *Critical management studies: A reader*. Oxford: Oxford University Press.

Gurevitch, Z. (2001) Dialectical dialogue: The struggle for speech, repressive silence, and the shift to multiplicity. *British Journal of Sociology*, 52:1, 87–104.

Halberstam, J. (1998) *Female masculinity*. Durham, NC: Duke University Press.

Hales, C. (1999) Why do managers do what they do? Reconciling evidence and theory in accounts of managerial work. *British Journal of Management*, 10, 335–350.

Hancock, P. (2008) Fear and (self)loathing in Coleridge Close: Management in crisis in the 1970s sitcom. *Organization*, 15:5, 685–703.

Handy, C. (1995) *Gods of management: The changing work of organizations*. Oxford: Oxford University Press.

Haraway, D. (1985) A manifesto for cyborgs: Science, technology and socialist feminism in the 1980s. *Socialist Review*, 15:2, 65–107.

Harding, N. (2002) On the manager's body as an aesthetics of control. *Tamara: Journal of Critical Postmodern Organization Science*, 2:2, 63–77.

Harding, N. (2003) *The social construction of management: Texts and identities*. London: Routledge.

Harding, N. (2007) On Lacan and the 'becoming-ness' of organizations/selves. *Organization Studies*, 28:11, 1761–1773.

Harding, N. (2008) The 'I', the 'me' and the 'you know': Identifying identities in organisations. *Qualitative Research in Organizations and Management*, 3:1, 42–58.

Harding, N., Ford, J. and Gough, B. (2010) Accounting for ourselves: Are academics exploited workers? *Critical Perspectives on Accounting*, 21:2, 159–168.

Harding, N., Lee, H., Ford, J. and Learmonth, M. (2011) Leadership and charisma: A desire that cannot speak its name? *Human Relations*, 64:7, 927–950.

Harrison, W.C. and Hood-Williams, J. (2002) *Beyond sex and gender*. London: Sage.

Hassard, J. and Holliday, R. (Eds.) (1998) *Organization-representation: Work and organizations in popular culture*. London: Sage.

Hawkins, B. (2008) Double agents: Gendered organizational control and resistance. *Sociology*, 42:3, 418–435.

Haythornthwaite, C. and Wellman, B. (1998) Work, friendship and media use for information exchange in a networked organization. *Journal of the American Society for Information Science*, 49:12, 1101–1114.

Heaney, S. (2004) *The burial at Thebes: Sophocles' Antigone*. London: Faber and Faber.

Hearn, J. (1992) *Men in the public eye*. London:Routledge.

Hearn, J. and Parkin, W. (1986) *'Sex' at 'work': The power and paradox of organization sexuality*. Brighton: Wheatsheaf.

Hegel, G.W.F. (1977) *Phenomenology of spirit*. Trans. A.V. Miller. Oxford: Oxford University Press.

Heidegger, M. (1926/1962) *Being and time*. New York: Harper and Brothers.

Hekman, S.J. (1999) *The future of differences: Truth and method in feminist theory*. Oxford: Polity Press.

Hester, J.D. (2004) Intersexes and the end of gender corporeal ethics and postgender bodies. *Journal of Gender Studies*, 13:3, 215–225.

Hird, M. (2003) Considerations for a psychoanalytical theory of gender identity and sexual desire: The case of intersex. *Signs: Journal of Women in Culture and Society*, 28, 1068–1092.

Hochschild, A.R. (1983) *The managed heart: Commercialization of human feeling*. Berkeley: University of California Press.

Hochschild, A.R. (1997) *The time bind: When work becomes home and home becomes work*. New York: Owl Books.

Hochwarter, W.A. and Thompson, K.W. (2012) Mirror, mirror on my boss's wall: Engaged enactment's moderating role on the relationship between perceived narcissistic supervision and work outcomes. *Human Relations*, 63:3, 335–366.

Hook, D. (2009) Restoring universality to the subject: Lacan's Kantian logic of sexuation. *Annual Review of Critical Psychology*, 7, 151–167.

Hühn, P. (1987) The detective as reader: Narrativity and reading concepts in detective fiction. *Modern Fiction Studies*, 33:3, 451–466.

Iedemam R., Degeling, P., Braithwaite, J. and White, L. (2003) 'It's an interesting conversation I'm hearing': The doctor as manager. *Organization Studies*, 25:1, 15–33.

Irigaray, L. (1985) *Speculum of the other woman*. Trans. G. Gill. Ithaca, NY: Cornell University Press.

Iser, W. (Ed.) (2000) The reading process: A phenomenological approach. In D. Lodge (Ed.), *Modern criticism and theory: A reader*, 189–205. Harlow: Longman.

Jacobs, A. (2006) *On matricide: Myths, psychoanalysis and the law of the mother*. New York: Columbia University Press.

Jameson, F. (1991) *Postmodernism, or, the cultural logic of late capitalism*. London: Verso.

Janesick, V.M. (1994) The dance of qualitative research design: Metaphor, methodolatry, and meaning. In N.K. Denzin and Y.S. Lincoln (Eds.), *Handbook of Qualitative Research*, 209–219. New York: Sage.

Jermier, J.M. and Knights, D. (Eds.) (1994) *Resistance and power in organizations: Critical perspectives on work and organizations*. London: Routledge.

Jovanovic, G. (2011) Toward a social history of qualitative research. *History of the Human Sciences*, 24:2, 1–27.

Judovitz, D. (2001) *The culture of the body: Genealogies of modernity*. Ann Arbor: University of Michigan Press.

Kark, R. and Weismel-Manor, R. (2005) Organizational citizenship behaviour: What's gender got to do with it? *Organization*, 12:6, 889–917.

Kikjuit, B. and Ende, J.C.M. van den (2010) With a little help from our colleagues: A longitudinal study of social networks for innovation. *Organization Studies*, 31:4, 451–479.

Knights, D. (1997) Organization theory in the age of deconstruction: Dualism, gender and postmodernism revisited. *Organization Studies*, 18, 1–19.

Knights, D. and Kerfoot, D. (2004) Between representations and subjectivity: Gender binaries and the politics of organizational transformation. *Gender, Work and Organization*, 11:4, 430–454.

Knights, D. and Willmott, H. (1989) Power and subjectivity at work: From degradation to subjugation in social relations. *Sociology*, 23:4, 535–558.

Knights, D. and Willmott, H. (1999) *Management lives: Power and identity in work organizations*. London: Sage.

Kociatkiewicz, J. and Kostera, M. (2012) The good manager: An archetypical quest for morally sustainable leadership. *Organization Studies*, 33:7, 861–878.

Korczynski, M. (2011) The dialectical sense of humour: Routine joking in a Taylorized factory. *Organization Studies*, 32:10, 1420–1440.

Korczynski, M. and Ott, U. (2005) Sales work under marketization: The social relations of the cash nexus? *Organization Studies*, 26:5, 707–728.

Kotter, J. (1990) *A force for change: How leadership differs from management*. New York: Free Press.

Kram, K.E. and Isabella, L.A. (1985) Mentoring alternatives: The role of peer relationships in career development. *Academy of Management Journal*, 28:1, 110–132.

Kristeva, J. (1982) *Powers of horror: An essay on abjection*. New York: Columbia University Press.

Lacan, J. (1977) *Ecrits: A selection*. London: Routledge.

Lacan, J. (1982) Feminine sexuality. In J. Mitchell and J. Rose (Eds.), *Feminine sexuality: Jacques Lacan and the école freudienne*, 27–57. Trans. J. Rose. London: Norton.

Lacan, J. (1998) *On feminine sexuality, the limits of love and knowledge, 1972–1973. Encore. The Seminar of Jacques Lacan. Book XX*. Ed. J.-A. Miller. Trans. B. Fink. New York: Norton.

Lacan, J. (2002) *Écrits: The first complete edition in English*. Trans. B. Fink. New York: Norton.

Lacan, J. (2007) *Seminar XVII: The other side of psychoanalysis*. Ed. J.-A. Miller. Trans. R. Grigg. New York: Norton.

Lacqueur, T. (1990) *Making sex: Body and gender from the Greeks to Freud*. Cambridge, MA: Harvard University Press.

Lam, M. (2004) The perception of inequalities: A gender case study. *Sociology*, 38:1, 5–23.

Larkin, P. (2003) *Collected poems by Philip Larkin and Anthony Thwaite*. London: Faber and Faber.

Law, J. (2004) *After method: Mess in social science research*. London: Routledge.

Law, J. (2006) *Making a mess with method. Version of 19th January 2006*. http://www.heterogeneities.net/publications/Law2006MakingaMesswithMethod.pdf, accessed 3 March 2012.

Leder, D. (1990) *The absent body*. Chicago: University of Chicago Press.

Lee, G.H. (2005) *Queer(y)ing health promotion: A critical analysis*. Unpublished doctoral dissertation, University of Leeds.

Lefebvre, H. (1991) *The production of space*. Trans. D. Nicholson-Smith. Oxford: Blackwell.

Lincoln, J.R. and Miller, J. (1979) Work and friendship ties in organizations: A comparative analysis of relational networks. *Administrative Science Quarterly*, 24, 181–199.

Linkman, A. (2011) *Photography and death*. London: Reaktion.

Linstead, S. (2000) Ashes and madness: The play of negativity and the poetics of organization. In S. Linstead and H. Höpfl (Eds.), *The aesthetics of organization*, 61–92. London: Sage.

Littler, C. and Salaman, G. (1982) Bravermania and beyond—recent theories of the labour process. *Sociology*, 16:2, 251–269.

Lloyd, M.B. (2005) Antigone and the state. *Political Theory*, 4, 451–468.

Lodge, D. (2000) Wolfang Iser—introductory note. In D. Lodge and N. Wood (Eds.), *Modern criticism and theory: A reader*, 188–189. Harlow: Pearson Education.

MacKenzie, R. and Forde, C. (2009) Rhetoric of the 'good worker' versus the realities of employers' use and the experiences of migrant workers. *Work, Employment and Society*, 23:1, 142–159.

Mankell, H. (2009) *The man who smiled*. London: Vintage Books.

Marks, L.U. (2000) *The skin of the film*. Durham, NC: Duke University Press.

Marks, S.R. (1994) Intimacy in the public realm: The case of co-workers. *Social Forces*, 72:3, 843–858.

Marshall, J. (1984) *Women managers: Travellers in a male world*. Chichester: Wiley.

Martin, J. (1990) Deconstructing organizational taboos: The suppression of gender conflict in organizations. *Organization Science*, 1, 339–359.

Martin, P.Y. (2006) Practising gender at work: Further thoughts on reflexivity. *Gender, Work and Organization*, 13:3, 254–276.

Marx, K. (1988) *Economic and philosophic manuscripts of 1844*. New York: Prometheus Books.

McCarthy, G.E. (2003) *Classical horizons: The origins of sociology in ancient Greece*. Albany: State University of New York Press.

McGregor, D. (1989) The human side of enterprise. In H. Leavitt, L. Pondy and D. Boje (Eds.), *Readings in managerial psychology*, 314–324. New York: McGraw-Hill.

McMurray, R. (2011) The struggle to professionalize: An ethnographic account of the occupational position of advanced nurse practitioners. *Human Relations*, 64:6, 801–822.

Menzies, I. (1960) A case-study in the functioning of social systems as a defence against anxiety. *Human Relations*, 13, 95–121.

Meriläinen, S., Tienari, J., Thomas, R. and Davies, A. (2004) Management consultant talk: A cross-cultural analysis of normalising discourse and resistance. *Organization*, 11:4, 539–564.

Mills, A.J. (1992) Organization, gender, and culture. In A.J. Mills and P. Tancred (Eds.), *Gendering organizational analysis*, 93–111. Newbury Park, CA: Sage.

Mills, A.J. and Murgatroyd, S.J. (1991) *Organizational rules*. Milton Keynes: Open University Press.

Mintzberg, H. (1973) *The nature of managerial work*. London: Prentice Hall.

Mitchell, J. (2000) *Mad men and Medusas*. New York: Basic Books.

Mitsuhashi, H. (2003) Effects of the social origins of alliances on alliance performance. *Organization Studies*, 24:2, 321–339.

Mulkay, M. (1993) Social death in Britain. In D. Clark (Ed.), *The sociology of death: Theory, culture, practice*, 31–49. Sociological Review Monographs. Oxford: Blackwell.

Neilson, I.K., Jex, S.M. and Adams, G.A. (2000) Development and validationof scores on a two-dimensional workplace friendship scale. *Educational and Psychological Measurement*, 60:4, 628–643.

Nietzsche, F. (1882/2001) *The gay science*. Cambridge: Cambridge University Press.

O'Doherty, D. and Willmott, H. (2001) Debating labour process theory: The issue of subjectivity and the relevance of poststructuralism. *Sociology*, 35, 457–476.

Ogbonna, E. and Wilkinson, B. (2003) The false promise of organizational culture change: A case study of middle managers in grocery retailing. *Journal of Management Studies*, 40:5, 1151–1178.

O'Leary, T. (2002) *Foucault: The art of ethics*. London: Continuum.

Pahl, R. and Spencer, L. (2004) Personal communities: Not simply families of 'fate' or 'choice'. *Current Sociology*, 52:2, 199–221.

Parker, M. (1998) Judgement day: Cyborganization, humanism and postmodern ethics. *Organization*, 5:4, 503–518.

Parker, M. (2002) *Against management*. Cambridge: Polity Press.

Parker, M. (2003) Introduction: Ethics, politics and organizing. *Organization*, 10, 187–203.

Parker, M. (2008) Eating with the Mafia: Belonging and violence. *Human Relations*, 61:7, 989–1006.

Parker, M. (2009) Pirates, merchants and anarchists: Representations of international business. *Management and Organizational History*, 4:2, 167–185.

Parker, M. (2011) *Alternative business: Outlaws, crime and culture*. London: Routledge.

Parker, M. and Cooper, R. (1998) Cyborganization: Cinema as nervous system. In J. Hassard and R. Holliday (Eds.), *Organization-representation: Work and organizations in popular culture*, 201–228. London: Sage.

Pateman, C. (1983) Feminist critiques of the public/private dichotomy. In S.I. Benn and G.F. Gaus (Eds.), *Public and private in social life*, 281–303. London: Croom Helm.

Patient, D., Lawrence, T.B. and Maitlis, S. (2003) Understanding workplace envy through narrative fiction. *Organization Studies*, 24:7, 1015–1044.

Patterson, O. (1982) *Slavery and social death: A comparative study.* Cambridge, MA: Harvard University Press.

Peirano-Vejo, M.E. and Stablein, R.E. (2009) Constituting change and stability: Sense-making stories in a farming organization. *Organization*, 16:3, 443–462.

Pendleton, A. (2003) Does privatization create a 'new breed' of managers? A study of the UK railway industry. *Human Relations*, 56:1, 85–111.

Pettinger, L. (2005) Friends, relations and colleagues: The blurred boundaries of the workplace. *Sociological Review Monograph Series*, 53, Issue Supplement s2, 37–55.

Pirsig, R. (1999) *Zen and the art of motorcycle maintenance.* London: Vintage.

Pollock, G. (2006) Beyond Oedipus: Feminist thought, psychoanalysis, and mythical figurations of the feminine. In V. Zajko and M. Leonard (Eds.), *Laughing with Medusa*, 67–120. Oxford: Oxford University Press.

Prichard, C. and Willmott, H. (1997) Just how managed is the McUniversity? *Organization Studies*, 18:2, 287–316.

Rabin, J. (1999) Organizational downsizing: An introduction. *M@n@gement*, 203, 39–43.

Ramo, H. (2004) Spatio-temporal notions and organized environmental issues: An axiology of action. *Organization*, 11:6, 849–872.

Rawlins, W.K. (1992) *Friendship matters: Communication, dialectics, and the life course.* Edison, NJ: Transaction.

Redman, T., Wilkinson, A. and Snape, E. (1997) Stuck in the middle? Managers in building societies. *Work, Employment and Society*, 11:1, 101–114.

Reed, M.I. (1989) *The sociology of management.* New York: Harvester Wheatsheaf.

Reed, M.I. (1992) *Rethinking organization.* London: Sage.

Reed, M.I. (2012) Masters of the universe: Power and elites in organization studies. *Organization Studies*, 33:2, 203–221.

Reedy, P. and Learmonth, M. (2011) Death and organization: Heidegger's thought on death and life in organizations. *Organization Studies*, 32:1, 117–131.

Rhodes, C. (2007) *Critical representations of work and organizations in popular culture.* London: Routledge.

Rhodes, C. and Brown, A.D. (2005) Writing responsibly: Narrative fiction and organization studies. *Organization Studies*, 12:4, 467–491.

Riordan, C.M. and Griffeth, R.W. (1995) The opportunity for friendship in the workplace: An underexplored construct. *Journal of Business and Psychology*, 10:2, 141–154.

Roan, A. and Rooney, D. (2006) Shadowing experiences and the extension of communities of practice: A case study of women education managers. *Management Learning*, 37:4, 433–454.

Ronai, C.R. (1999) The next night *sous rature*: Wrestling with Derrida's mimesis. *Qualitative Inquiry*, 5, 114–129.

Rose, J. (1982) Introduction 2. In J. Mitchell and J. Rose (Eds.), *Feminine sexuality: Jacques Lacan and the école freudienne*, 27–57. London: Norton.

Roseneil, S. and Budgeon, S. (2004) Cultures of intimacy and care beyond 'the family': Personal life and social change in the early 21st century. *Current Sociology*, 52:2, 135–159.

Ross-Smith, A. and Kornberger, M. (2004) Gendered rationality? A genealogical exploration of the philosophical and sociological conceptions of rationality, masculinity and organization. *Gender, Work and Organization*, 11:3, 280–305.

Rowlands, L. and Handy, J. (2012) An addictive environment: New Zealand film production workers' subjective experiences of project-based labour. *Human Relations*, 65:5, 657–680.

Rumens, N. (2008) Working at intimacy: Gay men's workplace friendships. *Gender, Work and Organization*, 15:1, 8–30.

Rumens, N. (2010) Firm friends: Exploring the supportive components in gay men's workplace friendships. *Sociological Review*, 58:1, 135–155.

Rumens, N. and Kerfoot, D. (2009) Gay men at work: (Re)constructing the self as professional. *Human Relations*, 62:5, 763–786.

Rzepka, C.J.(2005) *Detective fiction*. Cambridge: Polity Press.

Sabath, A-M. (2007) *Beyond business casual. What to wear to work if you want to get ahead*. Lincoln, NE: ASJA Press.

Said, E.W. (1978) *Orientalism*. London: Penguin.

Salih, Sara (2004) *The Judith Butler reader*. Oxford: Blackwell.

Salzer-Morling, M. (1998) Murderous ink: A case of rhetorical killing. *Studies in Culture, Organization and Society*, 4, 125–145.

Scarbrough, H. and Burrell, G. (1996) The axeman cometh. In S. Clegg and G. Paler (Eds.), *The politics of management knowledge*, 173–189. London: Sage.

Scarry, E. (1988) *The body in pain: The making and unmaking of the world*. Oxford: Oxford Paperbacks.

Schmidt, D.J. (2001) *On Germans and other Greeks: Tragedy and ethical life*. Bloomington: Indiana University Press.

Schneider, D. (1984) *A critique of the study of kinship*. Ann Arbor: University of Michigan Press.

Schwartz, H. (1987) On the psychodynamics of organizational totalitarianism. *Journal of Management*, 13:1, 41–54.

Scott, J. (2005) *Electra after Freud: Myth and culture*. Ithaca, NY: Cornell University Press.

Sedgwick, E.K. (1991) *Epistemology of the closet*. New York: Harvester Wheatsheaf.

Sedgwick, E.K. (2003) *Touching feeling: Affect, pedagogy, performativity*. Durham, NC: Duke University Press.

Seidler, V.J. (1994) *Unreasonable men: Masculinity and social theory*. London: Routledge.

Sennett, R. (2006) *The culture of the new capitalism*. New Haven, CT: Yale University Press.

Shildrick, M. (1997) *Leaky bodies and boundaries: Feminism, postmodernism and (bio)ethics*. London: Routledge.

Shilling, C. (1993) *The body and social theory*. London: Sage.

Sievers, B. (1994) *Work, death and life itself*. Berlin: Walter de Gruyter.

Siltanen, J. and Stanworth, M. (1984) The politics of private woman and public man. *Theory and Society*, 13:1, 91–118.

Silver, A. (1990) Friendship in commercial society: Eighteenth-century social theory and modern sociology. *American Journal of Sociology*, 95:6, 1474–1504.

Silverman, K. (1988) *The acoustic mirror: The female voice in psychoanalysis and cinema*. Bloomington: Indiana University Press.

Silverman, K. (1996) *The threshold of the visible world*. New York: Routledge.

Simmel, G. (1910/2007) The metaphysics of death. *Theory, Culture and Society*, 24:7–8, 72–77.

Sims, D. (2008) Managerial identity formation in a public sector professional: An autobiographical account. *International Journal of Public Administration*, 31, 1–15.

Sinclair, A. (2009) Seducing leadership: Stories of leadership development. *Gender, Work and Organization*, 16, 265–284.

Sinfield, A. (2004) *On sexuality and power*. New York: Columbia University Press.

Singh, D. (2006) *Emotional intelligence at work: A professional guide*. New Delhi: Sage.

Sinha, P.N., Inkson, K. and Baraker, J.R. (2012) Committed to a failing strategy: Celebrity CEO, intermediaries, media and stakeholders in a co-created drama. *Organization Studies*, 33:2, 233–245.

Sjöholm, C. (2010) Beyond pleasure: The other history of sexuality. In F. Söderbäck (Ed.), *Feminist readings of Antigone*, 173–194. Albany: State University of New York Press.

Skultans, V. (1999) Narratives of the body and history: Illness in judgement of the Soviet past. *Sociology of Health and Illness*, 21, 310–328.

Smart, C., Davies, K., Heaphy, B. and Mason, J. (2012) Difficult friendships and ontological security. *Sociological Review*, 60:1, 91–109.

Smith, W. (2006) Organizing death: Remembrance and re-collection. *Organization*, 13:2, 225–244.

Sobchack, V. (2004) *Carnal thoughts: Embodiment and moving image culture.* Los Angeles: University of California Press.

Sophocles (1982) *The three Theban plays: Antigone, Oedipus the King, Oedipus at Colonus.* Trans. R. Fagles. London: Penguin.

Sophocles (1988) *Oedipus the King, Oedipus at Colonus, Antigone.* Trans. D. Taylor. London: Methuen.

Sophocles (2008) *Antigone, Oedipus the King and Electra.* Trans. H.D.F. Kitto. Oxford: Oxford University Press.

Spee, A.P. and Jarzabkowski, P. (2011) Strategic planning as communicative process. *Organization Studies*, 32:9, 1217–1245.

Speer, S.A. (2005) The interactional organization of the gender attribution process. *Sociology*, 39:1, 67–87.

Spencer, L. and Pahl, R. (2004) Personal communities: Not simply families of 'fate' or 'choice'. *Current Sociology*, 52:2, 199–221.

Spencer, L. and Pahl, R. (2006) *Rethinking friendship: Hidden solidarities today.* Princeton, NJ: Princeton University Press.

Stein, M. (2007) Oedipus Rex at Enron: Leadership, Oedipal struggles, and organizational collapse. *Human Relations*, 60, 1387–1410.

Steiner, G. (1986) *Antigones.* Oxford: Oxford University Press.

Stenport, A.W. (2007) Bodies under assault: Nation and immigration in Henning Mankell's *Faceless Killers. Scandinavian Studies*, 79:1, 1–24.

Stewart, R. (1967) *Managers and their jobs: A study of the similarities and differences in the ways managers spend their time.* New York: Macmillan.

Strathern, M. (2005) *Kinship, law and the unexpected: Relatives are always a surprise.* Cambridge: Cambridge University Press.

Stroud, L. (2005) MMR—public policy in crisis: Whose tragedy? *Journal of Health Organization and Management*, 19:3, 252–260.

Sveningsson, S. and Alvesson, M. (2003) Managing managerial identities: Organizational fragmentation, discourse and identity struggle. *Human Relations*, 56:10, 1163–1193.

Taylor, C. (1992) *Sources of the self: The making of modern identity.* Cambridge: Cambridge University Press.

Taylor, F.W. (1911/2003) *The principles of scientific management.* Abingdon: Routledge.

Ten Bos, R. (2003) Business ethics, accounting and the fear of melancholy. *Organization*, 10, 267–285.

Thomas, R. and Davies, A. (2005) Theorizing the micro-politics of resistance: New public management and managerial identities in the UK public services. *Organization Studies*, 26:5, 683–706.

Thomas, R. and Linstead, A. (2002) Losing the plot? Middle managers and identity. *Organization*, 9:1, 71–93.

Townley, B. (2008) *Reason's neglect: Rationality and organizing.* Oxford: Oxford University Press.

Trethewey, Angela. (1999) Disciplined bodies: Women's embodied identities at work. *Organization Studies*, 20:3, 423–450.

Turner, B.S. (2008) *The body and society*. London: Sage.

Valsiner, J. (2006) Dangerous curves in knowledge construction within psychology. *Theory and Psychology*, 16:5, 587–595.

Van Dover, J.K. (2005) *We must have certainty: Four essays on the detective story*. Selinsgrove, PA: Susquehanna University Press.

Vogl, G. (2009) Work as community: Narratives of solidarity and teamwork in the contemporary workplace, who owns them? *Sociological Research Online*, 14:(4)4. http://www.socresonline.org.uk/14/4/4.html, accessed June 2012.

Wajcman, J. (1998) *Managing like a man: Women and men in corporate management*. Cambridge: Polity Press.

Wartenberg, T. (2007) *Thinking on screen: Film as philosophy*. London: Routledge.

Watson, T.J. (2008) Managing identity: Identity work, personal predicaments and structural circumstances. *Organization*, 15:1, 121–143.

Watson, T.J. (2009) Narrative, life story and manager identity: A case study in autobiographical identity work. *Human Relations*, 62:3, 425–452.

Webb, J. and Byrnand, S. (2008) Some kind of virus: The zombie as body and as trope. *Body and Society*, 14, 83–98.

Weber, M. (1930/2001) *The Protestant ethic and the spirit of capitalism*. London: Routledge.

Willmott, H. (1995) Managing the academics: Commodification and control in the development of university education in the UK. *Human Relations*, 48:9, 993–1027.

Willmott, H. (2000) Death: So what? Sociology, sequestration and emancipation. *Sociological Review*, 48:4, 649–665.

Wolfram Cox, J. (1997) Manufacturing the past: Loss and absence in organizational change. *Organization Studies*, 18:4, 623–654.

Young, I.M. (1990) *Throwing like a girl and other essays in feminist philosophy and social theory*. Bloomington: Indiana University Press.

Young, J. (2003) *The death of God and the meaning of life*. London: Routledge.

Young, M. and Willmott, P. (1969) *Family and kinship in East London*. London: Routledge and Kegan Paul.

Zald, M.N. and Lounsbury, M. (2010) The wizards of Oz: Towards an institutional approach to elites, expertise and command posts. *Organization Studies*, 31, 963–996.

Index

Printed in the United States
by Baker & Taylor Publisher Services